THEORY
OF KNOWLEDGE
AND PROBLEMS
OF EDUCATION

READINGS IN
THE PHILOSOPHY
OF EDUCATION

GENERAL SERIES EDITOR, HARRY S. BROUDY

THEORY OF KNOWLEDGE AND PROBLEMS OF EDUCATION

EDITED BY DONALD VANDENBERG

UNIVERSITY OF ILLINOIS PRESS
URBANA, CHICAGO, LONDON
1969

GENERAL SERIES PREFACE

Readings in the Philosophy of Education is a series of books each of which reprints significant articles, excerpts from books, and monographs that deal philosophically with problems in education.

The distinctive feature of this series is that the selection of materials and their organization are based on the results of a three-year project supported by the U. S. Office of Education and the University of Illinois. A team of philosophers of education with consultants from both philosophy of education and general philosophy scanned thousands of items. Their final selection was presented in a report entitled *Philosophy of Education: An Organization of Topics and Selected Sources* (Urbana, University of Illinois Press, 1967).

Unfortunately, not all college libraries are equally well stocked with the items listed in the report, and even with adequate resources, getting the appropriate materials to the student is a formidable task for the instructor.

Accordingly, several members of the original team that worked on the project agreed to bring out this series. The projected books are organized in two groups: One will devote a separate volume to each of the following problems in education: the nature, aims, and policies of education; curriculum; teaching-learning. The second group will be made up of a number of volumes each of which will bring together significant materials from one of the following philosophical disciplines: epistemology; metaphysics; value theory; aesthetics; and the philosophy of science. This volume belongs to the second group dealing with the problems of education in its epistemological dimension.

The first group of books will make available to the student some important and representative things that philosophers of education, utilizing the resources of epistemology, metaphysics, value theory, logical and linguistic analysis, social philosophy, philosophy of science, and the philosophy of religion have had to say about problems of education. Used as a set, these volumes are appropriate for the first course in the philosophy of education whether offered to undergraduates or on the master's level. Individually or in combination they can also be used in courses in administration, methods, principles, curriculum, and related fields.

Each of the volumes in the second group approaches the problems of education from one of the standard divisions of general philosophy, and individually or in combination they are suited to advanced and specialized courses. Some instructors may wish to use both types in their courses.

Donald Vandenberg, the author of this volume, was one of the original research assistants on the Philosophy of Education Project. His own work has explored the import of existentialism and phenomenology for the study of education.

HARRY S. BROUDY
General Series Editor

PREFACE

To classify and organize the writings included in this volume, I have accepted the fourfold division of educational problems of the original project. I find it to be as good as what I might invent. Some schematism is necessary to enable the talk to be about one thing at a time, readings are included that make the standard arguments against the schema, and inter-relations across the divisions are made in the introductory essays and in some of the readings. I have placed the materials on policy before rather than after those on curriculum because policy seems closer to aims, and curriculum seems closer to teaching and learning, rather than the reverse. From one perspective, policy is less general than aims and more general than curriculum. Placing considerations of policy before those of curriculum, then, puts the four main divisions in order of decreasing generality, according to this view. Because the authors of the selections do not confine themselves to the divisions of the schematism, users of this volume should have no difficulty in coming to their own just estimate of the alternatives in these issues. If they do, the schematism has fulfilled its heuristic function.

In selecting items, I have tried to employ the criteria of representativeness, significance, permanence, comprehensiveness, and uniqueness in respect to the style of treatment of the educational problem. I have tried to select according to the quality of the handling of the educational problem rather than according to strictly philosophical criteria because I feel that the norms of educational philosophy are logically independent of any one school of philosophical thought. I have tried to select primarily for quality and depth of treatment, but I enter the customary disclaimer to infallibility.

About three-quarters of these materials were collected at the University of Calgary and I would like to express my thanks to the library and the Department of Education Foundations there for the use of their facilities. Gratitude is felt toward the Cultural Foundations of Education division of the Department of Educational Services at Pennsylvania State University for a light teaching load while I was putting this volume together. I am also grateful for the stenographic assistance of Miss Karen Archer.

D. V.

CONTENTS

THE NATURE AND AIM
OF EDUCATION

Epistemology, the theory of knowing and knowledge, is relevant to the problems of ascertaining the nature and aim or aims of education in three ways: (A) Methodologically—how can one know what the nature of education is and what its aim or aims ought to be? (B) Substantively—what kinds of knowing or knowledge ought to be promoted in schooling? (C) Contextually—what ought to be the role of knowing and knowledge in the educative process in general, particularly in respect to non-cognitive learnings?

The questions are absurd. The answers are obvious. Science is the only method of knowing and its method yields the only valid knowledge. The obvious answers, then, are: (A) educational psychology, learning theory, personality theory, and sociology of education establish the only valid statements about the nature of education and its aims; (B) the scientific method of knowing and scientific knowledge ought to be acquired in schools; and (C) there ought to be the maximum amounts of knowing and acquisition of knowledge in schooling and all noncognitive factors should be subordinated to this end.

But what kind of statement is this: "Science is the only method of knowing and its method yields the only valid knowledge"? We will call this statement "Science." What kind of statement is Science? We are not questioning the worth of Science (nor of science). What *kind* of a statement is it? Is it, after all, a bit of scientific knowledge? Clearly not. It is something else; it is epistemological. To say Science is to make an epistemological statement because it concerns the nature of knowing and knowledge: Science cannot be known through scientific method and probably ought to be rejected because of its highly speculative nature. Because Science is philosophical, however, it follows that the "obvious" answers, rather than the original questions, are absurd. To answer A: If one accepts Science as making worthwhile sense, and if he goes to educational psychology, learning theory, theory of personality, and so on, to collect factlike statements about the nature and aim of education, he finds that a short trip in that direction is superior to a long one. A lengthy sojourn reveals that one has to choose between studies and theories that are based upon "data" collected from (1) quantified, statistical, "empirical" studies; (2) cats, rats, racoons, monkeys, mice, and pigeons; (3) clinical practice and case studies of real (if ailing) people; (4) laboratory investigations of very small groups of people; and so on to other kinds of "data" from which it is even more difficult to draw valid generalizations. A long trip reveals that one has to choose among "facts" and "theories" whose chief differences seem to be closely related to the *kind* of "data" employed. He finds that he has to choose statements about the nature of education according to his own preferences for kinds of "data," i.e., according to his own epistemological preferences and speculations. The question remains: Which kind of "data" yields the best knowledge about the nature and aims of education?

This question is easily transformed into its original form as A. As it stands it is not clear at all that the kinds of "data" yielded by scientific inquiries are able to supply an answer. Because it has to be qualified (Which kind of "data," *if any*, . . .), the obvious answer is absurd.[1] "Answering" the question this way merely begs the question. By the same reasoning, *mutatis mutandis,* the "obvious" answers to the second and third questions are equally absurd. They are no answers at all. As they stand, they state or suggest neither that the acquisition of the scientific method of knowing and of scientific knowledge is *educative* nor that subordinating noncognitive factors to their acquisition is *educative.* In other words, the "obvious" answers are *purely* epistemological in nature in spite of the fact that their speculative characteristics may be obscured in a culture that takes Science for granted, whereas the questions asked were *educational* questions with an epistemological accent. The answers are absurd because they are responses to kinds of questions different from those asked.

---

[1] What appears to have happened is this: The overweening prestige of science has promoted the illusion that it could solve everything. Then when it was turned to the study of education, what was studied became more and more reduced to fit the limits of the increasingly refined and confined methods of inquiry of the behavioral sciences until education became lost in the shuffle because nobody noticed the reductionism involved. This forgetfulness would be more tragic were it less comic.

The appropriate understanding of the three ways in which epistemology is relevant to the problem of ascertaining the nature and aim or aims of education, therefore, is to keep in mind that the three corresponding questions are part of the larger question: What is education? This is a larger question because its dimensions are metaphysical and axiological as well as epistemological. The theory of knowing supplies part of the answer but not all of it. Because philosophers of education have often tried to see things as a whole, their concern for the epistemological dimension of the nature and aim of education has often been subsumed within their concern for the axiological dimension. The issues of curriculum and teaching and learning have seemed to lend themselves more readily to epistemological inquiries than the issues of the aim and nature of education. Second, answers to the epistemological questions concerning the nature of knowing, truth, evidence, data, the given, and the objects of knowledge do not in and of themselves supply answers to educational questions. Fairy tales, fables, folklore, and fiction will remain educative regardless of their evidential and relative cognitive status. In their place they may have as much cognitive status as Science has in its place.

It does seem that Science (the speculative statement that science is the one and only method of knowing) has some cognitive status; so many people seem to find it so meaningful and true. We have spoken only of its worth. If it has some cognitive status, however, then it is simply untrue in its extreme form, for its very own cognitive status is *ipso facto* demonstration of its falsity. The self-falsifying proposition Science demonstrates the existence of philosophical knowledge, knowledge about knowledge. The alternative is that Science is an opinion, which also leaves the door open for the possibility of philosophical knowledge, for then there is the possibility of other kinds and degrees of knowing among which we find philosophical knowing. That is, if Science has some cognitive status, it makes sense to speak of philosophical knowing. If Science does not have any cognitive status, it does not bar the way to some other kind of philosophical knowledge. Then if it makes sense to speak of degrees of knowledge, it also makes sense to speak of the *epistemology of the epistemology of education* in reference to the area of inquiry opened up by the first question.

This meta-level inquiry *about* the epistemology of education is concerned with the nature of aims, their source or sources, and their derivation, justification, validation, and utilization within the educative process. This in turn involves some conception of the nature of education such that the meta-level inquiry is inseparable from the inquiry into the epistemology of education proper. The three selections chosen to illustrate the sort of responses that can be made to the first question, at any rate, deal with the second and third questions in addition to their primary concern with the first. This is probably as it should be in order to avoid certain errors, such as never getting to the matter that one started to think about, or losing one's self in free-floating talk. The first of these three, by Schwab, discusses the epistemic difficulties and the ensuing educational difficulties generated by attempts to derive views of the nature of education and its aims from various representative behavioral sciences, i.e., by attempts to omit epistemological considerations. Schwab indicates how in these cases something else becomes an inferior "epistemology" because the dimension cannot be omitted from the educative process. Schwab's article clears the way for the constructive suggestions of the diametrically opposed views of Dewey and Adler that follow.

The ways in which Dewey and Adler differ on the nature of educational aims is rather instructive. This difference is paralleled in their differences on the nature of education, the nature of knowledge, the nature of man, and the nature of the cognitive status attributed to philosophy and the philosophy of education. From within the much broader tradition of empiricism, positivism, and pragmatism that says Science, Dewey maintains, in a sense, that all thinking worthy of the name is scientific thinking. For Dewey *scientific thinking* is a redundancy. Philosophy of education cannot prescribe the aim or aims of education because, in a sense, it has no cognitive status. The best it can do is attempt to maintain a broad perspective and suggest things to be tried out—any aims enter into the educative process as hypotheses. By a curious twist, however, it can be said that Dewey, unlike others in the broader tradition, ascribes the same cognitive status to philosophic knowledge as he does to scientific knowledge: an aim derived from philosophic knowledge has no greater or less cognitive status than that of a hypothesis, since it is merely a suggestion to the teacher that hopefully broadens and deepens his foresight into the consequences of particular acts of teaching. In a sense, then, Dewey would equate philosophical knowledge and scientific knowledge. To understand this equation, however, one would have to understand Dewey's theory of knowledge and his entire program for the reconstruction of philosophy. It is nevertheless a valid equation when properly understood. Speaking equally broadly, Adler ascribes the cognitive status to philosophy and to the philosophical derivation of educational aims that might previously have been ascribed to Newtonian physics, or that might be ascribed to scientific knowledge by the lay public, by pupils in some kinds of classrooms, by some of the people who have been concerned with structure in the curriculum as of late, or, indeed, by some philosophers of education. Dewey sees both science and philosophy as highly uncertain and tentative; Adler sees philosophy as absolutely certain and dogmatic in a way that is very similar to the conceptions of science of some of the people who say Science. The methods which they advocate and employ for the derivation of educational aims differ accordingly. So do their views of the nature of education, of knowledge in general, and of other topics in philosophy and education.

If the preceding paragraphs have seemed rather long for introductory purposes, they have been so for the same reason that Dewey and Adler are juxtaposed at the beginning of the volume. The problems that these two selections pose when taken together (which, incidentally, might be the only proper way to take either—they constitute each other's antidote and taking them together thus prevents philosophical suicide) may very well be the entire field of the epistemology of education. The clever instructor or student can easily make them the gateposts through which the rest of the authors march. That this is the case can be partially seen in the next selection by Donohue. Donohue's effort to be the gate, to grasp both gateposts at once, is readily apparent when one recalls that Adler and Hutchins had approximately the same views. Although the precise debate between Hutchins and Dewey that Donohue refers to is probably as obsolete as silent movies, the features of

knowing that Donohue suggests probably ought not to be forgotten. The reader can easily discern for himself the way Donohue advocates retention of what he thinks is the best of each of
the traditions that Dewey and Adler stand for. Analogously, on
the meta-level the traditions represented by Dewey and Adler
probably ought not to be forgotten. The cognitive status of the
philosophy of education in its various phases probably ought to
remain an open and philosophical question. To avoid a bulky
inclusion of meta-level papers, some gateposts have been set up
so that the authors who spoke directly on education could begin
marching through them. To avoid begging the supernumerary
questions, however, we have tried to indicate them sufficiently
to permit a genuinely philosophical reading of the text. A vast
literature of over a hundred items is available on the nature of
philosophy of education, and much of it is relevant to our first
question concerning how one can know anything about the aims
and nature of education in its epistemological or any other
dimension. We have been arrogant enough to suggest that
Dewey and Adler are adequately representative for this volume.

Beginning with Donohue, the remaining selections in this part
of the volume respond to the second and third questions of the
first paragraph above. Concern for either the educational or the
epistemological aspect of the problems varies considerably. The
last selection by Broudy, Smith, and Burnett appears to approach the ideal blend of educational and philosophical involvement because a richer mixture of epistemology would be
uninteresting to teachers and a leaner mixture uninteresting to
philosophers of education. Be this as it may, the penultimate
selection by Peters partly gives stronger philosophical support
for some ideas explicated by Broudy, Smith, and Burnett, although the able reader will also gain ideas from Peters that will
enable him to criticize the last essay—and the reverse. This per-
tains to all the papers. Brettschneider's paper, for example, is
mostly a metaphysical support for the eventual epistemological
conclusion of the community criterion of truth suggested in respect to the selection of knowledge to be employed in education,
and one wonders what the acceptance of this criterion would do
to the interpretive use of knowledge of the last essay, or, on the
other hand, what an acceptance of the necessity of the interpre-

tive use of knowledge would do to the community criterion. Or
are they compatible? Or is Dupuis's criticism of this criterion
(in the next section) as it has been advocated in policy-making
better evaded with Brettschneider's organicism than with pragmatism? Or is the criticism more devastating to Brettschneider?
And so on and so on.

Whereas the last selection in this part of the volume is closer
to Adler's gatepost and Peters is somewhere in the middle,
Brettschneider is closer to Dewey's, particularly on the community criterion of truth. For Dewey's own view on the nature and
aim of education when he is speaking directly to the issues in
greatest detail, see the chapters on "Education as Conservative
and Progressive" and "Aims in Education" in *Democracy and
Education* (New York, Macmillan, 1916). Among other important discussions of these problems are Kingsley Price's "On
'Having an Education' " in the *Harvard Educational Review,* 28
(Fall, 1958), 320–37; and Marc Belth's second chapter in
Education as a Discipline (Boston, Allyn and Bacon, 1965).
Particularly germane as an overview is Frederick C. Wegener's
"The Problem of Knowledge and Its Consequences for Philoso-
phy of Education" in *Educational Theory,* 4 (April, 1954),
129–38, although it seems somewhat dated by its specific refer-
ences.

ON THE CORRUPTION OF
EDUCATION BY PSYCHOLOGY*

Joseph J. Schwab

The studies and speculations in psychology currently urged on educators for their guidance are marked by a radical deficiency. The deficiency in question has its roots in the old and familiar distinction between feeling and reasoning, the emotional and the rational, a distinction that colors current studies in psychology no less than it colored those of a century ago.

No serious exception can be taken to the sound use of such distinctions in general and to this one in particular. Any complex subject matter requires some differentiation into parts as a prelude to investigation, and the differentiation of our "inner" life into affective and cognitive components has been reasonably fruitful in inquiry. . . .

A distinction, however, can be misapplied. It may be used to expunge from attention one of the separated components. It may be so applied that, without evidence or reason, one of the components is systematically subordinated to the other. At the other extreme, the distinction may become so hallowed through usage that it is mistaken for a real difference, a natural boundary between one subject matter and another. It is the first and second of these misuses that characterize the collection of psychological theories currently being urged upon educators.

Based, as these theories are, on the traditional distinction between feeling and reasoning, we have reason to expect them to fall into three groups: theories concerning affect (emotion, drive, motivation); theories concerning reason or intellect; and a third group of theories concerned with the relations and interactions of feeling and thinking. Instead, theories on reason or intellect are virtually omitted, and the third group of theories is debased. No current theory of magnitude and standing deals with the intellectual as such. . . . Since there are no substantial

* Reprinted from "On the Corruption of Education by Psychology," *The School Review*, 66(Summer, 1958), 169–84. By permission of the University of Chicago Press. Copyright 1958 by the University of Chicago.

current theories on mature intellectual processes as such, there is little theorizing on the interrelations of intellect and emotion.

We have, instead, two other groups of theories. We have theories that are intentionally limited to the emotional side of behavior. These theories deliberately undertake a restricted study. They set aside all intellectual operations as subjects of later inquiry. Connections between intellectual operations and the emotional are, of course, excluded from investigation. Theories in the other group attempt to cover the "whole" person, the intellectual or cognitive as well as the affective or appetitive. These theories, however, fail in their effort to dispense with the distinction. Instead, they discover their "whole" by identifying only those intellectual aspects of behavior that are implied or suggested by the view of instincts, needs, appetites, or compulsions that serves as the principle or starting point for the theory.

In both groups of current theories, the rational factor is deficient, radically and frankly so in the first group, covertly in the second. The result of this deficiency when these theories are applied to the problems of education deserves our attention.

An ideal version of the radically incomplete theory of affect, did it exist, would provide a reasonably sound ground for treatment of educational problems. Such a theory would supply us with a working knowledge of the emotional springs and concomitants of behavior, while an analysis of the products of human intellect—science, solutions of practical problems, works of art—would provide us with knowledge of the operation of that phase of human activity. If each such body of knowledge were complete in its own way, the two could be combined, despite the fact that each is embodied in its own set of terms, for each would delineate half of an entire story. . . .

But theories of isolated parts applied to the parts *in vivo*—in their full, complex, interrelated status in the whole—are another matter. Then, the simplifications and modifications permitted by observation of the part in isolation may well fail to correspond to the condition of the part as it actually exists. The model is no longer a justifiedly incomplete model but a misleading one.

In education the inadequacies of theories of isolated parts are apparent. Here the human person exists *in vivo*. The classroom

is not a therapeutic chamber, and the average pupil is not a
mass of affect essentially isolated from all else by abnormality or
failure of emotional development. Instead, he is often a reasonably normal child and, as such, a complex one. In addition to
emotional   needs,   he   has   intellectual   wants   and   curi-
osities. . . . Moreover, the phrase "in addition" is misleading, for these intellectual needs, wants, and dynamisms are not
merely appended to emotional needs and dynamisms. On the
contrary, each modifies and modulates the other in reciprocal
interaction, and the complex person that emerges is a far cry
from the simplified model that is constructed when emotional
needs and processes are studied in isolation.

In addition to this fundamental inadequacy of a theory of
emotion in isolation, there is another inadequacy that is peculiar
to theories of emotion, whether isolated or not. It is simply that
the subject is so complex, is so difficult of access, and, above all,
exercises a fascination so urgent, that the most astonishing
simplifications, each plausible and each largely exclusive of the
others, are promulgated by investigators and accepted by parti-
san audiences. What is asserted about the emotional side of
personality is likely to suffer, then, not only from the isolation of
its subject matter, but also from a decidedly one-sided view even
of that isolated subject. Thus, at various times, the entire pattern of human behavior has been alleged to arise from and
center in just one such factor as sex, security, "we-ness," aggres-
sion, domination, self-realization.

To use such a theory as a principle of education is to risk two
successive forms of distortion. First, we are likely to adopt as
aims of education conceptions of effective behavior that are
themselves distortions. Then if we try to make our intellectual
aims coherent with them, these, too, become distorted. . . .

The second class of current theories involves more sweeping
dangers. These are the theories that recognize the incompleteness of their forerunners and attempt to repair the omission. In
such theories, learning and knowing, as well as feeling and
impulse, are treated, and in relation to one another. When such
theories are perfected, they will obviate the necessity for choice
between emotional and intellectual principles, since the distinction will have been removed or rendered innocuous. But they,

too, are as yet far from perfect and, indeed, still labor under the aura of the old sharp distinction in that they take affective factors as central: though a learning process is studied in relation to emotion and personality, it is an extremely incomplete and oversimplified version of learning. It is a version of learning that has gone beyond the memorization of nonsense syllables, the simple association, maze-running, and escape from problem-boxes, which the complexity of the subject forced upon earlier inquiries. But in no substantial degree does this version of learning yet include those complexities of intellectual activity that are visible in the mature products of scientific inquiry, of art, and of the process of deliberation. When such incomplete theories are used on their originating subject matter, no damage is done; but when they are imported into education and imposed upon its problems, the unavoidable result is a perverting of the intellectual aims of education to fit them to the simplified conception of learning embodied in the theory of personality.

How real this risk is can be seen from a closer examination of certain views currently used in this way. There are three that reflect, each in its own way, the consequences with which we are concerned. They are group dynamism, non-directivism, and autonomism.

Each of these names stands for two things: first, for a field of inquiry outside the area of education, but also for a doctrine of instruction arrived at by importing the terms of that inquiry into education and imposing them on its problems. Thus, as a field of inquiry, group dynamics is a study of the behavior of individuals in small groups and of the group character that emerges from the dynamisms involved. We may consider it as a branch either of sociology or of psychiatry, or as a field between the two. Non-directivism is a doctrine and a method in the field of psychotherapy. Autonomism is a moral-sociological doctrine on the origins of individual behavior in a structured society. We are not concerned here with these views as doctrines or as fields of inquiry. We are concerned with the form these views take as doctrines of education and with the consequences to intellectual aims that ensue when their principles are imposed on problems of education.

Group dynamism, as a doctrine of education, begins with the

fact that a large part of human work in our society (and perhaps in all societies) is done in groups. The doctrine then points out that work is not only done *in* groups, but it is done *by* the group as a group, rather than by individuals operating in their individuality. The group as a whole acquires a character from dynamisms that arise from the initial behavior of its constituents. This character determines what work is done, its kind and quality. Even where a task is assigned by the group to one of its members and is apparently done by him, it is not done by him in the same way or with the same outcome it would have had were he a member of another group. In short, once the group is fully formed, he has little or no status as an individual in his own right but only as a member of the group. It is the group that determines what will be done and, in effect, does it. And it is the group character, furthermore, that determines what is acceptable and unacceptable, good or bad, true or false.

From such a point of view, the first affective aim of education is to train persons to become willing and useful members of groups, to recognize the supremacy of group activity, and to distinguish between behavior that forms good groups and behavior that forms poorer (that is, less "groupy") groups. For such an education, discussion is a useful method because it takes place in a small group. The process of discussion becomes primarily the process by which a group is formed from its constituent atoms and through which it functions as a group. Discussion therefore becomes, first, the playing out of roles that stand in the way of group formation (catharsis), then the discovery of the rewarding warmth, security, and sense of strength that arise from the solidarity, the "groupiness," of the group, and from the relinquishment of private responsibility. After these stages, the function of discussion is to guard the integrity of the group and to perform work, intellectual or other, consistent with the integrity of the group.

From this last stage consequences arise that concern us. The integrity of the group becomes not only the affective *sine qua non* for efficient work but also the principle by which intellectual quality is determined. Whatever is done by way of intellectual activity must not destroy the integrity of the group. When terms are to be chosen for some inquiry or other, the subject and problem inquired into exercise some determining influence, since the group is seriously concerned with the subject and problem and intends to study the one and solve the other. But the group studies and acts as a group. If certain terms exceptionally apt for analysis of the problem happen to be terms that the group as a whole is not prepared to recognize and use, the terms are rejected. It is beside the point that some member of the group, as an individual, might have once valued them. It is beside the point that even as a member he may be touched momentarily by an awareness of their value.

The rejection takes place, not by vote or other summary action that explicitly invokes the solidarity of the group as the final criterion, but through the group process itself. The interplay of discussion will have established such rapport among the members of the group, such a recognition and acceptance of the character of the group as a working group, that terms, approaches, frames of reference alien to it are not likely to occur to one of the members. His is a member-mind, and its cogitation when faced with a problem is not an unrestricted exploration of possibilities but an exploration of possibilities acceptable to the group.

The very nature of inquiry, whether scientific or practical, is thus altered. It ceases to be a procedure whose ultimate measure is the completeness and verity of the knowledge acquired. It ceases to be a process whose fruits are measured by careful nurtured *diversities* of criteria. It becomes, instead, a procedure whose ultimate measure is the continuing and increasing solidarity of the group.

Test of a theory by its breadth of usefulness is changed into test of it against its usefulness in matters that interest the group. Deviance, idiosyncrasy, disagreement, and diversity—the means by which popular error is discovered and the germs from which new inquiries grow—are excised by the group-dynamical conception of education as threats to the integrity of groups.

Other, more specific, alterations in the character of intellectual aims of the curriculum could be traced: how science is given a subordinate role since its central concern for a subject matter is hard to reconcile with the group principle; how the fine arts are almost ruled out because of the largely private character of their enjoyment; how the curriculum becomes almost entirely a preparation for dealing with practical, localized problems. But enough has been said to make the main point: that by treating affective preconditions and outcomes of the curriculum as dominant, group dynamism alters intellectual aims, not by investigating the character of knowledge and inquiry, but by tailoring them to fit its doctrine of affective behavior.

In non-directivism, a similar subversion of education can be seen, aimed in another direction. This doctrine of education begins with the premise (as valid in its own terms as the starting point of group dynamism) that an individual human organism can employ no resources for intellectual or emotional growth that are not its own. The human organism cannot learn through the observation, imagination, or memory of others, nor recognize problems of behavior that it does not itself see and find ways to alter. Consequently, says this doctrine, the ruling purpose of education is to evoke and bring to recognition in each student the powers he himself may have. . . .

In such a view, the classroom becomes the situation in which individuals may find facets of their selves. A problem that arises for discussion (it may arise but not be proposed) is not treated as a problem to be solved but as an occasion for self-discovery. Each student is encouraged to conceive the problem in his own way, pursue it as he thinks best, and arrive at what is a terminus for him. The relative value of one or another formulation of the problem or one or another method of attacking the problem is not seriously discussed, since the value of formulations and methods lies, not in their effect on the inquiry, but in their potency as stimuli to the individual concerned.

It is easy to see that from such a position there can be no specified intellectual aims of the curriculum. Inquiry is what each individual does. Truth is what he is able to accept. A sound solution is one that satisfies an individual at the time it is arrived at. The important is what rouses and marshals *his* energies, the trivial that which leaves him relatively unmoved. True, there is a stubborn physical world that is not as permissive as the curriculum, and there is a common humanity. But the physical world must be discovered by the student through the pain it produces when account is not taken of it; its character as discovered through the accumulated experience of others cannot be imparted to him by instruction from without. And our common humanity will emerge only through processes initiated by each individual and only in the form superimposed by the unique characteristics of the particular human being involved.

Thus what begins as a theory of behavior transforms itself into an epistemological doctrine by tacitly ascribing to inquiry and knowledge a character that fits the original premises on behavior set forth in the theory. This doctrine does not pretend to be a theory of knowledge, but only a theory of learning. Hence it does not assert anything about truth and falsehood, validity and invalidity. But in its very silence on such matters, it illustrates the weakness of incomplete doctrines of behavior as principles of education. Without investigating the characteristics of knowledge as signs of the nature of learning and discovery, the doctrine sees no reason against inferring them from the limited characteristics of learning it has uncovered.

Autonomism as a doctrine of education is a current, romantic version of a commonplace opposition invented for inquiries in sociology: the opposition of individual and society. This doctrine begins with the fact that societies, crowds, and groups tend to impose their prevailing values on each individual through the institutions on which the individual must depend for his early nurture and protection. The doctrine goes on to point out that the values and attitudes imposed by society take no account of the individual's own wishes and needs, and, indeed, may attempt to stunt and eliminate them. Equally, society makes no objective estimate of the soundness of its own views and values. The doctrine then concludes that the continued existence of the individual and, further, the continuing survival of the society, require that some individuals somehow escape from the domination of society if they can—become each an "autonomous man." (It should be noted that the "autonomous man" is not the same as the "individual" of non-directivism. This individual is defined in its own terms: the person is the more individual as

he explores and develops his unique capacities. The autonomous man is defined in terms of what he is not: he is the more
autonomous the more he deviates from society. Hence, where
the "individual" studies himself to determine what he shall be,
the autonomous man is chained to society. He must continually
scrutinize it in order to determine what not to be.)

In such a view, education can be distinguished as "good" and
"bad." The bad system of education inculcates the values of a
society and acts as society's agent in subduing the individual to
it. Good education subverts the hegemony of society by aiding
the individual to escape from its dominion. The curriculum puts
heavy stress on sociology, therapy, practical training. Sociology
becomes the science that studies the operation of social institutions in order to inform the student of the stratagems by which
society seeks to incorporate him. To sociology are added the
therapy by which he is encouraged to rebel and the practical
training that will provide him with the tactics by which to
achieve and maintain his autonomy. Discussion takes no interest
in inquiries as such, either as object or subject. Discussion is
concerned primarily with understanding the operations of institutions as discovered by sociology and secondarily with proffer-
ing, through the example of the discussion leader, a model and
mentor of autonomy.

From the point of view of autonomism, some space in the
curriculum may be allotted to some of the other traditional
disciplines, but their character is transformed in order to make
them coherent with the predominantly normative and practical
character of autonomism. Mathematics and the natural sciences,
for example, cease to be enterprises addressed in their own way
to their own subject matter. Rather they are studied as symp-
toms or instruments of social action. Changes in problems or
principles in a discipline are considered not as attempts to
master subject matter, but as expressions of social trends or as
instances of individual escapes from social dominion. Galileo
serves as a famous example. In the same way, history becomes a
parade of events and an anthology of documents through which
the student can see competition for dominion among different
crowds, classes, or castes; or detect the operation of their propaganda. The arts are examined as evidence of social trends or as

monuments to an achieved autonomy. Since inquiry in all sciences other than sociology is externally determined by society, an examination of their methods as methods of inquiry is fruitless. And in sociology, since the character of its subject matter is taken as known absolutely (institutions and operations of subduction), as is its aim (to understand society in order to escape its dominion), an examination of what are alleged to be its various principles and methods is only a pointless intellectual game.

Thus, while group dynamism takes the group as its principle and while non-directivism establishes the uniqueness of the individual, autonomism canonizes adolescent rebellion. All three doctrines begin as normative or descriptive views of behavior and end by inventing an epistemology that tailors the intellectual aims of the curriculum to fit the terms of their incomplete theories of behavior.

What we have attempted to show can be summarized thus: many of the truths of current psychological studies are part-truths, and from part-truths dependable practical inferences cannot be drawn, however impeccable the logic may seem to be. . . . We may agree with the group dynamicist that men in our society work well in groups and are always, in some sense, members of groups. We may decide that work must, indeed, be done. But it does not follow that all work must take place in groups or that all learning should employ group dynamics. And certainly, it does not follow that what is learned shall only be that which is most adaptable to the group situation. For men are more than literal members of a literal group. In the first place, a given man is a member of many groups. Consequently, he brings to any one group whatever he garners from membership in others. Further, what he brings from one group to another he brings as *an individual.* . . .

In short, the fact that a man is always a member of a group, has kinship with other human beings, does not mean that he is that and that only. He is also a private person and an individual person, drawing on his numerous memberships and kinships in a way not precisely duplicated by any other person.

In the same way, we may agree with the non-directivist that

an individual human organism can employ no resources that are not its own. But it does not follow therefrom that he must be left to sink or swim as best he may. For he is also a person who can borrow from others and make what they give his own.

The patent cure for part-truths is, of course, whole truths. But this is a counsel either of perfection or of despair. The subject matter of psychology is enormously complex, and its students cannot be expected to emerge suddenly with the whole truth concerning it. Nor should we ask the psychologist to remain silent until the whole truth is in his hands, for larger truths in science grow from the conflict and conciliation of partial truths.

Nor does the cure consist of another half-truth, such as the dictum that psychology concerns only the means and not the aims of education. In the first place, sound truths about the human person tell us something about ends as well as means. What is soundly understood in the doctrine of non-directivism tells us that one aim of education may well be to help young people learn how to learn from others with greater freedom. What is soundly understood from group dynamics may properly suggest that one aim, among others, of education is to teach people how to work well with a diversity of persons and groups.

On the other hand, what is overstated or misunderstood in psychology can lead to errors about means that are just as serious as the errors about aims that they may suggest. It is no more sound a conclusion that all teaching should take place via group dynamics than it is to conclude that what is taught should be limited and subordinated to the teaching of "we-ness." Non-directive instruction is not the only *method* of teaching, any more than the aims suggested by the doctrine are the only aims.

A sound cure—no simple panacea—consists of recognizing half-truths for what they are and using them with an eye to their proper value and limitations. For the educational psychologist, this means three modifications of what appear to be his current tendencies. In the first place, he might well spend more time on his research and somewhat less on evangelisms for his imperfect formulations. Second, he might begin to talk more with others of his guild, bringing the several part-truths developed by different psychologists or "schools" into conflict and controversy directly with one another instead of through conflicting practices in schools and classrooms. Thereby, he would hasten the process by which the partial truths encompassed in doctrinaire formulations are brought together in more comprehensive and realistic structures. Third, he might pay much more attention to the common ethic of research that requires that one scrutinize one's work for its premises and assumptions, identify them, recognize their limitations and artificialities, and show forth these artifices and limitations so that all who read may note. . . .

Finally, since it takes two to make a corruption, there is a contribution to be made by the working teacher and administrator in our schools. They can bring common sense to bear on bright and shiny doctrines of behavior, the common sense that warns us that, about things as complex as the human person and human society, short and simple generalities must be either empty, false, or incomplete.

AIMS AS RELATIVE:
EDUCATION AS ITS OWN END*

John Dewey

If we now turn to the subjects from which are drawn the materials that are to be brought to bear upon educational problems, we are forced to recognize a fact already incidentally noted. There is no subject-matter intrinsically marked off, earmarked so to say, as the content of educational science. Any methods and any facts and principles from any subject whatsoever that enable the problems of administration and instruction to be dealt with in a bettered way are pertinent. Thus, in all that concerns the bearing of physical conditions upon the success of school work—as in the case of ventilation, temperature, etc., already mentioned—physiology and related sciences are sources of scientific content. In other problems, such as making budgets, cost-accountings, etc., economic theory is drawn upon. It may be doubted whether with reference to some aspect or other of education there is any organized body of knowledge that may not need to be drawn upon to become a source of educational science.

This consideration explains many phenomena in the present situation. It accounts for the rapid growth of interest in the development of scientific content for educational practices in so many different lines of activity. We have become only recently alive to the complexity of the educative process and aware of the number and variety of disciplines that must contribute if the process is to go on in an intelligently directed way. In accounting for the manifestation of enthusiastic activity on the part of some, the situation also explains the skeptical indifference of many about the whole matter. Not merely inert conservatives in the general public but many professors in other lines in universities have not been awakened to the complexity of the educational undertaking. Hence, such persons regard the activities of

* Reprinted from *The Sources of a Science of Education* (New York, Liveright, 1929), pp. 48–60, 70–74. By permission of Kappa Delta Pi, an Honor Society in Education, owners of the copyright.

those in departments of education as futile and void of serious meaning. . . .

Recognition of the variety of sciences that must be focused when solving any educational problem tends to breadth of view and to more serious and prolonged effort at balance of the variety of factors which enter into even the simplest problems of teaching and administration. The uncontrolled succession of waves of one-sided temporarily dominating interests and slogans that have affected educational practice and theory could thus be reduced.

In spite of the wide and indeterminate field of sciences that are sources of scientific content in education, there are certain subjects that occupy a privileged position. By common consent, I suppose, psychology and sociology hold such positions. The philosophy of education is a source of the science of education, but one less often recognized as such. We are, I think, habituated to thinking of the sciences as feeders of philosophy rather than of philosophy as a source of science. Philosophy is looked at by those who dignify it as a subject which analyzes critically the premises that are uncritically assumed in the special sciences, or else as a complete intellectual organization of their results. Others take a less respectful and perhaps more popular view of it, and regard it as a constantly vanishing quantity, dealing by way of opinion and speculation with matters that sciences have not got around to dealing with in a positive way. Personally, I think there is truth in both of these views, but that neither one touches the heart of the relationship of philosophy and science. There is in every subject at every time a serial progression from the more specific to the more general. The only distinction we can profitably draw is to say that science lies toward the specific pole and philosophy toward the general, while there is no definite line where one leaves off and the other begins.

It is because of this fact that there is a reciprocal relation between them, each feeding the other as a source. Were this the time and place, it could be shown from the history of the sciences, mathematical, physical and biological, that ideas originating at the philosophic end (general, often vague and speculative, if you please) have been indispensable factors in the generation of science. An examination of history would also show that there is no steady one-way movement; the movement from general to special is not one that has a definite conclusion that stays put. Specialized results recurrently get too set and rigid because of isolation due to the very specialization by which they are obtained. Fermentation and fructification then come in from the pole of general ideas and points of view. Specific results are shaken up, loosened and placed in new contexts.

The revolution in astronomical and physical science effected by Galileo, Descartes and Newton is a case in point. The controlling hypotheses were derived from philosophic ideas that seemed to their early contemporaries highly speculative. The idea of "evolution" was developed in philosophy before it made its appearance in biology. Metaphysical speculations regarding the relation of mind and body conditioned the creation and growth of physiological psychology.

These illustrations do not prove that the influence of philosophy as a source of science has been wholly to the good. On the contrary, there have been in every instance hang-overs from earlier philosophies which have been detrimental, and which have had to be eliminated from science with toil and pain. But aside from the fact that new general ideas have always played a part in finally getting rid of these hang-overs, it is an undeniable fact that the human mind works in this way, and that whether desirable or undesirable, it cannot be eliminated.

If we ask why this should be so, we are at once confronted with the rôle of *hypotheses* in every scientific undertaking, because of the necessary place they occupy in every intellectual operation. Hypotheses form a scale from more general to more specific, and at every point the more general ones affect the more specific. This fact of dependence is overlooked only because the more general one is so incorporated in the special and detailed ones that it is forgotten. Then some crisis in scientific development leads to its detection and revision. Physical science is at present undergoing precisely such a reconstruction.

Philosophy of education is, accordingly, a source of the science of education in the degree in which it provides working hypotheses of comprehensive application. Both "working" and "hypotheses" are important. It is hypotheses, not fixed and final principles or truths that are provided; they have to be tested and modified as they are used in suggesting and directing the detailed work of observation and understanding. They are *working* ideas; special investigations become barren and one-sided in the degree in which they are conducted without reference to a wider, more general view. This statement is particularly applicable in the early stages of formation of a new science. Physics, chemistry, biology, all have behind them a history that has put them in possession of relatively tested and solid general principles. Just because educational science has no such achievement of laws to fall back upon, it is in a tentative and inchoate state which renders it especially in need of direction by large and fruitful hypotheses. No matter how these are obtained, they are intrinsically philosophical in nature, good or bad philosophy as the case may be. To treat them as scientific rather than as philosophic is to conceal from view their hypothetical character and to freeze them into rigid dogmas that hamper instead of assisting actual inquiry.

It is sometimes said that philosophy is concerned with determining the ends of education while the science of education determines the means to be used. As one who is a philosopher rather than a scientist I might be inclined to welcome a statement that confers upon philosophy such an honorable position. Without a good deal of interpretation, it is, however, likely to give rise to more false than true conceptions. In this interpretation there are two important considerations.

In the first place, the notion easily gives rise to, even if it does not logically imply, a misapprehension of the relation of a philosophy of education to educational practices and direct experience in the field. In any vital sense it is these practices which determine educational ends. Concrete educational experience is the primary source of all inquiry and reflection because it sets the problems, and tests, modifies, confirms or refutes the conclusions of intellectual investigation. The philosophy of education neither originates nor settles ends. It occupies an intermediate and instrumental or regulative place. Ends actually reached, consequences that actually accrue, are surveyed, and their values estimated in the light of a general scheme of values.

But if a philosophy starts to reason out its conclusions without definite and constant regard to the concrete experiences that define the problem for thought, it becomes speculative in a way that justifies contempt. As far as ends and values are concerned, the empirical material that is necessary to keep philosophy from being fantastic in content and dogmatic in form is supplied by the ends and values which are produced in educational processes as these are actually executed. What a philosophy of education can contribute is range, freedom and constructive or creative invention. The worker in any field gets preoccupied with more immediate urgencies and results. When one begins to extend the range, the scope, of thought, to consider obscure collateral consequences that show themselves in a more extensive time-span, or in reference to an enduring development, that one begins to philosophize whether the process is given that name or not. What is *termed* philosophy is only a more systematic and persistent performance of this office.

What I have termed the contribution of "freedom," of liberation, is a necessary accompaniment of this breadth of survey of actual ends or consequences. The professional practitioner in any field, from a factory to a church and schoolhouse, is in danger of getting tied down, of getting habit-bound, compensating for this rigidity by impulsive excursions, undertaken according to temperament and circumstance, when routine becomes intolerable. I do not say that philosophers see life steadily and see it whole; complete achievement in this respect is humanly impossible. But *any one* is philosophical in the degree in which he makes a consistent effort in this direction. The result is emancipation. When this liberation is confined with the mind, the inner consciousness, of any one, it affords intense personal gratification, but it effects nothing and becomes specious. Its effect is found only in operation. For a philosophy of education this operation is found in enabling practitioners to carry on their work in a more liberal spirit, with escape from tradition and routine and one-sided personal interests and whims.

This contribution is made by way of the third function mentioned; namely, constructive imagination and invention. It is not enough to criticize the narrow limitations of accepted ends and values. This needful task is but the negative side of the function of suggesting new ends, new methods, new materials. In performing this office, provision of scope of estimate and liberation of mind comes to a head. As far as the philosophy of education effects anything important, this is what it accomplishes for those who study it. Ideas are ideas, that is, suggestions for activities to be undertaken, for experiments to be tried. The proof of the pudding is in the eating. The philosophy of education not only draws its original material as to ends and value from actual experience in education, but it goes back to these experiences for testing, confirmation, modification, and the provision of further materials. This is what is meant when it is said that its work is intermediate and instrumental, not original or final.

Our other point concerns the relations of science and philosophy with respect to means and ends. The statement as often made gives rise to misapprehension. It leads to the notion that means and ends are separate from each other, each having its own fixed province. In reality, ends that are incapable of realization are ends only in name. Ends must be framed in the light of available means. It may even be asserted that ends are only means brought to full interaction and integration. The other side of this truth is that means are fractional parts of ends. When means and ends are viewed as if they were separate, and to be dealt with by different persons who are concerned with independent provinces, there is imminent danger of two bad results.

Ends, values, become empty, verbal; too remote and isolated to have more than an emotional content. Means are taken to signify means already at hand, means accepted because they are already in common use. As far as this view prevails, the work of a science of education is reduced to the task of refining and perfecting the existing mechanism of school operations. Lack of efficiency, unnecessary waste, in the teaching of reading, writing, numbers, history, geography are detected so that they may be eliminated. More efficient methods of accomplishing the ends that already obtain are devised. This is good as far as it goes. But it overlooks a fundamental issue. How far do the existing ends, the actual consequences of current practices go, even when perfected? The important problem is devising *new* means in contradistinction to improved use of means already given. For "new means" does not signify merely new ways of accomplishing more efficiently ends already current, but means that will yield consequences, ends, that are qualitatively different. We can assign means to science and ends to philosophy only under the condition that there be persistent and unremitting interaction between the two. . . .

Education is autonomous and should be free to determine its own ends, its own objectives. To go outside the educational function and to borrow objectives from an external source is to surrender the educational cause. Until educators get the independence and courage to insist that educational aims are to be formed as well as executed within the educative process, they will not come to consciousness of their own function. Others will then have no great respect for educators because educators do not respect their own social place and work.

Such a statement will seem to many persons both absurd and presumptuous. It would be presumptuous if it had been said that *educators* should determine objectives. But the statement was that the *educative process* in its integrity and continuity should determine them. Educators have a place in this process, but they are not it, far from it. The notion that it is absurd springs from failure to view the function in its entirety. For education is itself a process of discovering what values are worth while and are to be pursued as objectives. To see what is going on and to observe the results of what goes on so as to see their further consequences in the process of growth, and so on indefinitely, is the only way in which the value of what takes place can be judged. To look to some outside source to provide aims is to fail to know what education is as an ongoing process. What a society is, it is, by and large, as a product of education, as far as its animating spirit and purpose are concerned. Hence it does not furnish a standard to which education is to conform. It supplies material by which to judge more clearly what education as it has been carried on has done to those who have been subjected to it. Another conclusion follows. There is no such thing as a fixed and final set of objectives, even for the time being or temporarily. Each day of teaching ought to enable a teacher to revise and better in some respect the objectives aimed at in previous work.

In saying these things, I am only recurring in another form to the idea with which I set out. The scientific content of education consists of whatever subject-matter, selected from other fields, enables the educator, whether administrator or teacher, to see and to think more clearly and deeply about whatever he is doing. Its value is not to supply objectives to him, any more than it is to supply him with ready-made rules. Education is a mode of life, of action. As an act it is wider than science. The latter, however, renders those who engage in the act more intelligent, more thoughtful, more aware of what they are about, and they thus rectify and enrich in the future what they have been doing in the past. Knowledge of the objectives which society actually strives for and the consequences actually attained may be had in some measure through a study of the social sciences. This knowledge may render educators more circumspect, more critical, as to what they are doing. It may inspire better insight into what is going on here and now in the home or school; it may enable teachers and parents to look further ahead and judge on the basis of consequences in a longer course of developments. But it must operate through their own ideas, plannings, observations, judgments. Otherwise it is not *educational* science at all, but merely so much sociological information.

The sources of educational science are any portions of ascertained knowledge that enter into the heart, head and hands of educators, and which, by entering in, render the performance of the educational function more enlightened, more humane, more truly educational than it was before. But there is no way to discover what *is* "more truly educational" except by the continuation of the educational act itself. The discovery is never made; it is always making. It may conduce to immediate ease or momentary efficiency to seek an answer for questions outside of education, in some material which already has scientific prestige. But such a seeking is an abdication, a surrender. In the end, it only lessens the chances that education in actual operation will provide the materials for an improved science. It arrests growth; it prevents the thinking that is the final source of all progress. Education is by its nature an endless circle or spiral. It is an activity which *includes* science within itself. In its very process it sets more problems to be further studied, which then react into the educative process to change it still further, and thus demand more thought, more science, and so on, in everlasting sequence.

AIMS AS UNIVERSAL: EDUCATION AS FORMATION OF GOOD HABITS*

Mortimer J. Adler

I have chosen to indicate the demonstration of the proposition which is central to the issue about principles in contemporary discussion. The Deweyites and progressives flatly deny what I am here affirming, and affirm, on the contrary, that the ends of education are relative and variable. Since the problems of education are practical, and since in every sphere of practical thinking, the ends are the first principles, it should be clear that from the resolution of this issue about the status of the ends, many consequences will follow with regard to the solution of all subordinate problems. In fact, I would say that every genuinely philosophical issue, between the educational opponents I have named, is crucially affected by whether the ends are absolute or relative, universal and necessary, or particular and contingent. . . .

The conclusion I am trying to prove can be stated in the following manner: The aim of education should be the same for all men (i.e. everywhere and always, in every mode of society, every condition of life, etc.). This proposition is identical in meaning with the proposition that the ends of education are absolute and universal, for what any practical process aims at are its ends; hence, to say that education always and everywhere (for all men) aims at the same thing is to say that it has the same ends. The words 'absolute' and 'universal' are thus seen to mean just what is signified by the words 'the same for all men.'

Furthermore, as we have seen, in any sphere of practical thinking, the ultimate ends are the first principles; hence, if the ultimate ends of education are absolute and universal, so too are the first principles of that practical thinking about education

* Reprinted from "In Defense of Philosophy of Education," The Forty-First Yearbook of the National Society for the Study of Education, Part I, 1941, *Philosophies of Education,* pp. 238–47. By permission of the NSSE, owners of the copyright.

which is educational philosophy. It will be noted, furthermore, that the proposition to be proved is practical rather than theoretic in its mode: It says what should be done, what education should aim at. To say that education *should* always and everywhere aim at the same objectives is equivalent to saying that its ultimate ends, truly determined *are* absolute and universal. Here we see an equivalence between what looks like a theoretic statement and a practical statement; but any statement of *what ends are* is only apparently theoretic, as its conversion into the practical form (what *should* be aimed at) reveals.

Finally, let me say that in speaking of the ultimate ends of education I am restricting my view to education as one phase of human activity among many others. The ultimate end of every phase of human activity, considered without differentiation, is happiness. The reason, then, why I do not say that happiness is the ultimate end of education is because that would fail to discriminate educational activity from political activity, domestic activity, the activity of every other human art, for all these aim ultimately at happiness, though each has an end or ends peculiarly appropriate to itself. Hence we must regard the ultimate ends of education not as final ends, without qualification, but as final only with respect to education as a special process and activity distinct from government, domestic management, etc. It follows, of course, that the ends which are final specifically for education, like the ends which are final for other special activities, must in turn be means to that which is the ultimate end of every and all human activity, namely, happiness. And it should be understood, as well, that if the ends of education are absolute and universal, so is the ultimate end of human life. Human happiness, truly conceived, *is* the same for all men, which, as we have seen, is another way of saying that what all men *should* aim at, as the complete objective of their lives, is the same.

The conclusion to be proved being clear, I shall now state the premises which are proximately probative of it. Here is the syllogism:

| *Major:* | Good habits (virtues) are the same for all men. |
| *Minor:* | Education should aim at the formation of good habits. |

Conclusion: Education should aim at the same objectives for all men (or, what is equivalent, the aim of education should be the same for all men).

Now, neither the major nor the minor premise is self-evident; hence we must proceed with their demonstration. From this point on we have two independent lines of proof, one converging on the major premise, the other converging on the minor. Let us consider the proof of the minor first.

The proof of the minor premise seems to involve the following propositions: (1) That men are born with various capacities which are undeveloped, (2) that in the course of life, human growth involves—more than certain physical developments—the development of native capacities for various kinds of activity, such intellectual activities as knowing and thinking and artistic production, such moral activities as desiring, willing, and social coöperation, (3) that the development of these various capacities for operation are habits formed by activities appropriate to the different sorts of capacity, (4) that habits can be either good or bad according as they conform to or violate the natural tendency of each capacity toward its own perfection, (5) that the betterment of men consists in the formation of good habits, i.e., the development of their capacities by good rather than bad habits, and (6) that education should aim at the betterment of men. By combining the last two propositions (5 and 6), we get the conclusion: Education should aim at the formation of good habits.

We are now required to examine the premises which enter into this conclusion. The two crucial premises are definitions, one the definition of education in its minimum terms, the other the definition of *good* with respect to habit.

The definition of education, in these minimum terms, is indisputable. This can be shown in a series of dilemmas. First, either education is a process whereby men are *changed,* by themselves or others, or it is not. Here the latter alternative is self-evidently impossible, for the meaning of education is absolutely incompatible with the denial of change. Hence we have the second dilemma; men can be changed by education *either* for better *or* for worse. This second dilemma is intelligible however "better" and "worse" be defined, whether there are objective (absolute and universal) standards of good and bad in human life, or only subjective (relative and variable) standards. Furthermore, there is no choice between the alternatives as stated, for both are equally possible: It is possible for education to change men for worse, as well as for better. But when we realize that education is a practical process, we realize that it cannot be defined except in terms of its end, or what it *should* do. Only if education were entirely natural could we define it in terms of what it is. That being so, our dilemma becomes a choice between saying that education should aim to change men for better or that it should change them for worse. Clearly the latter alternative is impossible, for all men, however else they differ in conceiving education, think of it as something good; and what aims to make men worse cannot be so regarded. Nor can it be said that good education is defined as education which aims at making men better, and bad education as education which aims at making men worse, for if education is itself understood as something good, then the phrase 'good education' is redundant and the phrase 'bad education' is strictly self-contradictory. Whatever makes men worse intentionally cannot be regarded as education at all, any more than a law which is intentionally unjust can be regarded as a law, for it is nothing but a disguised expression of tyrannical force. So just as a bad law is a law in name only, so bad education is education in name only. This excludes, of course, the circumstances in which education, rightly intended for human betterment, accidentally and unintentionally fails in execution. Hence we see that the definition of education as a process of human betterment, as activity which should aim to make men better, is self-evidently true. The foregoing discussion is not a demonstration of this definition; it is merely an explication of its basic terms 'education' and 'betterment,' which, when understood, enable us immediately to understand the truth of the definition.

Thus is established the sixth proposition in the series which I enumerated as relevant to the minor premise. But the minor premise was that education should aim at the formation of good habits. In order to pass from the truth of the definition (sixth proposition) to the truth of the minor premise, it is necessary to show that human betterment consists, in part if not wholly, in the formation of good habits. The first five propositions enumerated are directed to the definition of the good, as opposed to the bad, with respect to human habituation. Now we have a choice in procedure. 'Good habit' is a term in the major premise as well as in the minor. Hence we can establish the definition of *good* as to habit either in the context of proving the major, or of proving the minor. I shall take the former course, for reasons that need not be given. The proof of the minor is thus temporarily completed. I say *temporarily,* for its real completion depends on the analysis of good habits. For the time being, then, we shall regard human betterment as depending on the formation of good habits, and if it can be so regarded then it is clear that education should aim at the formation of good habits if it should aim at human betterment. The first five propositions enumerated have served the purpose of making this point intelligible, but they are neither self-evident nor proved. That must be accomplished in the proof of the major premise. Unless it is, the minor premise depends upon unverified assumptions about the possibility of a demonstrable distinction among habits as *good* and as *bad.*

I turn, therefore, to the proof of the major premise, and here we face two tasks: First, to show that all men have the same natural capacities; second, to show that for every capacity or power which can be habituated there is a natural basis for distinguishing between good and bad habituation. If these two things can be shown, the whole of the major premise will follow necessarily—that good habits are the same for all men. I shall undertake these two tasks in the order named.

(1) The conclusion to be proved (that all men have the same natural capacities) must first be interpreted. It does not mean that all men possess each of these capacities in the same degree, to the same extent. All of the facts of individual difference with respect to every measurable human ability are quite compatible with the proposition to be proved—that the fundamental abilities are the same for all men essentially, that every being born a man is born with the same set of powers, however limited in degree, or however much held in abeyance by pathological conditions, such powers may be. The proof is accomplished in the following syllogism:

Major:	All individuals having the same specific nature have the same natural powers or capacities.
Minor:	All individual men have the same specific human nature.
Conclusion:	All individual men have the same natural powers or capacities.

Now neither of these two premises is, strictly speaking, self-evident. Each must be proved. I shall return presently to what is involved in their proof, after I have accomplished the second task with equal brevity.

(2) What is to be proved here is the definition of a good habit as that development of a power or capacity which conforms to the natural tendency of that power or capacity. This proof depends upon the conception of the good of anything which can be perfected (which has potentialities capable of being actualized) as the actualization of its potencies. And this, in turn, depends upon the metaphysical conception of the good as convertible with being: Anything has as much goodness as it has being. Hence if a thing is naturally constituted by capacities to be developed, its ultimate good consists in their development, for thereby it has more actual being. Habits as developments of powers are perfections in so far as they increase and complete the being of the thing. But so far we can only say that whatever has powers subject to habituation is perfected by the formation of habits, without distinction among habits as good or bad, for any habit appears to be the actualization of a power, the development of a capacity. It is necessary, therefore, to go further and show that each power is itself a natural being, albeit an accident of the substance possessing it, and because it is natural can only be perfected by one mode of development. To do this, we must understand the metaphysical truth that every determinate potency is a tendency toward a certain actuality. Hence every natural power of man, being a determinate potency, tends toward a certain mode of actualization, a certain development. Now human habits without qualification are the development or actualization of human capacities for operation or activity, but habits are good only if they are developments conforming to the natural tendency of the power they develop.

This last point must be understood in a twofold manner. (*a*)

In the case of the intellect itself, which, as a power of knowing, naturally tends toward the possession of truth as its perfection, the habit of knowledge is good by reason of conformity to the natural tendency of the cognitive power, and the habit of error is bad by reason of violation of that tendency. If the intellect were indifferently a power of knowing and not-knowing, possession of truth and possession of error would be indifferently good as actualizations of the cognitive power. Knowledge (possession of truth) is a good intellectual habit only because the intellect is a power of knowing, not a power of not-knowing. (*b*) In the case of every human power, other than the intellect itself, the natural tendency of the power is toward that actualization of itself which conforms to reason. This follows from the subordination of all human powers, in their exercised acts, to reason itself. Hence, in the case of every power there is a natural tendency which habit can violate or to which it can conform; and in conforming, the habit is good; in violating, it is bad. Clearly, then, a man is not bettered simply by habit formation, for if the habits be bad they impede the development of his total nature by violating the tendency of his powers to their own perfection. In short, human nature, partly constituted by its natural potencies at birth, is bettered or perfected in the course of life only through the formation of good habits.

All of the analysis in (2) above (the definition of a good habit), can now be summarized in a single proposition: Every human capacity which can be habituated tends naturally toward a certain development and so, for each power or capacity, good habits are those which conform to the natural tendency of the power they develop. If now this proposition be combined with the conclusion of the syllogism in (1) above (all men have the same natural capacities), we are able to prove the major premise of the original syllogism. Thus:

Major: Every human capacity can be determined by habits which are good by conformity to the natural tendency of the power being habituated.

Minor: All individual men have the same natural powers or capacities.

Conclusion: All men are capable of having the same good habits.

This conclusion can be converted into the proposition: *Good habits are the same for all men.* This was the original major. Now if we combine that with the original minor—*Education should aim at the formation of good habits*—we get the conclusion which was to be proved, namely, *the aim of education should be the same for all men,* or *the ends of education are absolute and universal.* (In the light of the reasoning which establishes it, this conclusion is equivalent to the truth that the moral and intellectual virtues are the ends of education.)

The proof is completely *indicated,* but the demonstration is far from being completed. I can show its incompleteness easily by now enumerating some of the propositions which are involved in the proof of the original major premise—propositions which are either demonstrable and must be proved or which are self-evident but require their evident truth to be explicated. I say 'some' because the enumeration is far from exhaustive; but it will do to indicate how much remains to be proved before this demonstration can be completed. (1) Corporeal substances exist. (2) Corporeal substances are constituted as compositions of matter and form. (3) Corporeal substances differ essentially or accidentally, according as they are individuals of different species (have diverse specific natures) or as they are numerically distinct individuals having the same specific nature. (4) The essential distinction of substances is an absolute distinction in kind, without intermediates. (5) The distinction between living and nonliving substances is an essential distinction. (6) Living substances have vital powers which are essentially distinct from the potencies of inanimate things. (7) Man is essentially distinct from all other living things. (8) The essential distinction between man and brute as species in the genus animal is that man is rational and brute is irrational. (9) Only man can know intellectually and only man has free will. (10) Man has all the vital powers possessed by other living things (plants and brutes), and in addition has powers not possessed by them, i.e., intellect or reason, and will. (11) The vital powers of animals can be developed by the modification of instinctive determinations, but only human powers can be habituated. (12) Habit is the modification of a human power resulting from its rational and free exercise. (13) All men are of the same species, i.e., they have essentially the same nature, and differ *inter se* only in accidental respects, i.e., in such traits as complexion, weight, height, etc., or in the *degree* to which they possess characteristically human abilities, abilities common, *in some degree,* to all. (14) All men have the same vital powers, for the vital powers any living thing possesses are determined by its specific nature. (15) A vital power is a determinate potency and as such is a nature having a tendency toward a certain definite actualization. (16) The good is convertible with being. (17) The good of any imperfect thing (anything composite of potency and actuality, or matter and form) consists in the actualization of its potencies. (18) In the case of human powers, the actualization of potency is good only if it conforms to the natural tendency of that power to its own perfection.

Of these eighteen propositions, only two are self-evident, the 3rd and 16th. All the rest are demonstrable and can be proved. And of these, the 1st, 5th, 7th, 8th, and 13th are conclusions which must be demonstrated inductively. (Though some self-evident truths and some *deductively demonstrated* conclusions will occur in the a posteriori proof of these five propositions, the proof here must also rest upon certain evident truths known by *intellectual observation* of existing facts.) The remaining eleven propositions can be deductively proved. But in neither case does the work of demonstrating these sixteen propositions belong to the philosophy of education. These propositions are truths in metaphysics, the philosophy of nature and the philosophy of man (which will be recognized by the readers of this book as 'faculty psychology'). All of this knowledge is necessarily presupposed by the philosophy of education. It would not be difficult to prove, in terms of this presupposed knowledge, that the ends of (specifically human) education are absolute and universal. That, at least, should be clear from the foregoing indication of the demonstration as running backwards to its ultimate roots in theoretic philosophy. But, unfortunately, even more must be presupposed for a full understanding of what has been proved. For good habits are virtues. And the virtues are both constitutive and generative means with respect to the ultimate end of all human activity, happiness. Hence to understand what it means to say that the ends of education are the

virtues requires that one understand: first, the relation of the
virtues to happiness; then, the relation of the virtues to all other
goods constitutive of that whole of goods which is happiness;
then, the division of the virtues into two groups, intellectual and
moral; then, the analysis of both sorts of virtue, with respect to
their kinds, their order to one another, and their aetiology; and
finally, the relation of all the virtues *inter se*. All of this knowledge, being concerned with human goods to be sought, is practical and belongs to ethics.

Let me, in conclusion, repeat the definition of education
which I gave in the beginning, asserting then that it could be
demonstrated. It was: Education is the process by which those
powers (abilities, capacities) of men that are susceptible to
habituation, are perfected by *good* habits, through means artisti-
cally contrived, and employed by any man to help another or
himself achieve the end in view (i.e., good habits). In so far as
this definition implies that education should be the same for all
men (i.e., should aim at the same ends), its truth is proved by
the establishment of the proposition that the ends of education
are absolute and universal. To do that, as we have seen, requires
the whole of theoretic philosophy, and this is presupposed by
the philosophy of education. The definition also requires us to
understand what the several ends are and how they are related
to one another, for it is not sufficient to know simply that they
are absolute and universal. Such understanding would involve
the complete analysis of the virtues, in themselves, in relation to
happiness, to other goods, and to each other. At this point, the
whole of ethics is presupposed. And if we examine the definition
one step further we see that it calls upon us to understand the
means in general, and the social organization and employment
of these means, in the process of education-by-another whereby
the community cares for its members. At this point, a great deal
of political philosophy is presupposed. Hence by examining the
definition of education . . . we learn . . . the reasons why the
philosophy of education presupposes almost all of theoretical
philosophy, and most of practical philosophy. . . .

EDUCATION AS THEORETICAL AND PRACTICAL*

John W. Donohue

The question is this: What is the full register of human intelligence? Or, if speaking of intelligence seems to prejudge a philosophical issue, what is the full range of those activities commonly called intelligent and what are the implications of the evidence which in themselves they constitute? It will be understood I hope, that when hereafter I speak of intelligence I use the conventional shorthand term which, translated, means "man in his intelligent activity." There is no intention of hypostatizing the mind; it is not reason that thinks but men who use their intelligences in manifold ways.

The present question can be focused by dramatizing it as a confrontation of the two most widely heard American educational theorists of the past half-century: John Dewey and Robert Maynard Hutchins. We may think of each of them as responding to our question with an answer which is twofold, having an affirmative and a negative facet. Dewey would strongly affirm the value of pragmatic, problem-solving, instrumental intelligence. Together with this affirmation there would go the rejection as purely illusory of what Aristotle called the *nous theoretikos,* the power for a kind of thought whose truth has a criterion other than that of success in action. From Hutchins, on the other hand, we would get an affirmation of the value of the speculative activity of intelligence, that power which takes hold of real things by grasping their intelligible aspect. Together with this affirmation there would go, not so much a theoretical rejection of practical intelligence, as a neglect of it amounting to an effective dismissal. No doubt both our protagonists in certain places qualify those theses which elsewhere they systematically exaggerate for didactic purposes.

* Reprinted from "From a Philosophy of Man: Reflections on Intelligence as a Dyadic Function," *Educational Theory,* 9(July, 1959), 142–43, 146–50. By permission of the author and the editor of *Educational Theory.*

Here, however, we are simply employing Dewey and Hutchins as symbols of polar positions on the scope of intelligence. Each of these theories has a worthwhile point of view and without subscribing to every detail of their individual analyses, one can readily applaud the affirmations of both. But I would, for my part, deplore their negations or exclusions. In both cases, it seems to me that a concentration on a particular insight has meant the formulation of a theory of intelligence which is so strongly monistic in bent as to quite impoverish the concrete phenomena and to cover rather than discover certain of its implications. For this reason, therefore, I find each of these interpretations insufficient as an answer to the question proposed. The theory to which, instead, I would myself adhere, maintains that human intelligence is pluralistic in its function and that the vital apprehension of valid knowledge is, in the concrete order, polymorphic. Intelligence, so to say, has more than one note and more than one key. Its register embraces both instrumental and contemplative approaches to reality and each of these is genuinely fruitful.

If we turn for a moment to the psychologist we will be reminded that our cognitive experience first presents itself to reflection as a marvellously rich, though confused, complex. It enfolds sensation and imagination, each of them ministering to and neither of them identical with intelligence. It includes intuition, reasoning and memories as well as the making of hypotheses and systems. In the living person it takes on distinctive colorations from such factors as sex, age, habitat and individual history. It is often interwined with a profound affective disposition which, as Rousselot pointed out, itself heightens perception and provides man with a quasi-new "power of abstraction," a new formal object. Thus the optimist is stirred by and draws from all things their smiling aspect and the pessimist will say with Jaques in *As You Like It:* "I can suck melancholy out of a song as a weasel sucks eggs." [1] The psychologist himself may not be interested in analyzing this complex into its several factors for the sake of regrouping them thereafter in a synthesis.

[1] Pierre Rousselot, "Amour Spirituel et Synthèse Aperceptive," *Revue de Philosophie,* 16 (March, 1910), 225–40.

He may simply be content with delineating as accurately as possible the intellectual syndromes. It would seem defensible, however, for the philosopher to attempt such analyses so long as he makes his abstractions from actual experience and is not unmindful that, since the elements abstracted are never perfectly isolated in the concrete, the abstract formula is necessarily partial.

It is here proposed that one such analysis of our intellectual experiences confirms a celebrated thesis enunciated in the sixth book of the *Nicomachean Ethics.* According to that thesis the manifold expressions of human intelligent activity point to a fundamental division between two archetypical expressions of intelligence, the practical and the speculative, neither one of which can be reduced to the other. This does not mean a distinction between two minds but rather between two modes or manners of intelligent action. There is a practical valence of intelligence which shows itself in the arts and technics as well as in scientific experimentation and in the solving of not a few problems in human relationships. Moreover, the validation of all these ways-means or ends-means activities lies in their degree of actual success. But there is also another primary form of intelligent action for which it is nowadays somewhat hard to find a nonderogatory label since such terms as "speculative, theoretical, contemplative" are, in certain milieus at least, rather overcast. Let us call it, again for convenience's sake, the insightful or meditative intelligence—a prehensive power which can penetrate to a true, though not of course to an exhaustive understanding of things as they really are. When men think in this fashion they apprehend to comprehend and the knowledge generated may well be quite useful. Yet even if it were not, it would still be an immanent enrichment and a value or end in itself. The philosophical thinking, even of the strict experimentalist, involves refined expressions of this reflective function and it has its everyday actualizations in all those cases which indicate that often we do know more about nature than just its instrumental characteristics.

In a moment we shall consider some of those phenomena in a little detail, to suggest in a rudimentary way bits of the experiential evidence whose exigencies and hints are best accounted for by a theory of basic pluralism in the ways of knowing. . . .

Dewey, for one, would of course go much beyond this. For him all thought originates in necessity rather than wonder and all thinking is in some sense a problem solving. Not only would he explain in terms of its success the truth of that practical intelligence which is deployed in the ordering of concrete means to determined productive or ethical goals but he would reconstruct the whole philosophical explanation of experience from that base and dismiss whatever could not somehow be brought within this orbit. But my concern at this point is rather to advise those of an excessively rationalistic bent not to underestimate the mind's pragmatic role. If one lives in the past one may be inclined to nurture only a narrowly contemplative function of intelligence but if one lives in history one cannot ignore its operative power. For me the central intuition which is the nuclear value of the instrumentalist outlook is found in this reminder that reality is not completely disclosed by meditation —some of its facets must be approached in and through overt action—and that in any event the career of thought is indeed instrumental to the whole of human existence and loses its plenary richness if divorced from that existential context.

Once I have correctly perceived it, I do indeed know that the object across the room is a chair and there is no particular reason why I should say that this awareness is not knowledge or even that it is not useful. But I also know more about that chair when I sit in it. The example is trivial but there is another area in which the principle is enormously significant. For as Maritain has remarked the pragmatic intuition finds its fullest application in the moral order. There is a whole realm in which knowledge not completed by action is thin and unreal. Only the compassionate man, for instance, really knows what compassion is. It is no wonder that problems of human conduct were the ones that most engaged the mind and heart of John Dewey. Whenever he talks of knowledge the thought of its moral implications is not far away. Thus he observed in *Moral Principles in Education* that the whole business of the teacher is to see to it that the greatest possible number of ideas acquired by young people are so acquired as to become true motive forces of conduct. And in this he would have been understood by Emmanuel Mounier, the great French Christian Personalist, who wrote: "A thought which does not lead to a decision is an incomplete thought." [5] Not false, indeed, but incomplete.

The second half of the thesis I should like to maintain asserts that there is an authentic knowledge, a truth, which is not the child of practical activity and not expressed in operational formulae. Such a claim is obviously staked in highly contested territory under heavy fire from convinced experimentalists in general and positivists in particular. The latter, for instance, quite rightly suspect that to admit the possibility of meaningful propositions other than those verifiable by appeal to an activity of the bodily senses is to open the door to metaphysical and theological statements—something they most certainly do not wish to do. Conversely, a thesis like ours would be established, I suppose, if there were demonstrated the existence of a distinctive philosophical method which, while not that of the physical sciences, is still valid and even scientific in the broad sense of productive of knowledge. Instead of moving, as the physical sciences do, from explicit knowledge of one fact to explicit knowledge of another, philosophy as thus conceived would be the movement, under the intellect's own dynamism from implicit to explicit knowledge in one and the same case. But its starting point, the data from which its insights are drawn, would be experiential.

Since this whole matter of the range of intelligence is complex it is susceptible of a variety of approaches and of discussion at various levels of intensity with the temperatures varying accordingly.[6] I should like for my part here simply to underline two

[5] Emmanuel Mounier, *The Character of Man,* trans. Cynthia Rowland (New York, Harper and Brothers, 1956), p. 264.

[6] Logical positivism, for instance, is controverted in E. L. Mascall's little book, *Words and Images* (New York, Ronald Press Company, 1957). Again, the defense of a pluralism of ways of knowing has obvious links with the central position of immediate realism and for a succinct exposition of that view I cannot do better than bow to Parker's essay in the symposium, *Return to Reason* . . . or to R. J. Henle, S.J., *Method in Metaphysics* (Milwaukee, Marquette University Press, 1951). All these places argue that our cognitive interaction with the universe begins indeed with a sensory experience but that sense experience itself is more than the experience of sense-objects. For as Mascall puts the point: Perception is not identical with sensation but rather is "pri-

quite ordinary experiences which for me point inescapably to the acquisition of truth through a nonpragmatic function of intelligence. For I do not see that experiences of this sort can be adequately explained in operational terms nor yet explained away. "Nonpragmatic," does not, of course, mean "nonactive" for in these experiences one is not at all intellectually passive in the sense in which the seeing eye or a spinning tape recorder are passive. The knower is dynamic but his activity is immanent rather than instrumental and its fruits are secured without manipulations. The cases proposed here are no more than fragments suggesting the line a full-scale argument might take. One is the experience of the simple insight into intelligibility and the second is the experience of weighing values against each other.

Let us take first a homely illustration of the awareness of general truths in a concrete situation. Here is a woman dividing some apples because they seem too large to give to her young children whole. But as she does so, is she not simultaneously though unreflectively aware that any whole is greater, and necessarily greater than its parts? Does she not apprehend that pattern of intelligibility particularized in this existential gesture? Or take another example just as ordinary—seeing the point of a joke. After a number of press items had reported zoo experiments with simian finger-painters a wordless cartoon showed a picture gallery at the opening of a new exhibition. The walls were hung with swirling canvases and beneath one of them, the center of an attentive knot of bearded men and studious women wearing heavy glasses, stood the painter—a chimpanzee sporting a beret and clutching a cocktail glass. If you find it funny at all, you will do so in a glance. You will not ratiocinate, much less manipulate and if someone else fails to get the point explanations won't help much.

---

marily an *intellectual act,* an act in which the mind utilizes the phenomenon as an *objectum quo* and passes through it to grasp the concrete trans-sensible reality, whose nature is that not of sensible but of intelligible being." *Op. cit.,* p. 121. This may strike some of us as a very dark saying indeed. But in any case I am here bypassing these basic technical discussions for two good reasons. First, because I am not competent to improve upon the expositions I have just mentioned. And secondly, because the best that even a competent person could manage in a few pages would be an epitome of a complex argument and such epitomes are likely to misrepresent a case as much as to serve it.

There are other instances, still rather common but more significant, of this meditative insight. One finds it strikingly demonstrated in the frequent intuitions of artists and scientists. In these cases the truth seized does not originate in the process of verification and its meaning is not, or need not be verifiability. A careful study of the phenomena has shown that the creative intuition does often develop while the artist or scientist is struggling with a problem but the moment of insight is itself quite distinct from the hard business of working up the rich vein of experience out of which, in a flash of vision, the truth is drawn. Generally, in fact, this intuition comes in a period of relaxation when the thinker has turned to other matters or even reports that he was doing nothing. Subsequently it may be checked in practice—if, for example, it was the key to a procedure—or objectified in the finished poem, song, or picture. But this only confirms, it does not constitute the insight which in its purest form is a moment of self-validating knowledge precisely because it is a moment of sheer understanding: one has the answer because one sees that this is the way things are and must be. Quite similar is the apprehension of meaning in the events of our own personal history. This has both its everyday manifestations and others of a highly critical sort in the course of a successful psycho-analytic therapy. A generation ago, we are told, such therapy made much of "acting-out" on the grounds that this emotional reliving in analysis of past situations was the avenue to release from neurotic forces. Since the mid-twenties, however, the accent has been on the importance of a moment of insight when the patient suddenly understands the significance of matters he has been discussing for months.[7] There may, of course, be antecedent pragmatic tentatives on the part of the analyst seeking to set up a situation in which such insight can

[7] For instances of insight in the course of productive work, see the three papers, "Varieties of Insight in Humans," "The Period of Frustration in Creative Endeavor," and "The Nature of Insight," by Eliot Dole Hutchinson, which are reprinted in: Patrick Mullahy (ed.), *A Study of Interpersonal Relations* (New York, Hermitage Press, 1949), pp. 386–445. For the role of similar insight in analytic therapy see: Clara Thompson with the collaboration of Patrick Mullahy, *Psychoanalysis: Evolution and Development* (London, George Allen and Unwin, 1952), p. 240.

flower but the insight itself is quite a different thing. Ordinary life presents all of us with similar experiences and indeed the instant of vision which great art often affords the beholder is not dissimilar.

The second sort of common experience to which I would appeal is that in which intelligence is found not directing action but evaluating it and proposing goals antecedently. Often enough our lives confront us with a situation of choice which must be resolved in part by appraising different aims. In Dewey's ethical theory one knows the value of an end only in relation to the means. But if this were always true we could never appreciate a value in itself, or weigh one value against another, independently of whatever means, so as to conclude that value A is always superior to value B or that A is a real and B only a pseudo-value. Yet as a matter of fact we do just this with the conviction, besides, that we are dealing in aspects of truth. That is to say, we do decide that certain things are valuable whether people actually seek them or not and we do balance one line of action against another and appraise A as the better even though B may have been biologically and socially more successful.

Let us suppose that during the Korean war you had in a senior group two highly endowed young men. Both are drafted and one of them accepts the burden responsibly and goes off to die on some frozen plateau while rescuing wounded under fire. He leaves his parents a posthumous Medal of Honor to display on the piano. The other by a cunning but technically legal stratagem evades the draft and lives to play his own piano and to gratify the community with charming compositions. Whose was the better choice? On a strict pragmatic reckoning (which, to be sure, many a sincere pragmatist would not be willing to follow in this case) certainly the second man's since within a purely temporal perspective it is better for the individual to be comfortably and productively alive than honorably dead. It may be objected that if everyone followed the second example the nation would be imperiled and consequently even the individual's happiness placed in jeopardy. To which our student might not unreasonably reply that not everyone is smart enough to dodge the draft; that a limited Far Eastern War is not clearly an

imminent national peril and anyhow, why *should* he take considerations of patriotism and the larger context into account?
What antecedent imperative is there for esteeming either one of
these alternatives more than the other? Our point here, however, does not depend on which of these lines of reasoning is
wisest and best. The illustration can be built up with the sides
weighted in whatever way you wish. Like all illustrations it may
obscure as much as it illuminates. My point is that we do, as a
matter of fact, weigh one value against another before and apart
from pragmatic criteria and we do decide that generous altruism
is in itself better than cautious legalism; that a courageous
dedication is finer than a circumscribed prudence which refuses
commitment. Moreover, we are able to evaluate goals apart
from the means. As Brand Blanshard once suggested, the value
of a beautiful mountain-top view does not itself vary because in
one case you climbed by foot to see it and in the other you rode.

What these experiences all require, it would seem, is recognition of the fact that there are other than instrumental criteria of
truth; that sometimes at least we do know one action to be right
and another wrong; or one action to be better than another
antecedent to their observed consequences. One might, indeed,
argue that past experiences have provided me with a working
hypothesis in favor of generosity or that the area of consequences can be so enlarged as to prove that altruism is actually
always more successful than egotism. But this, I think, would
take quite some proving and in any case the very attempt to do
so, if carefully scrutinized, suggests a latent conviction independent of all pragmatic norms, about the superiority of what
most men would call the nobler choice. None of this is to deny,
of course, that disinterested knowledge can, once achieved, be
employed instrumentally but only to say that the way to its
acquisition is not the *via pragmatica*.

There is not a great deal of room left for indicating a few of
the educational reverberations of the position sketched here.
But then no great harm is done if these implications are merely
suggested rather than spun out in detail for they are not particularly arcane. They are, conventionally enough, of two sorts:
those which recommend certain fundamental attitudes and
others more specific. At the general level, for instance, I should

say that a simultaneous and equitable insistence on both the technical and the meditative functions of man-the-thinker means a rejection of all exclusivistic, "nothing but . . ." theories. If countless people testify to the existence of a certain range of experience, there must be no discarding of large chunks of this and no forcing of them into a uniform mold. To refuse process and the possibility of the intellectual control of that process is unsatisfactory. To diminish intelligence by admitting no more than its instrumental uses is equally unsatisfactory. One should rather hold, I believe, the difficult middle way which is defined precisely by its integration and harmonization of both these functions which singly find an exclusive accent in other traditions.

Pointing up these general implications by specific cases once again calls for troublesome choice. One can select only a few instances and after our earlier comments, we feel constrained to ask what relevancy the thesis here has for important current problems even though the more conventional applications are closer at hand and obvious.

One current problem is that of the content of secondary and collegiate education in this anxious hour of scientific and technological competition with the Soviet Union. Here my first comment only echoes what has been broadcast in dozens of declarations since the fall of 1957. That is to say, if one is to acknowledge the full register of intelligence then all its possibilities must be exploited—those for historical and literary skills, for artistic effort and philosophical thinking as well as those for mathematical, scientific and technical enterprise. All one-sided educational programs fall short of the ideal although a situation of crisis may make them essential for survival. For one who maintains a dyadic function of man in his intelligent action it is as necessary to cultivate the practical as the speculative intellect. It is not a question of choosing between a contemplative attitude and an active orientation but of holding both in an organic synthesis. I do not think that the experiences of historical, philosophical and theological thinking or the appreciation, as distinct from the production of art, find their *raison d'être* in the method of hypothesis, test and check. Conversely, neither do I believe that instrumental thinking finds its fulfillment in talk. It seems a pity, therefore, that so many young Americans fail to get either from their home or their school any thorough introduction to the methods and rewards of truly creative work. The adolescent may pick it up for himself by tinkering with a car, and adults with enough time and money may pitch into do-it-yourself activities. But in our schools there is, by and large, nothing even so good as what Eton is said to have. For in this English secondary school whose academic curriculum would terrify many an American collegian, there has been an honored tradition of creative extra-curriculars. These "drawing-schools" and "schools of mechanics" as they are called, provide a very sizable percentage of the student-body with some chance for serious wood and machine work; for clay modelling and pottery making; for painting in oils and water-colors. Apart from our technical and trade schools I am not aware that we do anything of equal caliber to an equal extent. Yet I am prepared to argue that this work-activity—which is an archetypical case of pragmatic intelligence—is profoundly humanistic. It nourishes both the individual and the social potentialities of man. It has resources of intellectual, moral and religious significance. Indeed, the concept of work can be widened to include the whole ethical endeavor. . . .

EDUCATION AS TELEOLOGICAL COHERENCE*

Bertram D. Brettschneider

Coherence is an ontological principle when it refers to the organizational togetherness of the parts of a spatio-temporal whole. It is the degree of togetherness established in the mutual relations between part-part and whole-part of any structured finite organismic entity. Nature is here construed as a community of organisms. Coherence is thus a comment on the degree of organization immanent in this community. It is a comment on the degree of organization immanent in both ontogeny and phylogeny.[1] It is applicable to the history of an individual organism, to the history of a species, and to the history of the universe taken from any vantage point you please.

The primordial universe of energy relations is infinite; finite groupings evolve from it through the inherent motion of energy. We may speak of different levels of organismic structures as does Alexander when he refers to the emergence of simple physical motion, matter as physical, matter with secondary qualities, life, and mind.[2] Emergence refers to the rearrangement of energy relations in such fashion that a new organization appears which is marked by a relatively high degree of stability or internal coherence.

The form of a coherently related system comprehends those relations which are logically possible in terms of the internal structure of the system. The structure of an organism thereby defines and delimits its capacity to function. To call a given level of systematized energy relations an organism is a comment on

---

* Reprinted from "Sketch for an Organismic Philosophy of Education," *Educational Theory*, 10(April, 1960), 133–41. By permission of the author and the editor of *Educational Theory*.
[1] "Ontogeny" and "phylogeny" are terms which have been appropriated from biology and used here in lieu of "particular" and "universal" respectively. Ontogeny refers to the unique spatio-temporal history of an individual organism. Phylogeny refers to the structural organization of a class of organisms as this has evolved in space-time.
[2] Samuel Alexander, *Space, Time, and Deity*, 2(New York, The Humanities Press, 1950), 52.

the uniqueness of the pattern of structure and function at that level of phylogenetic development as contrasted with the structure and function of organisms at a different level.

The universe, conceived as a community of organisms, reveals two aspects of coherence—a primordial and a consequent aspect. This double aspect of coherence exists through the necessity that each ontogenetic individual maintain itself by the capture and expenditure of energy.

The primordial aspect of coherence is the possibility of coherence which is formally implied in the inherent structural relations of each finite organism. As such it comprehends the normative and necessary relations which ought to obtain in the environmental and internal structural organization of the members of the community of organisms. On the other hand, the consequent aspect of coherence is the actual coherence relationship which comes to exist in the ontogenetic development of a given organism. As such, coherence is a statistical concept. As normative, the primordial aspect of coherence provides the standard for judgment of the consequent aspect. It thus prescribes the conditions of moral existence which are conceivable on the basis of possible relations into which an organism—when considered structurally from a phylogenetic viewpoint—may enter. Ontogenetic development thus realizes the possibilities which are inherent in the phylogenetic structure of the individual and which limit the ontogenetic organism's capacity to function.

The educative process is directly concerned with ontogenetic development. Education has its theoretical and practical aspects. Activity is practical when it results in a modification of behavior. The practical emphasizes the motor aspect of environmental control. Man has the potentiality to change his behavior and his environment in terms of individual or collective purposes. Before we act, we must understand the structural organization and possibilities of the environmental context in terms of which we are acting and reacting. Practical conation must be preceded by theoretical inquiry. In the theoretical attitude, the mind reviews the changes to be wrought in the structure of the environmental field.

The goal of our activity is to bring together the outstanding variables in a more effective coherent relationship than we have had heretofore. Methodologically, the first consideration after the recognition that we have a problem before us is an analysis of the given problematic field. This preliminary analysis involves the specification of the variables operant within the problematic situation, an analysis of the nature of the relations obtaining between these variables, and a statement of the possible alternative relations into which these variables may enter. This last step must do no logical or ontological violence to the given variables with which we are dealing.

This procedure takes into account the primordial aspect of coherence. The structure of our given variables provides us with normative legislation as to what relational possibilities may conceivably be involved in our subsequent practical activity. In a sense, this consideration of alternative relational possibilities serves the purpose of defining and delimiting the universe of discourse of our activity.

The primordial aspect of coherence is necessary as well as normative. In our preliminary inquiry we must examine the nature of the logical relations which hold between our given variables. The subsequent relations into which these variables may enter must not contradict the given logical matrix taken into account as the primordial aspect of coherence. . . .

The essence of the normative and necessary relations of the primordial aspect of coherence is sociality. Sociality refers to the mutual interaction and interdependence of structured organisms both in their environmental and internal structural relations. No structured organism can live in and by itself. It must constantly adjust itself to changing environmental conditions by developing structural modifications which serve to extend its control over its environment.

In this connection, George Herbert Mead makes a distinction between those organisms which are capable of establishing their own relational coherences by virtue of having greater differentiation of structure and those organisms which are incapable of such behavior. The latter are at the mercy of the elements, so to speak. Mead calls the former type of organisms "teleological" in their functioning, and the latter are "mechanical" in their functioning.[3]

A mechanical organism is one that may be defined in terms of other organisms whereas the teleological organism is one which defines other organisms with respect to itself. Mead offers the electron as an example of an organism which functions mechanically. "An electron is defined in terms of the fields of all other electrons as they are registered in its field."[4] The electron is thus a participant in and is dependent upon a process occurring outside of itself.

On the other hand, the teleological kind of functioning is one in which an organism participates in and constitutes its environment as an extension of its own striving for coherence. The occasion for such extension of the organism into its environment arises from the needs and demands of its internal structural organization. The internal structural relations of the organism function so that the process which is going on inside the organism becomes extended to the outside through a further elaboration of the process of meeting the need. Mead suggests by way of illustration that ". . . it is that which is sought which is present in the inner organic operation which controls the attainment of the outer object—thus, sexual stimulation is the inner reproduction of ova and spermatozoa."[5] In this way, the inner situation of the organism because of its lack of coherence has what Whitehead calls its "subjective aim." The subjective aim of the organism is comprehended by the primordial aspect of coherence in terms of which the organism makes demands for satisfactions which may be achieved from the outside.

This distinction between the mechanical and teleological kinds of organismic function finds the former more or less passive in achieving its structural satisfactions whereas the latter may be considered a more or less active function. The organism which functions teleologically goes out and gets what it is after. However, it should be noted that this distinction is not absolute.

[3] George H. Mead, *The Philosophy of the Act* (Chicago, The University of Chicago Press, 1938), p. 301.
[4] *Ibid.,* p. 302.
[5] *Ibid.*

There are situations where one organism may take an active role, and other situations where it may play a passive role. Whether an organism functions teleologically or not depends upon the nature of the external structural relations in which it finds itself and its capacity to produce some significant modification of these relations. In this way, an amoeba may play an active role in extending a pseudopod to engulf a food particle, but it may be helpless in resisting a change in the pH of its medium. The educative process may be conceived as an attempt to alter the functional behavior of children from mechanical activity to teleological.

The teleological manner of functioning suggests that an organism, if allowed to act unhindered, i.e., teleologically, is capable of positive action on its own behalf so that other organisms in the environment are utilized for their consequences. However, these other organisms do not rest idly, but impose a limiting condition on the action of the first organism. It is in terms of this mutual give-and-take of phylogenetic types that the primordial aspect of coherence may be recognized. This is what Alexander has identified as the process of natural selection making itself felt in the cosmos as a value principle. . . .

This formal, primordial aspect of coherence is normative because it is possible to conceive of sets of relations which best suit an organism in terms of its phylogenetic structure. This primordial aspect of coherence is likewise necessary for if the organism does not fulfill its capacity to function, it will cease to function actively. If it does not realize its capacity to function teleologically, the organism will perhaps succumb to the overbearing demands of some unforeseen set of relations.

Human societies take notice of this situation where these societies adopt policies which actively promote the education of the immature. Today, the alternative to education is intellectual subjugation by the propagandistic influences of dominant cultural interests. The introduction of advertising and public relations techniques into the American political arena, for example, is a cynical comment on the political amorality of those who seek to make mechanical objects of their fellows. The advertising and public relations technicians—these are not creative functions by any stretch of the imagination—are amoral agents in their reduction of mind to mechanical modes of function. On the other hand, the political interests which exhibit that mode of teleological functioning which seeks to make the minds of men mechanical objects exhibit a form of immorality which can only imply phylogenetic disvalue. Education is thus the supreme moral undertaking for man in terms of man's phylogenetic potential. The suppression of alternative sets of relational possibilities which tend to make mind a mechanical function constitutes the supreme mode of disvalue. . . .

The consequent aspect of coherence is empirical. It makes reference to the state of coherence which actually obtains in the course of ontogenetic development. This aspect is the realization of the possibilities contained in the normative nature of the primordial aspect of coherence.

The consequent aspect of coherence is statistical in effect. It cannot be supposed for a moment that every element of a coherent system of relations is in complete conformity with the total pattern of coherence. In the case of a magnetic field of molecules of oxygen, it cannot be supposed that every single molecule of the gas has actually turned parallel to the field like a compass needle. The coherence which is effected in the case of the magnetization of the field is vectorial or statistical. Although single molecules may constantly change their orientation with respect to the entire field, there is a preponderance of orientation in the direction of the field so that the observed coherence may be recognized as a magnetic field. As a statistical affair, coherence seems to emerge modally. It is not unlike the resultant of vectorial forces if the relational elements of coherence may be considered as vectors.

One characteristic of a statistical mode is that it is relatively stable and sluggish as compared to measures which are distant in magnitude from the parameter. As a statistical mode, the consequent aspect of coherence seems to be a conservative phenomenon which tends in the direction of establishing a relatively stable set of organismic relations. This stabilizing influence of coherence appears to be based upon the extreme difficulty of restructuring relations once a basically satisfactory coherence has been established.

The occurrence of a propitious set of environmental circumstances makes its recurrence more probable than the initial coming into being of a new event. As a result, a set of favorable circumstances tends to be retained at the expense of relations which prove to be detrimental to any given organism. The means whereby an organism is capable of determining, in some measure at least, its set of environmental relations is afforded by its particular mode of teleological functioning. Ontogenetic differences which are comprehended by the consequent aspect of coherence depend upon the efficiency of the organism in adjusting its particular teleological mechanism to its particular organismic field. The consequent aspect of coherence is thus concerned with what an organism actually does whereas the primordial aspect is concerned with what an organism can do.

In terms of the doctrine of coherence conceived as the basis for educational method, it has been suggested that the primordial aspect of coherence leads us to an analysis of the possibilities for relational reorganization of the variables present in our problematic field. A logical analysis of the matrix of relational possibilities serves to delimit the field to a few candidates for coherence. These remaining possibilities constitute hypotheses which are put to the test.

We put these several hypotheses to the test and then examine the results of what has actually come to pass. The consequent aspect of coherence takes note of the degree of error of prediction resident in the formal possibilities entertained in the primordial aspect of coherence. The primordial aspect of coherence is formal and theoretical. The consequent aspect is statistical and empirical. What elements of the primordial structure are not present in the consequent structure? Which hypothesis permits greater flexibility for subsequent use in the sense that it permits a greater number of statistical degrees of freedom?

Man's primitive endowments constitute the basis of his freedom. Man is free to select from among the possibilities open to him the type of relations he conceived as favorable to himself. The test of the efficacy of teleological behavior is afforded ontogenetically; a 'philosophy of life' is an analytic comment on the manner in which men utilize their freedom for action. Ontogenetically, the individual organism must maintain an equable balance between its own needs and the formal demands required of its phylogenetic type.

We seem to be involved in an implied paradox: the individual gains freedom to function as he surrenders his freedom to the necessity of formal considerations. This is what Alexander means when he calls freedom "self-determination." [6] We are free to act when we know the extent to which the self is restricted by formal as well as external factors. The self is free when aware of its delimited structure and nevertheless can act in terms of these limitations.

Whitehead similarly defines freedom in terms of our capacity to act as we are able to act. He says:

"The literary exposition of freedom deals mainly with the frills. . . . Freedom means that within each type the requisite coordination should be possible without the destruction of the general ends of the whole community. Indeed, one general end is that these variously coordinated groups should contribute to the complex pattern of community life, each in virtue of its own particularity. In this way individuality gains the effectiveness which issues from coordination, and freedom obtains power necessary for its perfection." [7]

In this sense, the statistical concept of 'degrees of freedom' may apply to the statistical nature of the consequent aspect of coherence. The greater the number of possibilities for action or degrees of freedom available to a phylogenetic type, the greater should be the probability that that organismic type may succeed in realizing its structural capacities in the ontogenetic development of individual organisms. Freedom is thus the ability to realize phylogenetic potential in the course of ontogenetic development.

This suggests that a man is not free when he casts a ballot in response to an impassioned campaign oration. He is free when he votes in terms of a rational analysis of the alternatives which have been presented to him in the course of an election campaign. In the latter case, he is making fuller use of his phyloge-

[6] Cf. Alexander, *op. cit.,* pp. 315–38.
[7] Alfred N. Whitehead, *Adventures of Ideas* (New York, The Macmillan Company, 1933), pp. 84, 86.

netic structural capacities. Education is the institutionalized process whereby man is liberated, i.e., whereby he comes to realize his structural potential and gains skill in its full use.

This paper is an essay in ontology. The problems of education are ultimately the concerns of ontology. The coherent individual constitutes the real and the goal of education is the development of real individuals. Coherence in its most significant terms refers to the felicitous coordination of the structure and function of an individual organism with the structure and function of the community of organisms in which he participates. In human valuational terms, this suggests that the individual should value coherently with the collective standard. This means that what is accorded status as real and valuable has been accorded social approval to a high degree.

This raises an interesting problem: if an educational system educates children to the point where their beliefs and attitudes are fully consonant with the accepted beliefs of the parent culture, then in what sense can it be said that the children are free? To put the matter another way, if a given set of beliefs is instilled without the children being trained in techniques of critical thinking, then it would follow that the children have been indoctrinated in the beliefs of a dominant segment of the culture. When propaganda is acritically accepted we are not free. In recent years, one of our major political parties has raised the cry that the American press is predominantly a one-party press. To the extent that the citizenry of our country have not been educated to form judgments on the basis of critical examination of data, their political judgments, for example, have some basis other than cognitive. The collective standard assumes the aspect of a political bandwagon; its appeal is emotional and qualitative rather than cognitive and rational. Where beliefs are founded on this basis we find a need for a reexamination of prevailing educational theory and practice.

Indoctrination, mimesis, and propagandizing are not actually implied as the consequences of the proposal of organismic philosophy that the collective standard should supply the criterion for the evaluation of all judgments. The collective standard refers to the dominant judgment of the community of inquirers with which the individual seeks coherence within any given frame of reference. The collective standard is an hypothesis that such and such a set of propositions is generally agreed upon by competent inquirers as providing the most effective knowledge that is available at a given time with respect to a given universe of discourse. That the collective standard is a temporarily accepted hypothesis implies that it has been put to the test of alternative hypotheses and the judgment has been empirically confirmed that this particular proposition is most adequate to explain the known facts at a given time and place.

In keeping with Charles S. Peirce's doctrine of fallibilism, we can never be certain that the hypothesis recognized as the collective standard is the best hypothesis. Each person making a judgment has the responsibility for determining the most adequate criterion for evaluating these judgments. The collective standard is constantly referred to as the standard for popular judgment. It is constantly undergoing revision and reevaluation in the course of this process.

The teacher has the moral responsibility of continually training the young and immature in the proper use of the collective standard as the criterion of judgment. The teacher's primary obligation is the development of a healthy respect for the correct use of the methodology of judgment-making as embodied in the primordial and consequent aspects of coherence. The teacher who develops the attitude that the collective standard is an hypothesis avoids the pitfalls of totalitarian indoctrination. Children who are properly trained in the methodology of judgment-making are thereby free.

EDUCATION AS INITIATION*

R. S. Peters

The distinction has previously been made between 'education' conceived of as an achievement and 'education' as covering a number of tasks. An educated man is one who has achieved a state of mind which is characterized by a mastery of and care for the worthwhile things that have been transmitted, which are viewed in some kind of cognitive perspective. The requirement built into 'education' that it should be of the 'whole man' implies the possibility of a man being trained in some more limited respect. In other words the concept of 'education' presupposes not only the development of beliefs but also the differentiation of mind in respects which can be developed to the exclusion of others. How, then, is the development of such a differentiated mind to be conceived?

There is a view about the development of mind, which has been very influential in England since the time of the British Empiricists (Locke, Berkeley, Hume), in which the development of the individual mind is regarded as a slow process by means of which generalized beliefs are acquired as a precipitate of individual experience. Atomic sense data, it was argued, are admitted through the inlets of sense. Gradually the individual mind, consisting of complex ideas and expectations established on the basis of the coexistence and constant conjunction of sense qualities, begins to emerge. The function of the educator is either to provide a suitable environment in which this individual development can proceed or to intervene more actively and implant the appropriate ideas in the mind of the child in accordance with some carefully articulated programme.

This rather botanical picture of the development of mind is correct in one important respect. It singles out 'consciousness' as the hall-mark of mind. The Greeks did not really have an explicit and articulated concept of 'consciousness.' Not that they

* Reprinted from *Ethics and Education* (London, George Allen and Unwin, 1966), pp. 46–51. By permission of George Allen and Unwin. Copyright 1966 by George Allen and Unwin.

thought of men as machines or failed to note that men lost consciousness from time to time; for conscious activity—especially that of reasoning—was regarded by them as a matter of great significance. Indeed Plato and Aristotle were so struck by the wonder of reasoning that they regarded it as a divine characteristic. But they did not stress the common core of consciousness in varied phenomena such as mathematical reasoning, purpose, pain, dreaming, and emotional states. Aristotle, for instance, singled out goal-directedness as the hall-mark of soul. This was exhibited at the plant, animal, and human level. The hall-mark of 'mind' was the imposition of plans and rules, associated with 'reason,' on this goal-directedness.

Historically the emphasis on private individual experience, in which consciousness was stressed as the hall-mark of mind, presupposed the development of individualism as a social movement; for the Greeks of the city-states lived in a public world of public feats and public concerns in which the term ἰδιώτης (idiot) disdainfully picked out the man who concerned himself only with private matters. Socrates, with his stress on individual self-knowledge and the care of the individual soul, was a moral innovator. With the conquests of Philip and Alexander of Macedon and the break-up of the small autonomous Greek states such moral innovation became systematized in the codes of the Stoics and Epicureans. The ideal of the self-sufficiency of the individual as a citizen of the world developed as a substitute for the much lauded self-sufficiency of the city-states. He must either discipline himself and purify his individual soul (Stoics), or slip through life unobtrusively by cutting down the possible sources of suffering (Epicureans). This led to an increase of interest in the will and emotions, and to an emphasis on the importance of individual consciousness.

This turning inwards was institutionalized by Christianity with its stress on personal salvation and purity of soul. Introspection vied with revelation as a source of knowledge. St. Augustine paved the way for Descartes' first certainty—Cogito; *ergo* sum. With Descartes the Platonic view of the soul and of knowledge was reinterpreted in the light of the rise of the mathematical sciences, but with a difference—the stress on the certainty of the individual's knowledge of his own mental states.

'Mind' was no longer simply associated with Reason; it was that inner world of consciousness to which each individual has private access and whose rational activity it is self-contradictory to doubt. The British Empiricists explicitly rejected Descartes' account of knowledge with its more precise rendering of Plato's innate ideas. Knowledge, they argued, was not spun out of the recesses of mind by the activity of reason; it was a precipitate left by sensory experience in the mind of the individual. But they implicitly accepted Descartes' emphasis on consciousness as the hall-mark of mind.

On this fundamental point surely both Descartes and the British Empiricists were right; for even if the importance of the Aristotelian criterion of goal-directedness is stressed, a distinction has to be made between behaviour in which there is consciousness of an end and in which means to it are seen or devised, and that in which, as in the case of plants, there is persistence towards an end without consciousness of it. If this distinction is not made minds could be attributed to machines; and one thing we know about machines is that mentality is not one of their attributes. The ideas and expectations of an individual centre of consciousness, however, do not develop as deposits out of an atomic individual experience. This is one of the misleading features of the empiricist account. On the contrary they are the product of the initiation of an individual into public traditions enshrined in the language, concepts, beliefs, and rules of a society.

A child is born with a consciousness not as yet differentiated into beliefs, purposes, and feelings. Indeed it is many months before consciousness of his mother as an entity distinct from himself develops. His 'mind' is ruled perhaps by bizarre and formless wishes in which there is no picking out of objects, still less of 'sense-data,' in a framework of space and time, no notion of permanence or of continuity, no embryonic grasp of causal connection or means-ends relationships. The sequence of children's questions—'What is it?', 'Where is it?', 'When did it happen?', 'Why did it happen?' mark the development of this categoreal apparatus. The differentiation of modes of consciousness proceeds *pari passu* with the development of this mental structure. For they are all related to types of objects and relations in a public world. The child comes to want things that there are means of obtaining instead of threshing around beset by unruly and unrealistic wishes; he comes to fear things that may hurt him, and to believe that things are the case which experience has confirmed for him. Later he comes to create predictability in his social world by stating his intentions and making promises, as well as to guide his behaviour through his grasp of the rules which he finds there.

In the history of philosophy Kant rightly achieved fame for outlining this structure of concepts and categories by means of which order is imposed on the flux of experience; this he attributed to an active reason at work in the experience of all individuals. Later on, in the early part of the twentieth century, the psychologist Piaget, much influenced by Kant, laboriously mapped the stages at which these concepts and categories develop. But neither of these thinkers speculated about the extent to which the development of mind is the product of initiation into public traditions enshrined in a public language. Hegel, perhaps, with his notion of 'objective mind' articulated in institutions, and Marx, with his stress on the social determinants of individual consciousness, were vividly aware of this social dimension of the development of mind. But for different reasons their accounts of mind failed to take root in the empirical tradition of Western thought and to correct the undue emphasis on individual experience. Indeed their collectivist, holistic approach to social phenomena tended to go to the other extreme of ignoring the importance of individual centres of experience.

The point is that consciousness, which is the hall-mark of mind, is related in its different modes to objects. The individual wants *something,* is afraid of or angry with *somebody* or *something,* believes or knows that *certain things are the case.* The objects of consciousness are first and foremost objects in a public world that are marked out and differentiated by a public language into which the individual is initiated. The learning of language and the discovery of a public world of objects in space and time proceed together. But the individual, as owner of experiences welded to each other in a unique life-history, represents a particular and unrepeatable viewpoint on this public world. As Leibniz put it, each one mirrors the world from a particular point of view. Furthermore, as he develops, he adds his contribution to the public world. His consciousness, as well as his individuality, is neither intelligible nor genetically explicable without the public world of which he is conscious, in relation to which he develops, and on which he imprints his own individual style and pattern of being. But that does not make individual consciousness any the less important both as the hall-mark of mind and as a centre of ethical concern.

The development of a structure of categories and concepts for picking out objects in a space-time framework and for noting causal connections and means-ends relations is only a stage in the development of mind. Further differentiation develops as the mastery of the basic skills opens the gates to a vast inheritance accumulated by those versed in more specific modes of thought and awareness such as science, history, mathematics, religious and aesthetic awareness, together with moral, prudential and technical forms of thought and action. Such differentiations are alien to the mind of a child or preliterate man—indeed perhaps to that of a pre-seventeenth-century man.

Each of these differentiated modes of thought and awareness is characterized both by a content or 'body of knowledge' and by public procedures by means of which this content has been accumulated, criticized, and revised. Each has its own family of concepts peculiar to it and its own distinctive methods of validation. In learning science, for instance, concepts such as 'mass,' 'force,' 'velocity,' and 'gravity' have to be understood, together with the procedures of experiment and observation by means of which hypotheses making use of such concepts are tested. All these are public. Many do little more than develop a familiarity with such a mode of thought together with a mastery of some portion of its body of knowledge. A few, however, develop this form of thought themselves to a pre-eminent degree and contribute themselves to the criticism and development of its content. But for all who get on the inside of such a form of thought and who make it, to a certain extent their own, the contours of the public world are to that extent transformed. The process of initiation into such modes of thought and awareness is the process of education.

The foregoing sketch of 'mind' and of its development has

been necessarily brief and selective. Its point should be obvious enough—to correct the conceptions of education that were derivative from the empiricist picture of mind and its development as well as to give an account of education that is consistent with the criteria that were made explicit. . . . The same sort of corrective is necessary also for the Kantian concept and its derivative in Piaget. For although a view which stresses the activity of mind in selecting from and imposing order on the flux of experience by means of a developing categoreal and conceptual structure is a great improvement on the *tabula rosa* or 'empty cabinet' view of the classical empiricists, it is still deficient if mental structure is regarded as innate or simply as the product of maturation. What is lacking is the notion that such a structure develops out of and as a response to public traditions enshrined in language.

EDUCATION AND THE USES OF KNOWLEDGE*

Harry S. Broudy, B. Othanel Smith,
and Joe R. Burnett

The terms "general" and "common," when used to qualify education, are related but not synonymous. Whatever the total population of a school studies is common in the sense that it is shared by all pupils. In this sense, our elementary school curriculum is regarded as common, and the school has been known as the common school. "General," on the other hand, refers or could profitably refer to a characteristic of the subject being studied. The general is the opposite of the specific or of the particular and is therefore more likely to be abstract than concrete. In this sense, mathematics is more general than geography, and geography more general than corn agriculture.

This book sets forth a theory of the curriculum that is general, that is, made up of general studies, but it also urges that it be common as well. The writers believe that in the scientifically based mass society, vocational training increasingly presupposes thorough grounding in general studies. One can expect that with automation reducing the number of unskilled jobs, the cognitive component of job training will rise in amount and level. Even now, careers at the technician level in mechanics and electronics require a secondary schooling comparable to that needed for college entrance. . . .

It cannot be repeated too often that in modern society every man's vocation requires specialization, while his roles as citizen and person demand that he be a generalist. Significantly, specialist and generalist roles in such a society . . . both look to cognitive products and processes of a quality hitherto expected from only a small minority of the population.

Because so much more in the way of schooling is demanded of so many more of our citizens, it becomes imperative to ask:

* Reprinted from *Democracy and Excellence in American Secondary Education*, pp. 44, 53–54, 61–65, 71–72. By permission of Rand McNally and Company. Copyright 1964 by Rand McNally and Company.

How can the secondary school of our time most economically deploy its resources? Can we fashion a curriculum that provides adequate basic education for both the specialist and the generalist roles? Can we avoid the waste inherent in overschooling and underschooling for these roles? Clearly, a further exploration of how schooling is to be used in these roles is needed before one can answer these questions.

The most usual, although not exclusive, meaning of the term "specialist use of schooling" is vocational use, inasmuch as it is with respect to vocation that most of us are likely to be specialists. How, then, do we use schooling on the job? Do we use it associatively, replicatively, interpretively, applicatively? How frequently is schooling used in these ways? Which use, if any, is the distinctive use? Does the level of occupational role affect the uses?

With respect to all four uses, schooling enters into the specialist's work from general and special education. General education provides the store of ideas and images from which some may be summoned for vocational purposes or in relation to vocational activity. For example, an architect's thoughts as he muses over the design for a nightclub might be affected by a long-ago reading of "In Xanadu did Kubla Khan/A stately pleasure-dome decree. . . ." Replicatively, the same architect uses his school learnings of reading and writing, and interpretively and applicatively, he uses some of his general education. Precisely because the studies are general, does this type of schooling have reverberations in all occupations or in the preparation for them. Special or vocational education, on the other hand, contributes knowledge and skill that are used almost exclusively on a particular set of behaviors required by a particular vocation or, at most, a small family of them. One of the problems we face is that some elements of general education, especially some of the content, can be taught with primary emphasis on only one of the four uses. When in general education we stress a use that is characteristic of the work of a specialist, we may be defeating the purpose of general education.

For example, the technical or the professional school tries to introduce into its curriculum tasks that the trainee can replicate on the job. This is the practice phase of the curriculum. Thus, in a school for draftsmen, the drawings assigned may closely resemble the drawings to be done on the prospective job; an auto-mechanics' school requires practice on automotive problems no different from those to be found in the contemporary repair shop. Professional schools devote a smaller proportion of time to tasks for replication than do technical schools. Only a small proportion of legal education, for example, is given over to the writing of briefs, courtroom procedures, and so on. However, items of knowledge, rules, and even modes of speaking and writing are included in legal training that presumably are to be used replicatively, that is, just as learned, and if one does not perfect these habits in school, one has to do it by practicing on one's clients.

General education in the secondary school cannot include practice on sample tasks of this or that occupation or of any set of occupations. Yet, we hear the argument that certain subjects should be taught in high school because they will be used in certain vocations, for example, mathematics in engineering, history in the teaching of the social studies, logical thinking in law, chemistry in medicine, and so forth. Presumably, they will be used replicatively (as taught) or applicatively (to guide the prospective practitioner in solving the problems peculiar to his job). But suppose such subjects are not so used by generalists, or even by specialists under ordinary circumstances, or in either case not so frequently as one might expect. Would this not make a difference in the way we organize these subjects for instruction in a program of general education?

One can begin the inquiry by noting that knowledge, as used vocationally, can take several forms. For example, one can teach it, as a teacher of chemistry uses chemistry to teach chemistry. An industrial chemist uses chemistry to solve industrial problems, making a new synthetic fabric, for example. A physician may use chemistry to understand the literature on a new drug. A research chemist may not teach chemistry or apply it to industrial problems; he may use it primarily to further chemical knowledge. Nevertheless, these people and others *might* use certain chemical apparatus or procedures in exactly the same way, for example, test tubes, Bunsen burners, wash bottles, and the like. In other words, their use of chemical skills may be the same, replicative, but their uses of the content can vary, even when used in relation to vocation.

An important characteristic of the specialist's use of a given segment of knowledge is its high selectivity. What is selected is dictated by his daily work. What is not relevant to it is not used and often forgotten; what is retained is retained as used. We are often ruefully surprised at how little of our schooling we actually use "on the job." For this reason, conscientious schools that follow up their graduates to inquire what courses helped them most in their work are usually disappointed or baffled by the responses. Either the number of courses mentioned is very small, thereby casting doubt on the value of the bulk of the curriculum, or many courses are cited as valuable but not by any sizable percentage of the graduates. Worse still, graduates impute to this or that inspiring teacher the reason for their success, although what he taught has no discernible conceivable connection with what the graduate is now doing. We would avoid this disappointment if we realized that by its very nature specialization has to be narrow, that the direct use of "general" studies by a specialist in his specialty is always small in volume and narrow in range, and finally that content is not all that is learned in school. Associative and unconscious uses of schooling defy easy identification by recall, but may operate powerfully nonetheless.

Thus, the expert may get by with a restricted set of symbolic skills. The reading, the mathematics (if any), drawing, note-reading, and so on, he uses are highly specific to the specialty. A first-rate chemist who cannot read Shakespeare or Proust might surprise us, but not very much, and surely there are many good auto mechanics to whom algebra is not even a meaningful word. This does not mean that as citizens the chemist or auto mechanic can get by without these items of knowledge or that having them might not affect their *interpretation* of their activities, even as specialists. It merely means that it is unlikely that these specialists make an applicative use of them.

Similarly with the conceptual store of content. The research or theoretical chemist, one would suppose, knows the basic conceptual structure of chemistry, and nowadays he had better be on reading and speaking terms with the basic concepts of physics and mathematics. Yet, in many chemical specialties, one can be ignorant of biology and economics with comparative safety. The modern surgeon likewise is probably more sophisticated in the sciences than were his forebears, but even so, the margin of tolerable ignorance is wide indeed. What one does not have to know about science to be a good surgeon would fill a large book.

On the other hand, the relevant knowledge is cultivated in as great detail as practice dictates. A professional chemist, for example, needs to know almost all there is to know about what has been done, what is being done, and what might be done within the bounds of his chemical specialty. He knows his field in detail and depth; he knows "who's who" in it, and how to appraise the import of every new piece of research. He himself may or may not contribute by research to the chemical domain; this depends on his chemical specialty.

To what extent is this theoretical competence required of the chemical laboratory technician? Or of the man who works on the control panels of an automated oil refinery?

A theoretical grounding in chemistry is desirable at the technician level, but it need not be as detailed or as sophisticated as that required of the research chemist. The knowledge needed by the technician is that which enables him to learn *about* the operations he is to perform in his work. These are guided by rules of procedure and manipulations with specific apparatus in specific situations. He uses courses in chemistry to *understand* what he is doing and why he is doing it. He does not use them to solve problems or to extend chemical knowledge. The technician uses his knowledge of *rules* applicatively but his knowledge of *chemistry* interpretively.

The specialist at all levels uses knowledge as a source of rubrics that enable him to classify a problem, to identify the causes of the difficulty, and to select a remedial procedure. . . .

The objection that not all of our citizens, or that a large proportion of them, do not use theoretical learnings in their work raises doubt as to the advisability of using high-school time for this kind of vocational training rather than about the importance of theoretical learnings. The writers can only reiterate that they do not look on the secondary-school curriculum as a means for job training, that is, for the applicative use of knowledge, but rather as the means to general education which exemplifies the interpretive use of knowledge primarily and its applicative use only indirectly.

The perspectival or interpretive use of knowledge has not been investigated as thoroughly as the applicative and replicative uses. For example, watching water boil, a child asks, "Why does the water bubble?" Father uses his schooling interpretively when he classifies the question as one to which two items he has remembered from his schooling are relevant: (1) molecules move faster when heated, and (2) water contains air. He may never have practiced or read the explanation he now devises; he cannot in all likelihood calculate or "do" problems involving heated liquids, although Boyle's Law might recur to him as of possible relevance. He cannot, on the spot, "apply" his knowledge to problems that require precise, detailed information. Yet he can follow such an application if made by someone else. This often is what we mean by "understanding," that we see how something to be explained (the boiling, seething of water) follows as necessarily true if a general principle (the molecular theory) is true. Why does a satellite have to attain a critical velocity to enter and stay in orbit? When does it pay for a prosperous corporation to buy up a company that is losing money? Why is it so difficult to solve the problem of agricultural surpluses? The well-educated citizen, as will be seen, uses his schooling *interpretively* in responding to these questions; the specialist uses it technically and theoretically to give precise and detailed solutions. He applies it in a sense and degree that a generalist does not.

As nonspecialists, however, we all use the results of schooling in other ways. Much is used associatively, as has already been pointed out, to supply a source of images and meanings that give to experience richness, variety, and no small amount of spontaneity. In the field of our specialties, we do not rely on associative hunches as a regular thing, although there are numerous occasions when we are grateful for their occurrence. A curriculum that treats the associative use of schooling with condescension is likely both to impoverish experience in general and to dry up prematurely the wellsprings of creativity. Testing procedures that disvalue the associative uses of learning affect the curriculum indirectly, insofar as they determine what is stressed in teaching and learning.

Some school learnings, especially those involving symbolic and manipulative skills, are used replicatively, . . . but they do not exhaust the replicative use of school learnings either for the specialist or the nonspecialist. Some content is used replicatively to anchor the interpretive frames that are used for orientation and perspective. Certain statements of fact ("There are fifty states in the Union."), certain generalizations ("Water freezes at 0 degrees centigrade."), certain hypotheses ("The universe is expanding."), and certain well-established theories (the atomic structure of matter) are all used replicatively as true assertions, even though the maker of these assertions has only the vaguest notions of how they were discovered or validated. A great deal of what John Dewey called "funded knowledge" is used by specialist and nonspecialist, but especially by the latter, in a replicative way.

Finally, the nonspecialist's way of using logical operations, as in critical thinking, differs in no significantly formal way from that of the specialist. The difference lies rather in the wealth of content each can summon. . . .

The important point is that in ordinary life the applicative use of knowledge is relatively rare. We do not solve many of our problems by thinking our way through them. On the contrary, we consult someone who has the solution for sale, or we look up the answer in some manual. Our behavior follows the law of least cognitive strain; we think no more than we have to.

. . . It is the specialist in the exercise of his specialty who is most likely to use knowledge applicatively, and even he does so only when confronted with problems that are not routine. The highest applicative use of knowledge is to expand knowledge itself, as in the work of the scholar and researcher. The generalist is satisfying the requirements of thinking and intelligence when he uses knowledge interpretively.

Why do we stress the relative rarity of the applicative use of knowledge? Because in educational thinking it has generally been taken for granted that it is the applicative use of knowledge that justifies schooling in general and the teaching of any subject in particular. At times the schools have operated on the assumption that a large repertory of facts, rules, and principles learned for replication on cue would automatically be used applicatively when the life situation became problematic. At other times, disappointed that automatic application of school learnings did not occur, the schools urged that the pupil be given practice in application, so that applying a piece of knowledge became a standard part of a lesson. These Herbartian applications, usually practiced on problems within a given subject, served as an admirable test of the pupil's understanding, but they did not guarantee that the learning would be used to solve nonschool problems.

This was due partly to the fact that life problems are "molar," that is, more complex and massive than problems in a single discipline like mathematics or physics or chemistry. It was also due to the technological complexity of our culture. In such a culture, one depends more and more on specialized problem-solvers who have the knowledge, tools, and skills required. In such a state of affairs, to justify a curriculum on applicative uses is neither practically nor theoretically defensible, unless it is the curriculum for the training of specialists.

Much of what in ordinary language we call application of knowledge is better regarded as interpretation, a process related to application but far less specific and detailed.

Experience becomes intelligible only as we categorize it, conceptualize it, or classify it. In other words, experience becomes intelligible and intelligently manageable insofar as we impose form upon it. But which forms, and from whence do they come?

The ultimate answer to this question is still a profound philosophical mystery, but for our purpose it is safe to say that every intellectual discipline, every science, every poem, and every picture is a source of forms or molds into which experience must flow and be shaped if we are to understand it at all. Our language is the great prefigurer or premolder of ordinary everyday experience; the sciences use molds or categories that allow us to understand our world in terms of atoms and electrons, galaxies and solar systems, acids and bases, causes and effects; our works of art enable us to feel the world as pervaded by human values.

Whenever we use our school learnings in these areas to perceive, understand, or feel life situations, we say that we are using our learnings primarily for interpretation, and not replicatively, associatively, or applicatively, although, strictly speaking, these uses do not necessarily exclude each other. There is a sense, however, in which the interpretive use of knowledge is the most fundamental of all, for without a prior interpretation of the situation we are not sure what we shall replicate, associate, or apply.

POLICY AND THE ORGANIZATION OF INSTRUCTION

The epistemology of educational policy is concerned with (A) the kinds of knowing and knowledge the pupil should acquire and (B) the process of formulating good policy. The first aspect focuses on determining the logical relations between accepted conclusions on the nature and aim of education, curriculum, and the educative process and items of policy when they are taken to be normative for policy. The second arises when none of these other areas is held to be normative for policy or when one attempts to determine which one should be considered most important to the consideration of educational policy and the organization of schooling.

In respect to A, it should be clear that Adler and Dewey, for example, both maintain that conclusions concerning the aim and the process of education, respectively, are normative for policy. They are normative but not themselves determinative of policy. Adler maintains that the aim is absolutely universal and necessary, but he also holds that policy is merely general and contingent upon the social and political philosophy of a particular society. The level of generality of policy is lower than that of the aim but higher than that of particular decisions within the actual teaching and learning situation. The latter have to take into account a number of factors that are not involved in policy decisions. Policy decisions also have to consider factors that are extraneous to the consideration of the nature and aim of education. Precisely how the thinking at the level of generality of policy is related to the more and less general levels of thinking of the aim and process is the problem of the epistemology of educational policy. Dewey maintains that policy is related to the educative process in somewhat the same way that aims are, but it is logically deducible from conclusions respecting the educative process only in that very broad sense of his in which everything conducted properly turns out to be education, to be part of the extended educative process. Policy "decisions" are hypothetical suggestions to be "validated" by their consequences in action. Then the articulation of why and how this should operate is the epistemology of educational policy. Neither Adler nor Dewey begins with conclusions concerning the kind of knowing or knowledge pupils should acquire and then proceeds to formulate policy by simple logical inference from the other conclusions, even if he does hold that these conclusions are of paramount significance to policy. Both require that the societal matrix be taken into account.

In respect to the process of formulating good policy it is uncertain if it is readily possible to accept either Adler's dictum that the aim determines the means or Dewey's that the means determines the end. One could advocate that conclusions concerning the curriculum should be considered normative for both means and ends as well as for policy. How curriculum can become decisive is indicated by Francis S. Chase in "Some Effects of Current Projects on Educational Policy and Practice" in *The School Review,* 70(Spring, 1962), pp. 132–47. Whether conclusions concerning curriculum *should* be decisive for policy is, of course, an open question. The point is that the issue between Adler and Dewey on the primacy of aim or process is also an open question. We are suggesting that curriculum, the third area, could be considered of paramount concern and normative for policy formulation and decision. Analogously, we are suggesting that perhaps the formulation of educational policy is the primary concern. Perhaps conclusions concerning policy should be normative for aims, curriculum, and the teaching-learning process rather than the reverse.

The attempt to decide at the level of policy which of the other three areas of education should be normative for policy is quite different from deciding the same question at the meta-epistemological level, as Adler and Dewey did, and from deciding upon policy and then proceeding by logical deductions to spell out the "logical implications" for the other areas. These matters would still be problematic and require an epistemology of policy. The primary questions, on the contrary, become: What knowledge is relevant to the formulation of good policy? What knowledge is useful and relevant to deciding upon a particular policy?

Although these questions may seem to be rather humdrum, they allow for the possibility of saying (1) only some of the relevant knowledge comes from philosophical conclusions about the aim, curriculum, and process of education, and (2) only some of that knowledge comes from epistemological considerations of these areas. The most relevant knowledge to the formulation of good policy might come from social philosophy, a nation's foreign policy, clinical psychology, inquiry into recent stock market trends, or, in fact, newspaper headlines. The last of these does not seem so odd if juxtaposed to the fact that particular items of policy are sometimes decided upon the basis of newspaper headlines during community controversies over sex education, "obscene" reading materials, etc. The epistemology of policy, then, is a matter of ascertaining the criteria by which one would recognize policy that was adequate according to relevant consideration and evidence. The attempt to measure the worth of a given policy against the norms and values of a given social philosophy, e.g., is quite different from ascertaining whether or not it agrees with and promotes a political party's campaign platform. The former might supply relevant evidence concerning the cognitive adequacy of an item of policy, the latter could not. Ascertaining the kind of difference between these two might be part of the epistemology of educational policy; ascertaining some answer to the prior question of whether or not agreement of educational policy with a social and political philosophy or with public policy constitutes valid evidence for good policy is definitely a larger part of the epistemology of educational policy. In general, the second aspect of the epistemology of educational policy has to do with the kinds of cognitive grounds that are relevant to policy and upon which such policy ought to be based. There is also the matter of generating specific recommendations from these grounds.

Further explication of this point of view appears in Clayton's selection that follows. Clayton's thesis is somewhat broader, for he argues that almost the whole of philosophy of education should become what we have called the epistemology of policy. Clayton's paper treats the whole current context of educational philosophy. It has not been edited in the belief that policy deserves as strong a case as aims, etc. Then, too, what he advocates has been a stronger force within philosophy of education than it now appears to be. It seems that the sort of emphasis he advocates ought to remain on the scene, if only to strengthen its opposition. At the very end of the paper Clayton cites the "social reconstructionists" of educational theory, who tried to come to grips with the epistemology of policy-making through the "method of practical intelligence." This method was not only a disciplined inquiry that would give to policy the kind of cognitive adequacy that the "reconstructionists" thought was desirable but was itself justified on the quasi-epistemological grounds of the sociology of knowledge. Although Clayton does not advocate a return to their efforts, more sympathy toward their efforts is possible after one sees what Clayton does advocate. Or perhaps one has to understand their efforts to grasp what Clayton suggests.

When the "reconstructionists" advocated the employment of the "method of practical intelligence" in actual policy-making, this was justified by the claim that the method was the method of democracy. This in turn was justified by an interpretation of democracy and democratic ideals. The interpretation of democratic ideals in turn was justified by an appeal to the sociology of knowledge. In other words, to some extent a number of important and avant-garde educational theorists employed the sociology of knowledge to justify certain procedures for policy-making and for certain policies themselves. In this employment the sociology of knowledge functioned as if it were a theory of the origin, nature, and validity of knowledge (as a quasi-epistemology), particularly in respect to the cognitive adequacy of social values. This will become clearer in the articles themselves.

In addition to the writings of the "reconstructionists" cited in the selections, are Raup's "The Community Criterion in Judgmental Practice" in the very first issue of *Studies in Philosophy of Education* (1960), pp. 4–39, and Stanley's *Education and Social Integration*. In general, they are difficult to excerpt from. We have, instead, selected items that discuss the sociology of knowledge in respect to what may very well be the major issue of educational policy: Should school policy reflect or reconstruct public policy? Can it reflect or reconstruct public policy? In its very nature, is school policy reflective or reconstructive? The sociology of knowledge is in some respects very well-suited to probe the basis for a perspective on these questions concerning whether the schools should attempt to perpetuate or improve the social order. This may be the central policy issue because many specific items of policy may often be decided according to preconceptions of the societal function of the schools in this respect. The opposing views are presented by Howie and Crittenden on Mannheim's and Durkheim's sociology of knowledge, respectively. If taken together they may not answer the questions, but they do raise them into explicit awareness. They are followed by Dupuis's critical exposition of the view of the "reconstructionist." As Crittenden indicates, Mannheim's view is the sociology of knowledge that is often referred to by educational theorists, as is more clearly indicated in Stanley's "Freedom and Education in a Corporate Society" in *Educational Theory,* 7(January, 1957), pp. 1–11. Crittenden's exposition of Durkheim intends to offer a balance, but actually Crittenden's paper raises a further question. Here are two "scientific" theories concerning the origin of knowledge and values in society. One concludes with "liberal" recommendations, the other with "conservative" implications. Have they escaped their own "sociology"? What about the sociology of the sociologist of knowledge? Can we simply say that Mannheim is a "utopian" and Durkheim is an "ideologist"? But what about us? It follows that the value of Dupuis's paper is his attempt to come to grips with the policy recommendations of the "reconstructionists" on epistemological grounds rather than from the viewpoint of an alternative sociology of knowledge.

THE RELEVANCE OF PHILOSOPHY OF EDUCATION TO QUESTIONS OF EDUCATIONAL POLICY*

A. Stafford Clayton

If concern with the proper role and business of philosophy of education were taken as an index of the vitality of the discipline, the evidences would point to considerable activity, if not growth, in the field of our efforts. As one reads the textbooks and articles of the recent past, it seems clear that a central and widespread search is being made for the distinctive place of philosophy of education in our culture today. Just what is it that the field of our study has to offer to an age facing momentous decisions concerning how to live together in a world caught up in a multitude of conditions and problems that men have not had to face before?

The conditions in the theory of education prompting this concern with the proper nature of our work are not difficult to discern. The general mood in the study of educational theory in recent years, characterized by some as a reaction against progressivism, by others as a failure of nerve on the part of creative liberalism, by some others as a period of consolidation of hard won achievements, and by still others as a time of incubation preparatory to the breakthrough of a new synthesis, has been hospitable to a renewed concern with the proper function of philosophy of education. It has been a period in which many reared within the dynamic years of progressivism's challenge have been reassessing their beliefs and convictions. For some this reassessment has led to a substantial reconstruction of commitment. Others have found that the continued restudy of the premises of educational theory has suggested the need for new emphases within the traditions that nourished them.

Movements of thought within philosophy and the social sci-

* Reprinted from "The Relevance of Philosophy of Education to to Questions of Educational Policy," *Proceedings of the Philosophy of Education Society* (1960), pp. 78–90. By permission of the author and the Philosophy of Education Society.

ences have also contributed to our search for what we should be about. The growth of philosophy of science and the formal analysis of meaning have centered attention upon the critical function of philosophy and advised educational philosophers to abjure speculation in favor of the clarification of protocol statements. Yet these movements within philosophy have led Paul Arthur Schilpp,[1] among others, to question whether philosophy in the dominant mood of the day has anything to say to our age. In as much as a vast number of his colleagues, as he sees it, concern themselves only with various aspects of linguistic problems, there is no widespread social effectiveness of philosophy in our day. But the historic role of philosophy is found in its search for wisdom concerning how to live together in a world in which the answers are not given in advance. In the social sciences not only has much criticism been given to the range of problems and the methods of social analysis, but also the theoretical structures involved have more and more received critical attention. C. Wright Mills,[2] for example, has been concerned with a widespread intellectual and moral uneasiness among social scientists as to the direction of their studies. To him the freeing and development of the "sociological imagination" which will enable us to achieve "lucid summations of what is going on in the world" is the great need of our time. Among other things this involves a focus upon the explicit troubles and the involvement of various publics in the public issues of modern society. In short, across the frontiers of the intellectual disciplines of our day men are being urged to come to grips with the pressing conditions and issues of social life.

With such conditions and movements of thought in mind we are here concerned with the bearing of our discipline on fundamental educational questions and issues of our time. This paper holds that philosophy of education as we know it today is in large measure irrelevant to the basic educational problems of the day. These problems and issues are seen as concerned with

---

[1] Paul Arthur Schilpp, "Does Philosophy Have Anything to Say to Our Age?", *The Bulletin of Atomic Scientists,* 15(May, 1959), 216–18.

[2] C. Wright Mills, *The Sociological Imagination* (New York, Oxford University Press, 1959).

the criticism and reconstruction of educational and social policies in the context of the pervasive and accelerated cultural changes of our decades. It is submitted that two main tendencies in philosophy of education have contributed significantly to the present irresponsibility of our discipline in regard to contemporary policy problems and that both of these movements involve restricted and parochial conceptions of the nature and role of philosophy of education. The paper will then try to suggest something of a broader conception of our discipline as it is brought to bear upon policy problems.

It seems to me that what philosophers of education have had to say in recent years contains two emphases which divert the relevance of our field from basic problems of educational policy. The philosopher of education, pushed back to a concern with his own grounds for saying something of significance to teachers and colleagues in the study of education, has found himself torn between two urges. On the one hand, he recognizes the demand to be clear and unambiguous in his formulations and to communicate his meanings with linguistic and logical precision. On the other hand, he needs to have something to say which is grounded in defensible premises and these, his interests suggest, are found in ultimate propositions involved in systems of philosophy. On the one side, dissatisfaction with the indeterminate and arbitrary character of much educational theory has led to an effort to disinfect our statements of their vague and imprecise overtones. On the other side, dissatisfaction with educational theories whose philosophical grounds are concealed or unexamined has led to efforts to explain how an educational theory is grounded in a system of philosophy. These urges and tendencies receive expression and support in two streams of thought bearing upon our conceptions of the proper function of philosophy in educational theory. Within one school of thought we are urged to carry the quest for clarity back to a concern with the formal network of meanings presupposed by an educational theory apart from its empirical claims. In the other it is supposed that we should trace educational choices back to ultimates about reality, truth, and value or deduce from the ultimate premises of a system its educational counterparts. On the one hand, the formal analysis of propositions is recommended;

on the other, we are to derive our educational choices from systematic differences in metaphysical, epistemological, axiological, or theological premises.

This paper takes the position that a point of diminishing returns is reached very soon in both of these tendencies. To become clear and precise as to what one is talking about is one thing, but to suppose that a philosophical theory of education must, as a logical priority, develop a formal analysis of the network of language and meaning is another. When the quest for linguistic and logical clarity is taken in the overly restrictive sense of the spelling out of the rules of meaning apart from empirical contexts, it becomes dissociated from the conditions with which a theory of education should be concerned. As a consequence, the operating theory of education involved in educational decisions is left without philosophical guidance and criticism. In brief, those devoted to formalistic analysis talk for the most part only to each other, not to the problems of schoolmen or those of the growing edges of educational theory.

A similar situation confronts us if we take the path leading to a direct and single-minded concern with ultimate differences between systems of philosophy. In this view it is supposed that differences between educational theories and the range of alternatives in a particular educational choice are in the last analysis expressions of idealism, realism, pragmatism, Thomism, humanism, and the like. The business of philosophy of education is to lead us to the ultimate parting of the ways over questions that have divided philosophers over the centuries. But the same consequence that follows from formalistic analysis awaits us here. The operating theory of education at stake in practical judgments in situations in time and place is frequently untouched by the direct reading off of ultimate philosophical presuppositions. When systems of philosophy are conceived as the fulcrum of educational decisions, many of the broader ranges of educational decisions are slurred over. Many aspects of the decisions of men and of schoolmen are not revealed within the systematic presupposition. Yet choices about policies are being made and frequently without attention to questions that permeate decision making. In short, philosophers of education when absorbed with the derivation of educational theories from differential ultimate premises speak primarily to each other rather than to the affairs of men.

To find these liabilities in these two common approaches in philosophy of education does not mean that both approaches have no appropriate place in our discipline. In regard to logical-linguistic analysis it is important to distinguish two types or phases. On the one hand, we can point to nonformal or contextual clarifications of meaning. In this kind of analysis the effort is to employ the skills and resources of semantical and logical processes as a situation in educational theory or practice is confronted. Such analysis undertakes the clarification of a human, social predicament. Within the context of the situation, it seeks what is fed into various appraisals of it, the conditions taken into account by those appraisals, and the probable outcomes of these judgments. The distinguishing characteristic of analysis at this level is its grounding in the empirical context of determinate situations and what is said about them. That this kind of analysis occurs within an empirical context does not mean that it deals only with narrowly and immediately practical situations. However, analysis of this type is concerned with the functions and meanings of terms in specific situations and with the purposes at stake in the human situation.

As distinct from analysis of this order, formal analysis seeks the linguistic-logical network of meaning in terms of which concepts are clarified apart from their empirical referents. It seeks to clarify the syntactic features and the logical geography of knowledge-claims rather than to add to knowledge or to check knowledge-claims against the concrete demands of situations. Gilbert Ryle's [3] analysis of the network of terms used to display the orders of meaning involved in talk about "mind" is in large part an example of formal analysis. Although in this work the various orders of terms are exemplified by references to common expressions and although the purpose is to correct "the dogma of the Ghost in the Machine," the analysis is of the formal orders of meaning, not of the current views of mind operating in determinate situations nor in terms of the theories and data of anthropological and psychological studies.

[3] Gilbert Ryle, *The Concept of Mind* (New York, Barnes and Noble, 1949).

My thesis is not that formal analysis is irrelevant to the tasks of philosophy of education. It is rather that, when formal analysis is taken as the model of philosophical inquiry or as a prerequisite of philosophical clarification of educational problems, attention to the substantive problems of an empirically grounded educational theory is minimized. The distinction between the two orders of analysis seems to me to be crucial. An educational theory appropriate to the problems and policy decisions of our time needs to be grounded in the skills and disciplines that promote the analysis of determinate human situations in which interests and values are at stake. The management of educational choices needs the aid of analysis that will make clear the kinds of relationships that pertain between policies on the one hand and on the other the conditions of American life, the best knowledge that can be mustered from the advances in science, and the values of a free people. Informal or contextual analysis devoted to these purposes clarifies key components of an educational theory. The function of formal analysis seems to me to lie largely in the systematization and consolidation as well as in the criticism of the achievements of the more nonformal analytic processes. Undoubtedly philosophers of education have a responsibility for the refinement of educational concepts and relationships when abstracted from their empirical referents. But the larger scope of the philosophical task and the need for disciplining educational decisions as to policy suggest a derivative rather than a logically primary role of formal analysis.

On the other side of our concern with influences which reduce the relevancy of our discipline to the educational conditions and problems of our time, much of the common concern with systems of thought has restricted and confined the role of philosophy of education. It is frequently taken for granted that our proper business is to deduce from systems of ultimate premises their educational counterparts or to infer from a stated educational point of view the ultimate postulates of a philosophical system. This view is subject to two criticisms. It involves an oversimplification, with consequent distortions, of the relations between particular educational choices and ultimate premises, between an educational theory and final philosophical convictions. It also presupposes that the decisions of teachers as to what is preferable in the situations confronting them are made more defensible by tracing their choices in some sense back to expressions of systems of philosophy. This leads to the neglect of large ranges of the tasks of a philosophical approach to educational problems and thus limits the way in which philosophy of education might be brought to bear on the actual problems of the educational situation.

In regard to the charge of oversimplification, it seems helpful to distinguish two kinds of relationships that may be involved when it is affirmed that a particular educational concept to be held more defensibly needs to be traced back to its more fundamental premises. In one kind of relationship the educational concept is so implicated logically in a theory of knowledge, reality, or value that its meaning is dependent upon the system of thought of which it is a logically necessary expression. To be distinguished from this logically tight relationship of implication is the situation where an educational concept may be interpreted within a more inclusive order of generalization or abstraction but is not a logically necessary implication of that abstraction. The first relationship is that of a logically necessary premise or implication; the second, that of a consistent but corollary or contingent belief or inference. As an example of the distinction in educational theory, consider the conception of growth as the inclusive end-in-view of education. If one affirms the educational conception of growth as the continuous reconstruction of experience, one must also affirm the proposition that human experience is the authoritative source of norms and criteria for the appraisal of its own processes. That is, Dewey's conception of growth involves the logically necessary postulates of his experimental empiricism. However, an expression of a policy about how to group children in school is not, as I see it, a direct and unitary expression of a philosophical premise or set of premises. Judgments concerning the grouping of children involve a host of empirical and situational considerations and appraisals not directly deduced from a single guiding philosophical concept or position. Such judgments must be related to a range of sensitivities to conditions and consequences and may be suggested by more inclusive generalizations but are not direct logical implications of a philosophical premise or of a general philosophy.

On the view that a philosophy of education is an expression of a system of philosophy the tendency is to read off without careful discrimination all aspects of an educational theory as expressions in one way or another of philosophical systems. On the view taken in this paper a large range of educational judgments involved in an operating theory of education may be consistent with various philosophical premises but not derived exclusively and necessarily from them. Educational judgments of this order need to be disciplined in the sense that their consequences are seen and tested and that a consistent direction of an educational program is maintained. But this discipline is derived not from a particular system of philosophy or the contrasts between them but from a more general philosophical-mindedness appropriate to the examination and building of policies within the conditions and values of a particular social order.

The second difficulty with a direct and pervasive concern by philosophy of education with traditional philosophic systems concerns the way in which this presupposition conceals large ranges of our appropriate tasks. In the first place, it is doubtful that the most pressing educational problems of our day will be solved by treating them simply as expressions of historic systems of philosophy. The continuities and discontinuities in the moral and intellectual basis of modern life indicate a broader range of considerations. In the second place, public education in a free society needs a community of persuasion about matters of common policy. Systems of philosophy in their historic expressions contribute only secondarily, if they do so at all, to the creation of an operating agreement for the direction of educational decisions. Third, a range of concerns that ought to be opened for consideration in the design and criticism of public policy is neglected in the emphasis upon established systems of thought. In large measure an educational theory ought to be tested by how it brings into the open and examines new problems and promotes a continuous and cooperative attack upon them. Current movements in systematic philosophy of education are in this sense unproductive.

This does not mean that systematic expressions of philosophic positions are irrelevant to philosophy of education but
that the character of the relevance is a part of the problem of
developing a grounded educational theory. Certainly the educational theorist is nourished by his participation in a particular
philosophical tradition, and his awareness of alternatives to his
own ultimate commitments is a measure of his profundity.
Furthermore, one need not assume a disjunction between the
contributions of philosophical systems and the achievement of a
theory of education. At least some pervasive decisions as to
educational policy are contingent upon preferences concerning
the ultimate grounding of educational concepts and derive their
fuller meaning from being interpreted within a framework of
higher abstraction. But that the decisions of teachers as to what
is preferable in the wide range of situations confronting them
are made appreciably more defensible by tracing their choices in
some sense back to expressions of systems of philosophy seems
doubtful.

It is proposed then that philosophy of education come directly to grips with problems of educational and social policy.
One reason for its doing so is largely strategic. Decisions concerning the quality and direction of educational policies are
continually being made and should be made more critically and
defensibly. Furthermore, philosophy of education when focally
concerned with questions as to educational policy would be
more closely attuned to the common concerns and problems of
schooling. But, more than this, in a democratic society where
the directions of educational policy are not established at the
top and passed down only for acceptance and execution, we
need to develop common agreements about policy and appropriate means for the growth of operating agreements which give
unity and direction to common efforts. This does not mean that
a policy-centered philosophy of education would necessarily
radically increase consensus in the sense of unanimity in educational theory. However it does mean that disagreements would
appear and be managed in a new light. An agreement as to the
sources and character of different policy persuasions is itself
part of the wisdom needed in a theory of public education.
Although philosophy of education has resources most appropri-

ate to the building and refinement of an operating basis of public policy, it has not matured as a scholarly discipline contributing to this community of purpose. In this sense we have been overly concerned with our qualifications and interests as philosophers rather than sufficiently concerned to see philosophy as an enterprise at work with the problems of men.

To this point in this paper we have been concerned with how several of our philosophic interests have contributed to the irrelevance of much of our work to the order and direction of educational decisions. We have proposed that philosophy of education focus on the study and development of educational policies in the context of the demands of the current educational and social situation. We have indicated the need for an educational theory expressing a common persuasion about the management of schooling in a democratic society. In such a society, although we treasure the profound differences as to ultimate philosophical commitment which characterize the life of free men, yet we are bound together in a quest for operating procedures and value-directive propositions promoting a free and humane social order. The quest for a range of agreement and for a way to manage disagreements concerning the major directions of the public welfare comes into focus as a primary task of an educational theory.

Although part of the task of a policy-centered philosophy of education is to spread out the range of policy-problems needing study, we can suggest something of the scope and nature of the task by pointing out three aspects of the philosophic undertaking in matters of policy.

In the first place, some of these questions indicate areas of common concern where the search for some substantial direction in decision making is presently experienced. The question, "How should children be grouped in school?" not only indicates a commonly recognized educational problem, but its exploration involves judgments about pervasive conditions of modern life, the values of a free people, and the bearings of educational policies upon different interpretations of the public welfare. Many other questions commonly confronted by teachers today pose philosophical considerations in policy forming. How should teachers report to parents concerning the growth of children? Should the school be responsible for all aspects of the child's growth, or for selected aspects, or for narrow range of intellectal abilities? Such questions not only represent current problems calling for decisions. To deal with them adequately calls for profound consideration of the normative dimensions of our way of life.

In the second place, current treatments of some aspects of modern educational decisions have as yet paid little attention to their bearings upon an examined theory of democratic education. For instance, much attention has recently been given to the education of the talented and to the need in our time for high levels of proficiency in those areas where the cold war and the race for ascendancy in the space-age have shown us to be deficient. Profound questions as to national public and educational policy are involved but have not received the attention from a philosophical point of view which they merit. Should talent, excellence, or superior performance be broadly construed or restricted to certain kinds of academic abilities, or to what is currently rewarded, or to socially prestigeful activities? A philosophically minded approach to what is involved in this question would be interested in identifying narrow and restrictive notions of talent which, when presupposed in policy proposals, distort or negate other values of a democratic life. For example, one of the values which a free people has found to be a deep ingredient of the good life is the opportunity of the individual to engage in socially significant work. Yet, not only do many of the conditions of modern life limit or deny the realization of this value on the part of many, but policies instituted in the name of certain otherwise worthy purposes may reinforce the conditions which we deplore. We need comprehensive analyses of policies relative to manpower, the selection and development of talent, the way in which a democratic society manages its occupational needs in relation to the other values in a maximal life-opportunity for all. The contribution of a philosophically minded approach to policy problems of this order would be to infuse current discussion with the fuller range of value considerations which are frequently squeezed out by other pressures.

In the third place, some ranges of policy problems are not

sensed or opened up to public discussion through present efforts, interests, or demands upon the school. Or, if the conflicts between policy proposals are in part articulated, their bearings upon the full extent of educational policy have not been indicated. Unexplored but emerging areas of policy problems of this order might be exemplified by what is at stake in the fuller development of the evolutionary hypothesis within the life sciences and its consequences for educational theory. The present state of conflict in this regard is probably shown in controversy over the teaching of evolution and pressures concerning the treatment of the principle in biology textbooks. Despite recent treatments of evolutionary theory in popular magazines, the situation in public education has not changed appreciably since the Scopes incident. Yet beyond immediate questions about the inclusion of evolution in the instructional program of the school are profound questions of educational policy concerning the control of the life process in the interest of human values. The biological and behavioral sciences have increasingly described and made available to human decision the processes which were earlier unknown and uncontrollable by human purpose. The geneticists have been telling us of late that human progress is not ingrained within the evolutionary principle but that mutations in the human species can not in the long run be left to chance if the welfare of future individuals is adequately sensed and prized. However, the attitudes, beliefs, and existing value patterns of individuals and institutions are hardly ready for the responsibilities which our new knowledge indicates. What is proper responsibility of the school in regard to those areas in which reliable knowledge conflicts with the traditional views of large segments of the people? Involved in this whole matter are fundamental questions concerning the freedom of learning, religious freedom, and the moral responsibilities of the school for the fullest welfare of the individual.

This suggestion of the range of concerns of a policy-oriented approach to a theory of education indicates that policy problems when basically explored cut deeply into the fabric of American life. The exploration of what is at stake in them involves the clarification and judgment of competing claims as to what ought to be done in the context of the continuities of cultural movements and norms and the discontinuities of modern conditions and achievements. The philosophic mind has a range of intellectual resources to bring to the analysis, systematization, and adjudication of policy problems. These skills and habits brought to the center of attention as they engage the policy problems of the day constitute a common philosophical discipline at work in developing an educational theory. Philosophy of education thus gets down to cases in regard to the educational situation but develops its cases not primarily in terms of ultimate systems or of formal linguistic-logical analysis but in terms of a potentially common philosophical method, specified in what philosophers do, not merely in terms of the products or doctrines of their particular positions.

In this perspective the proper and pressing business of philosophy of education is to undertake the exploration of policy questions so that the assumptions made by different proposals are inquired into and value-involved preferences are identified and made to yield their credentials. Since, as this paper has argued, assumptions are not all of the same order, the philosophic mind sorts them out so that the distinctions between them are available. Some of the things assumed by policy proposals are matters of fact to be tested by empirical evidences or the convergence of lines of empirical evidence. Other things taken for granted involve such selection and interpretation of grounds and evidences that the value framework of the interpretation is focal. Here the determinate grounds for the proposals being examined are interwoven with the network of value generalizations that express certain appraisals and interests. Still other assumptions refer to the logically necessary premises of world-views, or, on the other hand, to postulates involved in intellectual frameworks more or less independent of or common to differential systems of ultimate premises. When assumptions are taken as single monolithic entities apart from their place and function in situations where policies are at stake, human deliberations are deprived of the means of deciding the extent and character of conceivable practical agreements. In contrast, when a situation involving policies is explored in terms of different levels of assumptions, a public means for a cooperative judgment of what ought to be done is available. This does not mean that a single encompassing theory of public education will be derived directly from the kind of situational analysis here suggested. However it does mean that the quest for a common theory of schooling would have an opportunity for continual refinement. Moreover, as the different orders of assumptions and value-involvements of conflicting policy proposals are scrutinized, a process of systematization of policy and of adjudication between competing policies becomes open to study.

If it be granted that the relations between a policy proposition and its fundamental assumptions are plural and of various orders, the systematic character of a theory of education is seen in a new light. To reduce statements of educational policy to expressions in some sense or other of traditional schools of philosophical thought is one thing. To search for order, consistency, and a harmony of valuations in policy statements at different levels of inclusiveness and between various areas in which appraisal and choice are crucial is another. A systematic treatment of policy propositions means inquiry into how the meaning of one depends upon the meaning of the others, and inquiry into the full range of interests and values that ought to be included in a considered judgment of the direction of public life. For instance, in the area of religion and public education profound differences in ultimate premises as well as in practical policies have recommended the separation of church and state as our historic, although by no means unquestioned, policy. I do not mean to challenge the wisdom of this policy as a means of managing the divisive issues of religious and theological systems of thought. But we have also averred in our society a conception of religious freedom in the context of the freedom of speech, assemblage, and inquiry, and this means that each grows in freedom as he communicates and searches freely and responsibly in the context of diversity. Existing policies interpreting the separation of church and state—that religion is a private rather than a public matter, that parents may send children to the school of their choice, and that the school is to be neutral as to religious preference—do not square with the value we place upon the freedom of the learner to search, to inquire cooperatively, and to speak. Questions which probe the moral and political and general cultural consequences of what is held to be

sacred by some ecclesiastical group or authority are deleted
from textbooks and the curriculum. My point is that a concern
with the systematic aspects of an educational theory would
attend to the full range of educational values of a society of free
men. It would seek to bring these into an interrelated order of
policy propositions and problems to be inquired into and tested
in terms of their bearing on the inclusive interests and values of
the democratic society.

   In what has been said about the philosophical responsibility
in matters of public and educational policy, I do not mean to
imply that we have only to read off the meaning of agreed-upon
democratic values for a program of education. On the contrary,
the adjudication, not the mere reconciliation, of conflicting interests and interpretations calls for philosophical examination
and appraisal of existing policy alternatives and the creation of
new ones. A defensible educational theory needs the philosophic
scrutiny of the grounds and evidences alleged to recommend
certain policies. It needs the philosophic weighing of the outcomes of policies as they fulfill different purposes. The examination of assumptions differentially integral and imperative to the
interests and purposes of various points of view is most appropriately a task of philosophical statesmanship. The claim which
philosophy of education makes as a unique and central discipline in educational theory is not justifiable, it seems to me,
primarily in terms of the doctrines espoused because of a feeling
of certainty about ultimate premises. Philosophy's centrality in
an educational theory is justified rather, I think, by its role in
the examination and explication of what is at stake in conflicting
policy proposals. It is a matter of identifying and constructing
and bringing to bear upon policy formation the skills, habits,
and intellectual-moral resources of the philosophical mind. I do
not mean this in the gross or overly simple sense of an application from the outside or of a veneer to cover up hidden preconceptions. I mean to point to the integrity of the disciplined mind
that will listen and take the role of the other, make distinctions
and follow their significance, recognize and appraise the bearing
of evidences, and probe assumptions in their different dimensions. Adjudication without these ingredients is arbitrary and
opportunistic, and differences in the quality of adjudicative
judgments should themselves be objects of study.

The term "adjudication" has been chosen deliberately. As used here, it refers not to a narrowly legalistic process of arriving at judgments. It suggests the process whereby the relevance of evidence, of selected postulates, of discriminatory valuations, and of alternative social consequences is discovered in a situation containing conflicting purposes claimed to express what ought to be done in the public interest. It suggests a different approach to the study of value considerations from those commonly employed in philosophy of education. As I see it, inquiry into the ingredients and grounds of policies which are to guide us in determinate situations does not mean that we must first come to agree about the nature and status of values as existential entities. In my view, the solutions of questions concerning the relativistic or absolutistic status of values are not logically indispensable premises to the objectification of certain value propositions in the management of human situations. In an educational theory devoted to policy study we can be concerned with the way in which some values cast judgment upon the character of human choices without presupposing that in the last analysis values are either emotional expressions, or a hierarchy of goods dictated by the essential nature of man, or evaluated wants. The point in the educational situation is that a determinate direction in public and educational policy must be achieved and should be developed in the context of the study of who proposes what policies with what interests in mind in the anticipation of what consequences. Inquiry into the situation in which value propositions operate is thus distinguishable from other levels of abstraction in the study of values. It is acknowledged that alternative systems of philosophy with their different value theories might articulate differing educational policies. They might also, in larger measure than we commonly conceive, concur. More significant, as I see it, is the opportunity to see whether the differences make any difference and, if they do, whether they are negotiable in terms of the claims and consequences of the human situation.

I mean to suggest that it is the judicial act, the process of adjudicating the interests of the determinate human situation, that may well serve as the model for the disciplined act of reflection in an emerging educational theory in our day. In a sense we need to do for the act of adjudication what Dewey did for the logical analysis of the method of scientific inquiry. I am not suggesting a disjunction between two alternative methods, although in the weighing of various values and interests one is called upon to do things which the scientist in his more strictly controlled acts of judgment can minimize. I am suggesting that much that has been done in the study of "the discipline of the practical judgment" [4] and in the analysis of the cleavages in the democratic tradition [5] seems to me to serve the reorientation of philosophy of education to the study of policy. At least, attention to the role of philosophy of education in the determination of educational and social policies would lead us into inquiry into adjudication as a human undertaking rather than the more limited conceptions of the role of philosophy which we have earlier indicated.

This paper has endeavored to explore, not to define, the role of our discipline in regard to policy questions. It has suggested that the reorientation of philosophy of education toward problems of social and educational policy would meet the educational needs of the day more adequately than other and, as I see it, more restrictive views. Its purpose has been not to present a comprehensive or exhaustive analysis of this reorientation but to explore in part what might accrue if we were to meet more responsively the policy demands made upon the teaching-learning situations of our culture. At least, it seems to me that I can tell the difference between teachers who have been led to a concern with policy problems and those who think of philosophy of education in other terms.

[4] R. Bruce Raup, et al., *The Improvement of Practical Intelligence* (New York, Harper, 1950).

[5] William O. Stanley, *Education and Social Integration* (New York, Bureau of Publications, Teachers College, Columbia University, 1953).

MANNHEIM'S SOCIOLOGY OF KNOWLEDGE AND EDUCATIONAL POLICY *

Marguerite R. Howie

Mannheim's epistemological approach to a planned society is through his sociology of knowledge. As a theory, it seeks to analyze the relationship between knowledge and existence. An historical-sociological research, it seeks to trace the forms which this relationship has taken in the intellectual development of mankind. It is concerned with "unmasking" the various ways which objects present themselves to the subject according to the differences in social setting.

His epistemological approach does not provide a blueprint for a utopia, therefore, I interpret him to be a realist possessing utopian thought. His analysis of utopian thought is in quest of reality. . . .

Mannheim views the control of the collective unconscious to be one of the major problems of our age. Historically oriented in the religious world view, control of the collective unconscious became fractionalized in the upsurge of political outlooks that came into dominance with the split in clerical domination that accompanied the Protestant Reformation. Attempts to interpret and to analyze collectively experienced events are basic in the thinking of Adam Smith and Karl Marx.[10] Marx's theory of class struggle evidences awareness of the unconscious collective motivations which had always guided the direction of thought. It is in opposition to the party science manipulation of the collective unconscious as expressed in Marxism that Mannheim develops his thought levels from the noological stage to the level of collective consciousness. It is in this last stage that political sociology synthesizes thought into collective consciousness.

* Reprinted from "Karl Mannheim and the Sociology of Knowledge," *Journal of Education,* 143(April, 1961), 55, 57–61, 64–68. By permission of the editor of the *Journal of Education.*

[10] Karl Mannheim, *Ideology and Utopia* (New York, Harcourt, Brace and Company, 1951), p. 37.

In preliterate societies where the same meanings of words, the same ways of dedicating ideas are inculcated from childhood into every member of the group divergent group processes cannot exist. Only when horizontal mobility is accompanied by intensive vertical mobility, i.e., rapid movement between strata in the sense of social ascent or descent, is the belief in the general external validity of one's own thought-forms shaken.[11] According to Mannheim, vertical mobility is the decisive factor in making persons uncertain and skeptical of their traditional view of the world. It is not until we have a general democratization that the rise of the lower strata, which formerly had no public validity, enables it to acquire validity and prestige.[12] When the stage of democratization has been reached, the techniques of thinking and the ideas of the lower strata are for the first time in position to confront the ideas of the dominant strata on the same level of validity.[13] Although the lower strata, i.e., the feudal peasant, possessed opinions, their validity was unrecognizable as it lacked political status.

In every society there are social groups whose special task it is to provide an interpretation of the world for that society, i.e., the "intelligentsia." In medieval society the clergy monopolized intellectual thought. It possessed the power to sanction the ontology and the epistemology implicit in the prevailing mode of thought. In such a hierarchical position it was remote from the open conflicts of everyday life, insensitive to the opinions of the masses, and removed from any obligation to reckon with the same.

The dual influences of the Protestant Reformation and the Industrial Revolution liberated the intellectuals from the church and the modern, free "intelligentsia" emerged. The free "intelligentsia" recruits from constantly varying social strata and life situations. With democratization varying social organizations or the larger world of varying strata compete for favor of the public. Monopolistic thought becomes passé. . . .

Investigating the cognitive process from a sociological point of view, men became aware of the collective unconscious, the

[11] *Ibid.*, p. 6.
[12] *Ibid.*, p. 7.
[13] *Ibid.*, p. 8.

motivations which guide the direction of thought based on external causations. The theory of external causality is based on the assumption that an external situation can call forth an inner reaction. Such reactions are reflected in the collective mentality of the group or the collective unconscious. Mannheim interprets these polaristic mentalities as being either ideological or utopian.[17]. . .

The ideological mentality is the collective conscious of the ruling group. Its members become so interest bound that they are unable to see the real conditions of society. The word ideology means the opinions, statements, and propositions, and systems of ideas are not taken at their face value but are interpreted in the light of the life situations of the one who interprets them.[18] The concept of ideology in historical perspective is rooted in the distrust and suspicion which men everywhere evidence toward their adversaries: Bacon's theory of the "idols"—idols, phantoms, the preconceptions that were idols of the tribe, the market, or the theatre.[19] During the Renaissance period the thought of the palace was one thing; the thought of the public square was another.

The utopian mentality is representative of "thinking among certain oppressed groups." [20] These groups are so strongly interested in the transformation of a given condition of a society that they unwittingly see only those elements in the situation which tend to negate it. They are not concerned with what really exists; rather in their thinking, they already seek to change what exists.

Developing a philosophy of consciousness was synonymous with the social and political democratization. Prior to such democratization, collective mentality was at the "noological" level. Using man's conception of the world as an example, men viewed "world" as existing independently of the individual: "The word 'world' exists only with reference to the knowing mind, and the mental activity of the subject determines the form in which the world appears." [21] Only when the total conception

[17] *Ibid.*, p. 36.
[18] *Ibid.*, p. 54.
[19] *Ibid.*
[20] *Ibid.*, p. 36.
[21] *Ibid.*, p. 59.

of ideology is seen in historical perspective does class ideology, class consciousness, develop. Ideological thinking could not develop until the feeling of nationalism was really born. The "folk" of primitive society was replaced by the "class" of medieval society; the "class" of medieval society was replaced by the "nation" of modern society. The independent system of meanings in regard to levels of society vary from one historical period to another. The types of collective conscious, the types of social and political levels are determined by the historical flux.

Historically speaking, the ideologists were a group of French intellectuals who rejected metaphysics and sought to base the cultural sciences on anthropological and psychological foundations (e.g., Condillac). The concept of "false consciousness" actually originated with Marx. The problems of "false consciousness" occur whenever the genuineness of a prophet's inspiration or vision is questioned either by his people or by himself.[22] Inadvertently, the term ideology acquired a new connotation as it was redefined by the politician in terms of his experience. As such, ideology becomes a method of research.[23] As a method of research it has the twofold function of showing the interrelationship between the intellectual point of view held and the social position occupied; of combining such a non-evaluative analysis with an epistemology. The non-evaluative conception of ideology is not concerned with which of the opposing parties has the truth on his side but the consideration of the approximate truth as it emerges in the course of historical development and out of the complex social process. There is no guarantee of dominant values or ideas—one position is not regarded as impregnable and absolute. The theme of this non-evaluative study of ideology is the relationship of all partial knowledge and its component elements to the larger body of meaning, and ultimately to the structure of historical reality.[24] . . . So it is with understanding the mentality of an epoch, for facts do not exist in isolation, but in an intellectual and social context. Mannheim's quest for reality lies in the

[22] *Ibid.,* p. 70.
[23] *Ibid.,* p. 79.
[24] *Ibid.,* pp. 84–87.

"unmasking" of ideas in their historical-social setting through ideological and utopian analysis.

His analysis accepts the collective unconscious but rejects the party science ideas of Marx. While he admits to social and political determinants of knowledge, he rejects the idea of a science of politics. Political conduct, according to Mannheim, is concerned with the state and society in so far as they are in the process of becoming. It is concerned with a process in which every moment creates a new situation. As such, it is difficult to formulate general laws in a situation where now forces are incessantly entering the system and forming unseen combinations. The observer does not stand outside of the realm of the irrational, but is a participant in the conflict of forces. Likewise, the observer's mode of thought is bound up in political and social undercurrents.

Mannheim cites general types of political currents that are the determinants of knowledge. Bureaucratic conservatism which turns all problems of politics into problems of administration; historical conservatism which cannot be managed by administration but admits to "construction by a calculated plan"; liberal-democratic bourgeoisie thought which demands scientific politics (parliament, electoral system, League of Nations); the socialist-communist current based on the theory that the state of productive relations determines the political sphere; and the fascist theory which admits to a power élite—all are but theories. As theories, even communistic theory, they are in the process of becoming and therefore cannot become a science of politics; they cannot set up an "a priori."

In conceiving theory as a function of reality, Mannheim posits that theory leads to a certain kind of action. Inadvertently, action changes the reality, or in case of failure, forces us to a revision of the previous theory.[29] Socialist-communist theory, according to Mannheim, is a synthesis of institutionalism and a determined desire to comprehend phenomena in an extremely rational way.[30] It is based on the interdependence of economics, class and ideology: the political sphere in any so-

[29] *Ibid.*, pp. 112–13.
[30] *Ibid.*, p. 114.

ciety is based on and is always characterized by a state of productive relations; changes in this economic factor are closely connected with class relations; and it is possible to understand the inner structure of the system of ideas dominating men at any period and to theoretically determine the direction of change or modification of this structure.[31] Revolution, an intention to provoke a breach in the rationalized, interrupts Marxian thought and prevents Marxian ideology from perceiving the true interrelationships as they actually exist, and thus defeats the system. Marx's theory, like the others, attempts to manipulate the masses. Conservatives, liberals, and socialists operate on the theory that there is an interrelationship between events and configurations, through which everything, by virtue of its position acquires significance.[32] The Fascists use social psychology as a technique for manipulating the masses.[33] The liberal-democratic bourgeoisie carry on the class struggle through the parliamentary process. These levels of thought (antithesis), all points of view in politics, are but partial points of view because historical totality is always too comprehensive to be grasped by any one of the points of view which emerge out of it.[34]

The problem, then, is whether or not it is possible for different styles of thought to be fused into one another and to undergo synthesis. Mannheim contends that it is possible: "Every concrete analysis of thinking which proceeds sociologically and seeks to reveal the historical succession of thought-styles indicates that styles of thought undergo uninterrupted fusion and interpretation." [35] His re-examination of the basic thought-forms, utopia and ideology, reveals that the former has the greater possibility of synthesis. . . .

Historically, utopian mentalities have evidenced themselves in three forms: (1) those of the middle ages which originated in the depressed forms of society and advocated the "spiritualization of politics"; [38] (2) liberal-humanitarianism based on idea

[31] *Ibid.*, p. 115.
[32] *Ibid.*, pp. 122–23.
[33] *Ibid.*, p. 125.
[34] *Ibid.*, p. 134.
[35] *Ibid.*, pp. 136–37.
[38] *Ibid.*, p. 190.

as a goal—that "other realm" which absorbed in our moral
consciousness inspires us as a goal—becomes bound up with the
process of becoming, i.e., free will, undeterminate and uncon-
ditioned; and (3) the materialistic orientated utopia based on
force—that a realm of freedom and equality will come into
existence in the remote future when there is a breakdown of
the capitalistic culture.[39] Each of these forms is instrumental
through revolution. Mannheim's thesis is dependent, not upon
revolution, [but] upon progressive development at the conscious
level. Collective consciousness enables man to plan such a
synthesis. The result would never be static but always in process,
always in movement, based on constant planning to meet the
needs of the historical movement. In this movement, education
would be the motivating force, the bond between all intellectuals (those whose task it is to provide an interpretation of the
world for that society) no matter what the strata.[40]. . .

In the process of historical development, man has experienced three stages of psycho-social development: [66] (1) man at
the stage of horde solidarity is relatively homogeneous and his
behavior is ultimately enforced by tradition and fear; (2) man
at the stage of individual competition is capable of competitive
thinking, a subjective rationality (to calculate chances from
one's own point of view) not necessarily the fundamental relationships between cause and effect in society as a whole; (3)
man at the stage of the super-individual group solidarity at
which individuals are compelled to renounce their private interests and to subordinate themselves to the interests of the larger
social units. "The individual is beginning to realize that he must
plan for the whole of his society and not merely parts of it; that,
further, in the course of this planning, he must show a certain
concern for the fate of the whole." [67] It is here that man has
arrived at a stage of planning.

Mannheim considers that modern danger lies not in the planning but lack of it. His thesis is that the same tensions which are

[39] *Ibid.,* p. 198.
[40] *Ibid.,* p. 139.
[66] Karl Mannheim, *Man and Society in an Age of Reconstruction*
(New York, Harcourt, Brace and Company, 1941), pp. 66–70.
[67] *Ibid.,* p. 70.

causing such distress in economic life are also at work in the cultural sphere. As a result, the planned society has the responsibility for providing an atmosphere where freedom may reach the level of self-determination. (1) Our cultural life is exposed to certain dangers, as long as democratic mass society is allowed to function without control. (2) Our cultural life encounters greater dangers when dictatorial governments supplant liberal forms. (3) "These social causes which bring about cultural disintegration in a liberal society, themselves pave the way for dictatorship." [68] From Mannheim's point of view, "the task of the intellectual élites is to inspire the life of the culture and to lend it form, create a living culture in the different spheres of social life." [69] In the three stages of psycho-social development . . . sociological freedom expresses itself differently. In the initial stage, freedom expresses itself in direct action on and reaction to the stimuli of the surroundings. In the second stage, man is benefited by his inventions and becomes more and more independent of natural conditions. His increased demand over his immediate aims becomes the most valued expression of his freedom. Although technique (invention) frees man from the harnesses of nature, it subjects him to the social coercion which competition entails. It is in the third stage, then, that mankind becomes increasingly entangled in the network of social relationships which he has created.[70] The self-deterministic character of the new conception of freedom creates the desire to control the social surroundings as far as possible. The advances that have been made in the social technique have reached the stage where man can conduct social affairs from key positions according to a definite plan. Human mentality has reached the third stage in the phychological transformation: from the symbol as a mere substitute goal in the first stage, to the symbol as the driving force for spontaneous group-integration in the second, and finally to the third stage where the symbol becomes the rigid symbol of the organized group.[71]

[68] *Ibid.*, p. 80.
[69] *Ibid.*, p. 82.
[70] *Ibid.*, pp. 370–75.
[71] *Ibid.*, pp. 132–33.

In the stage that we have just reached, we have the choice of planning in a healthy society which we ourselves have chosen. To plan a healthy society, we have need to recognize the opportunities as well as the dangers. . . . Mannheim considers the major opportunities of our age to be (1) that an integrated science of man may enable us to understand clearly the causes of maladjustment and to plan a society that removes the extremes of the same; (2) that mankind has the possibility of implementing democracy by the use of efficient social techniques; (3) that we may think for and plan for humanity as a whole; (4) that once collective responsibility is realized, commonly accepted tensions may be subsided; and (5) that new weapons reduce the military significance of national boundary lines.[72]

Aware that experiments may miscarry, Mannheim posits that improvement is possible only if the experimenter can clearly state what he wants; he can only try again if he knows exactly what he wanted and why he failed before. In realistic manner, he selects the following guiding values or goals toward which there may be democratic planning:

1) planning for freedom, subjected to democratic control;
2) planning for plenty—full employment and full exploitation of resources;
3) planning for social justice rather than absolute equality, with differentiation of rewards and status on the basis of genuine equality rather than privilege;
4) planning not for a classless society, but for one that abolishes the extremes of wealth and poverty;
5) planning for cultural standards without "leveling down"— a planned transition making for progress without disregarding what is valuable in tradition;
6) planning that encounters the dangers of mass society by coordination of the means of social control by interfering only in the cases of institutionalization or moral deterioration defined by collective criteria;
7) planning for balance between centralization and dispersion of power;
8) planning for gradual transformation of society in order to encourage the growth of personality: planning, but not regimentation.

[72] *Ibid.,* p. 70.

As I interpret Mannheim, the "whole" plan seems significant.[76] The avoidance of fragmentation is necessary. To accomplish agreement or at least "loyal opposition," a plan must fulfill certain preconditions: It must be consistent; it must be acceptable to a majority. The twofold functions of the reconstructed ruling class are: (1) to visualize and define the principles and objectives of democracy in industrial society; (2) to devise practicable ways and means to attain its ends by reforms and mass consensus.[77]

Throughout Mannheim's works a ruling élite, solicited from the intellectual potential in all classes and strata of society, is cited as the democratic power group. I understand their power to be functional, that of interpreting the socio-historic epoch and guiding democratic planning accordingly. He expresses his democratic theory of power thus: "Democracy, rightly understood, implies a theory of power aimed at defining ways of distributing and controlling communal power for maximum security, efficiency, and freedom." [78] These are but the external prerequisites for a new society. His *Diagnosis of Our Times* is founded on the premise that no society can survive unless basic values, institutions, and education are integrated with one another. It seems to me that he considers education as the instrument for accomplishing these ends. Social science replaces custom as the source for the remaking of man.[79]

Specific educational responsibilities of the social sciences as explicitly stated are:

[76] See Karl R. Popper, *The Poverty of Historicism* (Boston, Beacon Press, 1957), pp. 55–104. He refutes the possibility of predicting historical developments which may be influenced by the growth of knowledge. He attacks the holistic quality of the sociology of knowledge because of its methodology of re-designing society as a whole. Popper considers the holistic method as impossible because in application it would resort to the expediency of piecemeal improvisation. Such expediency, Popper contends, causes the planner to do things he did not intend to do. The vastness of the scale and scope of the planner's task makes it impossible to be activistic on an "all or nothing at all" basis. Hayek in *The Road to Serfdom* also questions planning on the grounds that the scope is too vast for a whole or world view. No strata able to view society is able to view it as a whole at any given moment.

[77] Karl Mannheim, *Freedom, Power, and Democratic Planning* (New York, Oxford University Press, 1950), p. 107.

[78] *Ibid.*, p. 45.

[79] *Ibid.*, pp. 173–98.

1) "Social education . . . aims at creating a balanced personality in the spirit of real Democracy; individuality should not develop at the expense of the community sentiment." [80]
2) Social science in the place of workable tradition will assist democratic planning in three directions: it will clarify (a) the democratic idea of co-ordination; (b) the making and re-making of human behavior, i.e., social and psychological means of conditioning man (c) the pattern of democratic behavior, conscience, and personality as ends of democratic planning.[81]

Education as the groundwork for the remaking of man, the remaking of culture (as I interpret the remaking, it is from a universal concept of culture rather than from the traditional geographic perspective), according to Mannheim, must accept new tasks. An outline of his explicit responsibilities for education follows.

1) "The school may . . . perform its special tasks by intensifying and systematizing social experience—a function that the various compartments of social life can hardly perform." [82]
2) The school as an agency for change "will have to give up its older, purely scholastic character, the more it takes over the functions neglected by other social institutions. The school will have to become more homelike, more like a workshop, more like the community, as the family, workshop and community shed their educational functions. Children will have to find in school what the home has lost, perhaps because both parents work and eat out. The more fugitive the atmosphere of the two or three generation family, the more the school environment must embody and seek to impart the humanization qualities that formerly characterized good homes. . . . The task of the school is to show how to learn more efficiently from life, how to draw correct conclusions from experience, how to become one's own educator." [83]
3) The special function of the school in a democratically planned society will be to interpret all phases of life in terms of democratic experience, ". . . to show the different ways of starting a family, educating the young, transacting business, spending leisure, et cetera." [84]
4) Continuity in the educational scheme: "that young people

[80] *Ibid.*, p. 175.
[81] *Ibid.*, p. 176.
[82] *Ibid.*, p. 247.
[83] *Ibid.*, pp. 249–50.
[84] *Ibid.*, p. 250.

may have in the context of their own organizations experience which is in miniature that of the wider community in which they will in a fuller measure soon participate. . . . Such a policy should help to develop co-operation, tolerance, self-reliance, joint responsibility, and especially the feeling that every person counts." [85]

5) That the educational process will not become fragmentary, adult education is influential as "post-education and re-education for those who wish to keep abreast of scientific advances and swift social changes." [86]

6) The people's university to offer "permanent refresher courses for managers, technicians, ultimately for all, and especially for people in their thirties, is in keeping with our characterization of the need in a dynamic society for continuous adult education to keep everybody mentally alert and enable them to meet the modern requirements of democratic citizenship." [87]

7) Responsibility to man's quest for freedom: ". . . freedom in a planned society should not be judged in terms of the absence or presence of bureaucracy and regulation, but in terms of the common good and the best use of individual potentialities, intelligence tests, interviews, expert observation of physical and mental development and dispositions, and expert guidance of vocational choices in agreement with planned and predictable developments—and at the same time provision of unplanned sectors which give scope to people of specific gifts or aspirations—may serve man's quest for freedom in a planned world." [88]

The new patterns of democracy proposed by Mannheim in his "Third Way" as opposed to the alternatives of "laissez-faire," Total Regimentation, Communism, or Fascism concentrates upon the monumental significance of planning the transition needs which is as decisive a factor as mapping out a distant future. His guiding principles for democratic planning can help the administrator to assess the merits of single forms and decisions in the reconstruction process. . . .

For Mannheim, then, ideas that do not exist in the social situation, ideas that transcend social realities are the content of

[85] *Ibid.*, p. 252.
[86] *Ibid.*, pp. 253–54.
[87] *Ibid.*, pp. 257–58.
[88] *Ibid.*, p. 284.

ideologies. Therefore any reorganization in the social structure, any reconstruction are the efforts of groups that were utopian minded. It is they who have reached the level of collective consciousness needed to plan a democracy.

DURKHEIM'S SOCIOLOGY OF KNOWLEDGE AND EDUCATIONAL POLICY *

Brian S. Crittenden

There is a trend in the history of recent educational theory which gives special interest to a study of Durkheim's sociology of knowledge and its bearing on his theory about the role of the school in society. In the face of radical changes in the structure of modern society, and the condition of crisis thus involved, a number of theorists have argued that the school should be the primary instrument for deliberately reshaping the social order according to a desirable pattern. . . . In justification of their claims, some of the leading exponents of this position both in England and the United States [1] have, in fact, appealed to the type of sociology of knowledge which Durkheim proposes. It will be instructive, therefore, to examine the implications which a sociology of knowledge, such as Durkheim's, holds for a philosophy of knowledge, and to determine whether or not Durkheim himself finds that it lends support to a reconstructive theory of the school. . . .

How does one go about the task of defining education in a satisfactory way? Durkheim suggests that a careful analysis of the role of education in contemporary and past societies must first be made. This will then reveal the common elements which constitute the essential definition. In its general form the function of education in any society has two characteristics: it is both one and manifold. Under the first aspect its purpose is the same for all the members of the society. Every society, however differentiated, has a core of common ideals in virtue of which it coheres as a unity. As his sociology of knowledge has already

* Reprinted from "Durkheim: Sociology of Knowledge and Educational Theory," *Studies in Philosophy and Education,* 4(Fall, 1965), 207, 239–51, 254. By permission of the author and the editor of *Studies in Philosophy and Education.*
[1] E.g., Sir Fred Clarke, Karl Mannheim (in England), and Theodore Brameld, R. Bruce Raup (in the United States).

argued, these ideals differ from one society to another.[175] Under the second aspect there are as many different kinds of education as there are groups within the total society. The existence of specialized occupation in a society ipso facto creates different forms of education. If one wished to find a society in which the educational system is absolutely homogeneous and egalitarian, it would be necessary to return to the most primitive form, in which the structure had not yet been affected by the division of labor.

Durkheim understands education, whether one considers its characteristic of unity or multiplicity, as being entirely a process of socialization. He follows the distinction . . . between man as an individual and as a social being. The former refers to the private mental states and events of one's personal life, the latter is the 'being' formed in the individual through the influence of group systems of ideas, beliefs, sentiments and practices. It includes both the collective representations (the ideas common to the society as a whole) and the values held by particular sub-groups within the society. It is the forming of the social being (with its double aspect of unity and variation) that is the *distinctive* role of education. The individual is born egotistical and asocial; through education he is fashioned into a social being. Thus Durkheim reaches his definition of education: ". . . the influence exercised by adult generations on those that are not yet ready for social life. Its object is to arouse and to develop in the child a certain number of physical, intellectual and moral states which are demanded of him by both the political society as a whole and the special milieu for which he is specifically destined." [176]

Durkheim stresses that education does not simply develop certain native capacities. "It is not limited to developing the individual organism in the direction indicated by its nature, to elicit the hidden potentialities that need only be manifested. It

[175] Emile Durkheim, *The Elementary Forms of the Religious Life: A Study in Religious Sociology,* trans. J. W. Swain (London, Allen and Unwin, no date), pp. 116–17.
[176] Durkheim, *Education and Sociology,* trans. S. D. Fox (Glencoe, Ill., Free Press, 1956), p. 71.

creates in man a new being." [177] Even the tendency to improve
one's intellectual powers comes from the particular social conditions, not from nature. On the one hand, man's innate predispo-
sitions are extremely general. On the other, he needs very
specialized skills, a precisely defined character and set of values
in order to live in society. It is the role of education to bridge
this gap. At this point Durkheim recalls his general theory on
the relation of the individual and the social group. The two
terms imply one another. It is especially through the institution
of education that society enables the individual to grow as a
truly human being.[178] Hence he strongly opposes theorists like
Kant, Mill, Herbart, and Spencer for casting educational theory
in terms of the individual and a universal human nature, thus
supposing that education could add nothing essential to the
work of nature. Such a position finds use only for the science of
psychology and neglects the disciplines which, because of education's profoundly social character, are most fundamental for
its understanding: sociology and history. Durkheim agrees that
psychology is important for establishing the appropriate means.
But the goals are determined primarily by sociology, and because of this it must influence even the discussion of the means.

Durkheim is merely expressing his sociology of knowledge
when he insists that the body of ideas and values which guide
the institution of education and which it conveys is strictly
relative to each society. He states his thought in this way: "If
our modern education is no longer narrowly national; it is in the
constitution of modern nations that the reason must be sought.
. . . The man whom education should realize in us is not the
man such as nature has made him, but as the society wishes him
to be; and it wishes him such as its internal economy calls
for." [179]

Durkheim's attitude to a reconstructive theory of education
has, for the most part, already been implied in the foregoing
discussion. Now its main features will be emphasized and made

---

[177] *Ibid.*, p. 72. He thinks of education as an elaborate act of initiation which, like the religious initiation ceremonies, involves a new
creation. See p. 126.
[178] *Ibid.*, p. 78.
[179] *Ibid.*, p. 122.

explicit. The first question is the extent to which Durkheim considers that the educational institution *can* be deliberately changed. Although it is difficult to know in every context whether he is referring to what can be done rather than what ought to be done, his general position is expressed in this way: "Institutions are neither absolutely plastic nor absolutely resistant to any deliberate modification." [180] He stresses the dependence of the education system on other social institutions such as religion, the political organization, the level of development in science and industry. It can no more be changed at will than the structure of society itself. Hence the limits within which deliberate change in the system of education is possible are set ultimately by the impersonal social forces which shape the actual conditions of society at any time. To return to his favored example, an individual or group could not have used the school institution to transform the Roman world according to the present ideal of individuality. "There is no man who can make society have, at a given moment, a system of education other than that which is implied in its structure." [181] In his discussion of suicide Durkheim asks whether education might be the instrument for changing the conditions responsible for the present high rate. His conclusion is that such is not possible; to think otherwise is "to ascribe to education a power it lacks. It is only the image and reflection of society. It imitates and reproduces the latter in abbreviated form, it does not create it. Education is healthy when people themselves are in a healthy state; but it becomes corrupt with them, being unable to modify itself." [182] For the pedagogical system to function in opposition to the prevailing social system is for Durkheim "some incomprehensible miracle." Apart from any other reason, the very antagonism would rob it of its desired effect. He points out, however, that when the objectives of education conform to those of the society its influence is considerable. This it derives both from the psychological and intellectual condition of the child in rela-

---

[180] *Ibid.,* p. 33.
[181] *Ibid.,* p. 94.
[182] Emile Durkheim, *Suicide, A Study in Sociology* (Glencoe, Ill., Free Press, 1951), pp. 327–73 [*sic*].

tion to the teacher and the moral authority of the latter in virtue
of being the representative of society.[183]

The characteristic ideals of the society as a whole are not
automatically and necessarily reflected in all its institutions. At
certain times, particularly when the society is changing rapidly,
the system of education may be out of harmony with its real
needs and values. This is the situation in which Durkheim
claims that education not only can but ought to change. The
criterion and goal of educational practice is the ideal of man as
currently accepted by the society. The customs and ideas which
determine this type are products of the common life of the
society at its present moment of existence and throughout its
history. It is the moral duty of educators to promote social
cohesion and consensus by forming individuals according to this
type and by communicating the ideas which underlie it.

The ideal of man which Durkheim finds is characteristic of
contemporary society stresses the values of common humanity
rather than those of nationality or class. He insists, however,
that this is not to be confused with the idealistic theory of a
universal human nature. The ideal of humanity is imposed by
the collectivity not because of any intrinsic worth but because,
in the present conditions of a highly differentiated society, it is
the only basis on which the indispensable social cohesion can be
realized. Society has made the general human type, rather than
that of a nation, into an ideal only because this is demanded by
its present structure. Among the values which support this ideal
Durkheim suggests "respect for reason, science, ideas and sentiments which are at the base of democratic morality." [184]

At the present time, he finds that the institution of education
is at many points not in harmony with the ideal and needs of
society.[185] Hence a reconstruction of the educational system is
demanded. This, of course, is the task which can and should be
performed by pedagogy as Durkheim understands it. . . .

Pedagogy is never called upon to construct an entirely new
system of education. The fact that many parts of our culture
have endured for a long period creates the presumption that

[183] *Education and Sociology,* pp. 85–90.
[184] *Ibid.,* p. 81.
[185] *Ibid.,* p. 103.

they have been meeting vital needs. They do not disappear suddenly. "It is neither possible nor desirable that the present organization collapse in an instant; you will have to live in it and make it live. But for that you must know it. And it is necessary to know it, too, in order to be able to change it. For these creations ex nihilo are quite as impossible in the social order as in the physical order. The future is not improvised, one can build only with the materials we have from the past." [186] Thus Durkheim's educational theory attempts to be neither revolutionary (or utopian) nor conservative. He notes that the classical educational theorists, like Rousseau, are frequently revolutionary (or at least utopian in Karl Mannheim's sense). They are useful for a sound pedagogy because they at least express some aspect of the spirit of their time. However, the value of their ideas for planning the future development of education must be judged according to whether the causes which have produced them are "bound up with the normal evolution of our society." [187]. . .

Despite his recognition of a deep moral crisis in modern society and of the need for social reconstruction, it must be stressed that Durkheim does not cast the school institution as a principal agent of reform. His pedagogical theory always assumes that one can discover in a society a commonly accepted ideal of man. Whatever this ideal may be, the educational system as a whole not only ought not, but cannot, effectively act against it. Although Durkheim recognizes that it is possible for particular schools to pursue a different ideal, he judges such action as morally undesirable. "It is idle to think that we can rear our children as we wish. There are customs to which we are bound to conform; if we flout them too severely, they take their vengeance on our children. . . . Whether they had been raised in accordance with ideas that were either obsolete or premature does not matter; in the one case as in the other, they are not of their time and, therefore, they are outside the conditions of normal life." [192]

It is evident from Durkheim's general theory that, if there is

---

[186] *Ibid.,* p. 145.
[187] *Ibid.,* p. 150.
[192] *Ibid.,* pp. 65–66.

no commonly accepted ideal of man for a given group of people, one cannot speak meaningfully of that group as a society, and therefore as having an educational system. If the common ideal is severely threatened (as Durkheim considers is the case in contemporary Western society), the consequent confusion and indecision will be inevitably reflected in the institution of education and the general body of teachers. Thus Durkheim remains consistent with his theory of the school as the microcosm of society.[193] It follows from the nature of this relationship that when the need for reconstruction penetrates to the very roots of the society the school cannot take the leading part in this process. His conclusion is that education "can be reformed only if society itself is reformed. To do that, the evil from which it suffers must be attacked at its sources." [194] . . .

What is the relationship between Durkheim's educational theory and his sociology of knowledge? In the first place, the general consistency is evident. In the preceding discussion this was seen in the development of his definition of education as an almost exclusively socializing process, in his emphasis on the basic role of history and sociology in educational theory, and in his insistence on the need for the constant adaptation of the school to changing social conditions.

His conclusions about the reconstructive role of the school seem to be not only consistent with, but also logically entailed by his sociology of knowledge. If the prevailing values of a society define the goal which the school system ought to serve, and if the prevailing values are determined by underlying social forces, then these conclusions must inevitably follow. In fact, it is not merely that Durkheim draws logical implications about the nature and practice of education from his sociology of knowledge. Under many aspects it is itself an educational theory. Since the collective conscience, as Durkheim understands it, determines what shall be accepted as true and good for a given society and hence is the ultimate bearer of moral authority, it is the source and goal of all acceptable pedagogy in the society. The school system is simply a specialized instrument of the collective conscience.

193 *Ibid.,* p. 131.
194 *Suicide,* p. 373.

Durkheim does not deviate from his position of social relativism. Provided that the educational system forms the individual according to the prevailing type, it is helping him to grow as a "truly human being." It follows, of course, that Durkheim has no way of passing judgment on the commonly accepted ideals of his own or any other society. If they are commonly accepted, they are ipso facto true and good for that society. Thus the goal of education in Greece and Rome, "to subordinate oneself blindly to the collectivity," [198] was good because that was the ideal of the society. Presumably, for the same reason, Durkheim could not have criticized the type of man being formed by the schools of Nazi Germany.

Pedagogy, in its primary function of prescribing what education ought to do, simply applies the conclusions reached by "the science of public opinion" (what, for Durkheim, is essentially sociology). The role of the science of public opinion will be critically discussed in the final section. Here it need only be noted that its use in relation to education is fully consistent with and illustrates his general theory. He asks three questions of fact: What are the common values of this society? [199] What values are being pursued by the institutions of education? Are these two sets of values essentially the same? Then he makes the moral judgment: If there is a discrepancy, the system of education should be reconstructed so that its values are identical with those which prevail in the society as a whole. However, the science of public opinion (and therefore pedagogy) performs descriptive and explanatory functions; of itself it does not establish or justify normative principles. Thus, in the final stage of his argument he must assume either that the values which are commonly held ought to be accepted in the society, or that the values which express the objective needs of society at a given time are those which ought to determine behavior in that society. These assumptions demand a justification which lies beyond the scope of the science of public opinion (and pedagogy) as Durkheim understands it.

[198] *Education and Sociology,* p. 78.
[199] As was seen earlier, this may require a distinction between the apparently common and the genuinely common values; but this is precisely the competence claimed for the science of public opinion.

Durkheim's conclusions about the role of the school in society seem to be thoroughly consistent with his sociology of
knowledge. As long as there is a clearly defined collective
conscience, knowable at least to the social scientists, one can
speak of the school as reconstructing society, without compro-
mising the sociology of knowledge. In effect, the school is
reconstructing the practice of society by reflecting its theoretically held values. However, it is precisely when the latter are
disrupted and uncertain in a time of crisis that the school, apart
from acting in an arbitrary fashion, has no legitimate ground of
authority from which it might even begin the work of reconstruction. Moreover, if the real determinants of knowledge and
values in a society are non-rational, substructural social forces,
then the school not only ought not, but cannot, initiate the
process of social reconstruction. A criticism of Durkheim's
theory of education must, in effect, be a criticism of his sociological theory. Hence, finally, some observations on this latter
will be made, restricted to the aspects under which it involves a
philosophy of knowledge.

The foundation of Durkheim's theory is found in his interpretation of social reality—the concept of the collective conscience.
He rightly emphasizes that social reality belongs essentially to
the psychological order, that it cannot be explained by a reduction to its material conditions. However his position seems to be
incorrect on the crucial point of the relationship between the
mental life of the individual and that of the group as a whole.
Consider his argument from analogy. . . . In itself, this argument is incapable of proving that collective representations
stand in the same relation to individual representations as a
living organism to its component parts, or the mental life of an
individual to his physical organism. But even as an illustration it
is deficient. The principal elements of the analogy can be stated
in this way: the mental life of the individual is to his physical
organism as the collective conscience is to the individual mental
lives which compose the group. There seem to be two basic
defects in this comparison. First, the substratum of the psychological phenomenon in one case is a physical composite, in the
other it is psychological. The analogy would perhaps be more
accurate if Durkheim were arguing that just as the mental life of

an individual is not reducible to his physical organism, so the culture of a society cannot be explained in terms of its physical environment or material forces. Secondly, individual mental life is characterized by psychological activity of a kind not found in the collective conscience of which it is claimed to be a component part. Only in individual mental life is there a self-reflective subject, capable of conscious thought processes, of choosing, and taking responsibility for action. Durkheim strongly rejects the idea of a group mind conscious of itself as such. Yet this is the logical conclusion of his analogy.

Because society is made up of a large number of widely differing individuals existing in an extremely complicated pattern of relationships, Durkheim concludes, ". . . it is not surprising that a higher life disengages itself which, by reacting upon the elements of which it is the product, raises them to a higher plane of existence and transforms them." [201] This, of course, is simply an implicit application of his argument from analogy. He is, in effect, assuming a principle, without either theoretical or empirical demonstration, that in all cases the more complex is necessarily superior. [202]

In his second theoretical argument, Durkheim attempts to show that moral and speculative concepts could not possess their characteristics of necessity and universality unless there were a collective moral authority from which they are derived. An adequate critique of this argument would involve the exposition of an alternative theory of knowledge. Here, at least certain implications of Durkheim's argument can be pointed out. First, it accepts Hume's assumption that the individual can perceive only discrete objects. Of himself he can form generalized images, but is not capable of grasping, by his own powers of observation, insight, and reflection, essential (that is, necessary) connections between things. Secondly, it does not allow that the characteristics of necessity and universality depend on the connection between a concept and, say, physical reality. They are derived from a factor extrinsic to this reality: the moral

[201] *The Elementary Forms of the Religious Life*, p. 446.
[202] Emile Durkheim, "Représentations Individuelles et Représentations Collectives," *Revue de Metaphysique et de Morale*, 6(1896), 299.

authority of the collective conscience. If Durkheim is consistent in this argument he must hold that an external natural world is unknowable. All a person can know is the social reality of which he is a part. In relation to the individual the collective representations are social a priori forms and categories which are always interposed between him and the postulated physical reality.[203] Thirdly, the argument raises problems of inconsistency within Durkheim's general theory. In the discussion of his thought it became clear that although he is theoretically committed to the socially relative nature of all truth, his position is in fact not unequivocal. The objectivity of a collective representation is guaranteed because it is collective. Yet Durkheim adds immediately that the generalization and persistence which this involves are not without "sufficient reason," that if an idea is commonly accepted it means that individuals are constantly verifying it by their own experience. Moreover, he admits that a few concepts are established by critical, scientific tests.[204] Although Durkheim insists that the number of such ideas is very small, they nevertheless introduce a serious difficulty for the argument he has proposed in order to establish the existence of the collective conscience. It means that at least in some cases the truth of an idea is ultimately not derived from collective acceptance, but from its being an accurate account of external material reality as tested by everyday experience or scientific method. Durkheim does not examine this other concept of truth, but attempts to avoid the problem by claiming that concepts which are scientifically tested differ only in degree from the others.

Even if Durkheim's observations are presumed to be accurate,[205] his epistemological conclusions about the categories and other speculative concepts are not justified. The question of the historical genesis of ideas is not identical with that of their epistemological status. This is even implied in Durkheim's own theory. Here, the truth of a concept or ideal depends on its being a collective representation, irrespective of whether it de-

[203] Cf. P. M. Worsley, "Emile Durkheim's Theory of Knowledge," *Sociological Review*, 4(July, 1956), 49.

[204] *The Elementary Forms of the Religious Life*, pp. 435–37.

[205] For a criticism of the accuracy of Durkheim's empirical evidence see Worsley, *op. cit.*

rives ultimately from a social fact or an individual experience.[206] Moreover, he recognizes that logical categories differentiate themselves from the social mould and become autonomous.[207] He does not claim, therefore, that in contemporary society, speculative concepts are necessarily reflections of the social structure. Hence, if his theory about the origin of concepts is to have any significance for their present epistemological condition, he must argue that the truth and meaning of these ideas are still dependent on the social conditions in which they originated. . . .

Presuming that there are some members of the society who hold moral values which seriously deviate from those of the collective conscience it seems that they may reasonably ask Durkheim why they ought to obey the dictates of the collective conscience. Now the answer to this question does not come from the science of moral opinion itself. This is evident in Durkheim's own thought. . . . He argues that the very possibility of ethics depends on the existence of the collective conscience as the ultimate moral authority. It is in effect what religions have always personified as God. Whatever may be said about the adequacy of this argument, it is clearly an attempt to give a reasonable justification for his ethical theory and is presupposed in his science of moral opinion. The validity of the ethical conclusions reached by means of the latter ultimately depends therefore on Durkheim's theory of the collective conscience. And we have argued that this theory involves a form of complete social relativism in ethics. Unlike reconstructive educational theorists, such as Mannheim, Raup, and Brameld, who appeal to the sociology of knowledge, Durkheim does not compromise its ethical relativism by introducing, either surreptitiously or by design, any moral ideal for which universal validity is claimed. For this reason his whole system is more consistent and his prescriptions for the school's reconstructive role in society far more limited.

[206] "Représentations Individuelles et Représentations Collectives," p. 295.
[207] *The Elementary Forms of the Religious Life,* p. 444.

CONSENSUS, POLICY MAKING, AND TRUTH *

Adrian M. Dupuis

The theory of social consensus affords a method for the solution of many of the perplexing problems in the area of human relations. That this theory should receive wide support among educational philosophers seems reasonable since many of these conflicts originate in the schools. Extreme nationalism is kept alive through the medium of education; overemphasis on competition often begins in school or at any rate may be further accentuated by the school; racial and religious conflicts sometimes find their origin in school situations and practices. Thus the involvement of education in the problems of life seems to enhance the popularity of this theory among teachers as well as educational theorists.

The most complete exposition of the theory of consensus applied to education is found in *The Improvement of Practical Intelligence* by Raup and associates.[1] Their work explores the fields of knowledge which bear most directly and fruitfully on the formation and validation of the kinds of judgments which are necessary for resolving social conflicts. In fact, it seems that the authors make the theory of consensus the cornerstone of their theory of knowledge. Apparently, for them, the development of this outlook and method should have first claim upon the resources of all educational effort.[2]

According to these theorists, the areas with which consensus is concerned are the making of decisions and policies, the reconstruction of norms and beliefs and finally the changing of ideologies. Thus it would seem that consensus is primarily concerned with value judgments rather than judgments of fact.

* Reprinted from "Social Consensus and Scientific Method," *Educational Theory*, 5(October, 1955), 242–48. By permission of the author and the editor of *Educational Theory*.

[1] R. Bruce Raup, George Axtelle, K. D. Benne, B. Othanel Smith, *The Improvement of Practical Intelligence* (New York, Harper Brothers Company, 1950).
[2] *Ibid.*, p. 283.

Then the answer to the question, "How do we know what is right or wrong in a given situation?" or to the query "How do we know what to do or how to act under certain conditions?" is to be based not only on the facts of the case, but also to be subject to the consensus of all those who will in any way be affected by the decisions, policies, changed norms and ideologies. The crux of the problem seems to lie in the relation of factual judgments to the practical (value) judgments of those employing the facts in a problematic situation.

A judgment, according to Raup and associates, is settling some issue, resolving some indeterminate situation by deciding the response appropriate to the particular situation. Thus motor skills do not involve judgmental behavior because there is no unresolved situation where there is opportunity for deliberation and choice. Judgmental behavior, then, is only found in situations which involve the solution of problems.

In judgmental behavior, there are four "phases": [3] the optative, the indicative, the contemplative, and the normative. The question may be raised, namely, how does the scientific method come into play? The answer is that it enters into judgmental behavior only in the indicative phase. In other words it is concerned with the survey and assessment of the existing state of affairs. When the indicative phase is compared with the other three phases it appears to be the least important. For example, the optative phase which is concerned with the clarification of common purpose or the desired state of affairs is given more emphasis because all activity is goal-directed activity. The contemplative phase which represents the attempt to fit the facts and ideas employed to the claims of the situation as a whole obviously is of greater importance than the indicative, since it states that the ideas and facts must be suited to the situation and not vice-versa. The normative phase, which is concerned with making the plan and putting it into action, is probably the most important since the whole process is primarily designed to result in some cooperative action in the solution of problems.

For the development of a theory of knowledge, and this

[3] Words in quotation marks are terms used by the various authors cited.

seems to be the purpose of the authors, the third phase probably contains the key step in the process as far as claims to knowledge are concerned. For example, they state that we may have all the facts about population trends, but these facts are of no value unless there is consensus about the educational objectives of the society in which these facts are located. The facts themselves are to be obtained by the scientific method, but that is the extent of the use of empirical procedures. Actually the scientific method is a subsidiary method and the acceptance or rejection of facts and their use is subject to the uncoerced consensus of all those involved in the whole problematic situation.

This emphasis on the whole situation and its place in the judgmental process can be noted all through *The Improvement of Practical Intelligence*. Facts never stand on their own, so to speak, but are always part of a situation with a unitary character. Any analysis or division of the whole situation into its parts may unduly emphasize one aspect with the result that the entire analysis becomes inadequate. The possibility of introducing new perspectives which will increase the utility and adequacy of practical judgments is not thereby excluded, but the authors nevertheless maintain that fullness and integrity of the whole situation are so necessary to the adequacy of judgment that deliberate and planned attention to its mediation is one of the most important phases of the judgmental process.[4] . . .

The theory is further developed in Theodore Brameld's *Patterns of Educational Philosophy*. At this juncture, it may be well to describe some of the important aspects of the "new epistemology." To begin with, emphasis is placed on "goal-seeking" in the knowing process—the goals themselves condition the functions which are needed for achieving the goals and the functions, in turn, condition the goals. Thus far, this appears to be the same as Dewey's conception of the interaction of goals and functions. But going beyond Dewey, Brameld maintains that we must decide, here and now, exactly what these goals are and how they affect the knowing process. When a decision regarding the definability of these goals has been reached through consensus, it must be kept in mind that as goals they

[4] *Ibid.*, p. 108.

are not the immutable and eternally fixed goals of the absolutist but rather the "definable wants" that man attempts to satisfy. Brameld puts it in these words, *"the truth of those experiences most vital in the social life of any culture are determined not merely by the needful satisfactions they produce, but also by the extent to which they are agreed upon by the largest possible number of the group concerned. Without this factor of agreement or consensus the experience is simply not 'true'."* [5] The scientific method is only one aspect of the more pervasive and more fundamental method, consensus, which is primarily concerned with goal-seeking and "future-making."

Certain knowledge principles are, therefore, basic to truth-seeking, viz.: (1) Goal-seeking is a determinative characteristic of modern man and the basic goals of our culture can and should be defined and recognized as interrelated and integral parts of a more comprehensive cultural design; (2) These goals, both social and individual, are motivated by the "unrational" drives which are expressed in conscious and organized channels; (3) Though ideologies tend to crystallize, there are always at work "utopian forces" which impel cultures to modify and reconstruct themselves. These knowledge principles put the major emphasis on the social and cultural environment and the "unrational" drives rather than on objective evidence. It follows that the act of agreement is indispensable to truth, for even though we may possess scientific evidence we must ultimately agree or disagree in regard to the relation of these facts to our goals. It is this agreement or disagreement by which "truth" or "falsity" is determined. An ideology is then a consensus which has been achieved, while a utopia is the striving for consensus not yet achieved.

The second knowledge principle mentioned above, namely, the role of the "unrational" in the knowing process, also seems to further differentiate the scientific method from the theory of consensus, since the "group mind" tends to project its own wants and desires upon the objective world and in that sense recreate or reconstruct the world to its own liking. Contrarily, it

---

[5] Theodore Brameld, *Patterns of Educational Philosophy* (New York, World Book Company, 1950), p. 456. (Italics mine.)

is the aim of the scientific method to enable both individuals and groups to come to know the world as it is and not as the group mind projects it. This same difference in approach between the scientific method and the theory of consensus seems to hold with regard to the strong utopian strain which calls for a new "sociology of knowledge" or as Brameld puts it, "a new epistemology of culture." [6] Again the scientific method does not purport to describe and explain the objective world *as we would like it,* but rather *as it is.* But the advocates of consensus maintain that scientific method and logic are only aids in constructing a utopia in so far as they are useful in testing the pertinence of any particular culture at a given time.

Another interesting aspect of the new epistemology is the role which the "group mind" plays in the knowing process. Brameld maintains that the group mind "thinks" in much the same manner as an individual thinks, though there is no mystical group mind which exists independent of individual minds.[7] The group mind has, generally speaking, greater difficulty attaining reflective judgments, because it is more profoundly affected by social and economic forces than by logic and scientific data. The individual mind on the other hand, is able to isolate and analyze more objectively the forces which affect it from without. Furthermore, the group mind serves as an end in so far as individuals may join the group to achieve certain goals in unison with others which they could not achieve as individuals. The group mind also serves as a means for achieving the widest possible consensus regarding goals, norms and ideologies. The means are always democratic and aim to build group minds which express social consensus of the majority. The minority is heard through its representatives and as a last resort, through its right of advocacy, i. e., the right to revolt against the majority.

A final point which follows from the above is the distinction between knowledge and truth. Knowledge, according to Bra-

[6] *Ibid.,* p. 455.
[7] Group mind may be exemplified by the attitude of certain groups of people toward Negroes and Jews. The entire group holds the same views regarding these racial or ethnic minorities. Also, the reverence for certain symbols, customs, etc. may be regarded as examples of the manifestation of "group-mind."

meld, designates the body of *agreed upon* experiences which have been part and parcel of past and present cultures, i. e., it is the equivalent of the group mind since it contains the ideological content from which any new content must be constructed. But knowledge can degenerate, especially when it lags behind change, and cannot therefore be equated with truth. Truth is "any social consensus about the dominant goals and means to the reconstructed culture." [8] Thus truth is the achievement of the group mind in the process of working toward a goal or in the possession of that goal. Truth, then, is not determined by objective evidence but by social consensus. Even judgments of fact are colored by the a priori beliefs of the group mind since factual judgments are only useful and meaningful when they are employed in connection with some normative action. "Brute facts" no longer have independent existence since all factual knowledge passes through the group mind, so to speak, and only after the group mind has agreed upon it, does it become real knowledge. In other words, the noumena can never be known.

Some may argue that the theory of consensus is merely another formulation of the criterion of "intersubjective testability" used in the sciences.[9] As one of the most important criteria of the scientific method, it is a more precise statement of what is often called "objectivity" in scientific endeavor.

However, the term "intersubjective" seems to imply that some degree of consensus is necessary before a scientific proposition can be considered true. This does not appear to the writer to be the correct interpretation. What does this criterion require of propositions? This principle makes it a basic requirement that all propositions, hypotheses, theories etc., which claim to be scientific must be capable of test by anyone who is intellectually capable and properly trained in the methods of scientific research. This test need not be a direct, complete test, but confirmation or "disconfirmation" must at least arise from some indirect test. For example, if a scientist states that a certain

[8] *Ibid.*, p. 470.
[9] For a formulation of "Intersubjective Testability" see Herbert Feigl and May Brodbeck, *Reading in Philosophy of Science* (New York, Appleton-Century-Crofts Inc., 1953), p. 11.

remote star has a certain temperature, his assertion is capable of indirect test only, for obviously such a proposition is not capable of direct test since no human being could directly "take the temperature" of such a star because of its extreme heat and distance. In fact, the more indirect the test is, the more accurate it is, since the grosser inaccuracies arising from sense perception are usually removed.

It seems obvious that this criterion excludes knowledge which is arrived at by intuition or revelation. Also, emotive statements are excluded, because they are incapable of intersubjective test of any kind. It is true that the processes involved in intuition etc., may be the objects of scientific study, as is done in psychology, but this does not make the processes themselves valid means of arriving at scientific knowledge. One of the main difficulties involved in attempting to validate the knowledge claims of intuition and similar processes, is stating these experiences in such a manner that they can be put to the intersubjective test. However, it must be kept in mind that the criterion of intersubjective testability does not forbid the use of the emotive (poetic) function of language; it merely asserts that such statements are not to be considered scientific propositions. One can give as much freedom and latitude to purely emotive statements as one wishes, as long as one does not claim that these statements are scientific propositions.

There is, however, considerable controversy as to whether or not such processes as empathy, instinct, extra-sensory perception, religious intuition and the like are non-cognitive simply because the statements which are derived from such processes cannot be put to the "intersubjective test." For example, mystics may experience the divine and science cannot demonstrate that these experiences have no claims in the cognitive domain.

If purely emotive statements of the type mentioned are non-scientific, *a fortiori,* statements which are logically incapable of test, are excluded. For example, the existence of a spiritual soul cannot be proved by scientific method, since by definition, a spiritual soul is a non-scientific construct.

To continue the discussion concerning the degree of similarity of consensus and intersubjective test, it may be pertinent to discuss Brameld's concept of truth-seeking as social consensus. In this connection he quotes C. S. Peirce as follows: "The opinion which is fated to be ultimately *agreed to by all who investigate is what we mean by truth. . . ."* [10] As it stands, this quotation seems to assert that consensus is essential to truth. However, examination of the entire passage would demonstrate that Peirce asserts that objectivity (intersubjectivity) determines consensus and not vice-versa.

"They (scientists) may at first obtain different results, but as each perfects his method and his processes, the results are found to move steadily together toward a destined centre. So with all scientific research. Different minds may set out with the most antagonistic views, *but the progress of investigation carries them by a force outside themselves to one and the same conclusion.* This activity of thought by which we are carried, not where we wish, but to a fore-ordained goal, is like the operation of destiny. No modification of the point taken, no selection of other facts for study, *no natural bent of the mind even can enable a man to escape the predestinate opinion.* This great hope (law) is embodied in the conception of truth and reality. The opinion which is fated to be agreed to by all who investigate is what we mean by truth, and the object represented in this opinion is the real. That is the way I would explain reality." [11]

By fate, Peirce does not mean a supernatural determining force, but merely that which is sure to come true, e. g., we are all fated to die. Peirce goes on to explain that it may appear as though he is defending a position which makes reality depend ultimately upon what is thought about it. But reality is, he maintains, independent of what you or I and any finite number of men may think about it, even though it is not necessarily independent of all thought. So if truth were crushed, it would rise again and the opinion which would finally result from investigation would in no way depend on how anyone may actually think about it.[12]

It seems that the statement of Peirce points out the fundamental difference between consensus and intersubjective testability. Intersubjective testability is a method for determining the *hic et nunc* acceptability of scientific propositions, hypotheses and theories based on available empirical data. It is in no way

[10] *Ibid.,* p. 456. (Italics Brameld's.)
[11] C. S. Peirce, *Collected Papers,* Vol. 5, No. 407, p. 268. (Italics mine.)
[12] *Ibid.,* No. 408.

implied that the consensus of scientists makes the proposition true or false, though the *adoption* of any proposition, hypothesis or theory is a result of social interaction. But the act of adoption does not put the stamp of truth or falsity on them.

The use of Peirce's argument and the minor emphasis placed on the facts of the case in the four phases (moods), seem to indicate that all propositions, hypotheses and theories are true or false only in so far as they are agreed upon or not agreed upon.

Another item which causes difficulty in the analysis of the theory of consensus as described by Raup and Brameld, is the failure to distinguish clearly the psychological aspects of their theory of knowledge from the purely epistemological (logical) knowledge claims. However, this difficulty may be remedied in the future as the literature on the subject deals more and more with such logical considerations. At present, most of the literature on the subject deals with classroom situations and controlled laboratory experiments such as those done by Lewin and his associates at the University of Iowa and the laboratories in human dynamics at the Universities of Michigan, Chicago, Minnesota and elsewhere.

The purpose of this essay was not to determine whether schools, communities, and nations should attempt to train people to work together for commonly agreed-upon goals. The pragmatic value of cooperative effort has been demonstrated, while the ill effects of lack of cooperation among individuals and nations are quite apparent. But unless the fundamental principles and the claims to knowledge involved are clearly understood, the remedy may ultimately be as undesirable as the evils which it proposes to correct. For example, social consensus may easily degenerate into the tyranny of the majority which is still tyranny, although it may not always be as ruthless as that exercised by one or a few members of a society.[13] Furthermore, social consensus, as a criterion of truth is inadequate since it represents only one aspect of "truth-seeking," omitting such others as correspondence and coherence.

[13] Fred N. Kerlinger, "The Authoritarianism of Group Dynamics," *Progressive Education,* 31(April, 1954), 169–73.

IDEOLOGY AND EDUCATIONAL POLICY *

Donald Vandenberg

The increasing distrust of vaguely expressed political and social ideals that is perhaps best symbolized by the title of Daniel Bell's *The End of Ideology* has made it increasingly difficult to relate educational problems to societal problems with any degree of logical or scientific warrant. But is this distrust of political and social philosophy, this distrust of ideology, merely another ideological proclamation? What accounts for our hesitancy to venture into thinking about the educational development of persons who are capable of alleviating or resolving contemporary societal difficulties? Is this hesitancy due to the indirect support of education resting upon suppressed premises, i.e., upon an ideology?

From certain *facts* such as another nation's technological accomplishments or an increased proportion of people attending or wanting to attend college there follow *no* schooling recommendations at all without additional premises because it is not clear that or why nations should compete technologically nor is it at all clear as to what is the best preparation for college. Although there is a widespread opinion that there was nothing philosophical about Sputnik I and subsequent policy making in education, it is characteristic of ideologies, by definition, to fail to recognize their own value commitments as such. On the contrary, it makes as much sense to say that the fundamental philosophical event of the century was Sputnik I, for never before had the problems of men, of how to live together, been thrown into such sharp focus. . . . What Sputnik I demonstrated beyond the power of words is the necessary and inescapable unity of the world and human life thereon.

It also established that the fundamental problem, educational and otherwise, is the alienation of people from each other. If

* Reprinted from "Ideology and Educational Policy," *Journal of Educational Thought,* 1(April, 1967), 38–50. By permission of the author and the editor of the *Journal of Educational Thought.*

one wishes to reflect upon the problem of the educational
development of the kinds of persons that can resolve or alleviate
present difficulties, he is confronted with formulating an educational program that can contribute to the reduction of alienation
between men. The implications of Sputnik I would then fall into
the non-cognitive dimensions of the schooling process, within
the moral aspects of educating. If this is so, there has been very
little response thus far to an alleged crisis in education stemming
from events on the international scene. If the problems are
indeed non-cognitive, one does not quite know how to understand what has happened. No matter what foreign policy the
nations may adopt to suit the exigencies of the more or less cold
war, from that policy nothing is entailed for school policy. This
is true in any case. It is particularly valid if the educational
development of people should be directed to balance or amelio-
rate the existing state of affairs. If the general problem is how to
live together, in other words, this problem can be approached in
different sectors of experience in ways that may even be logically incompatible: foreign policy decisions concerning how to
live together possess neither logical nor ideological entailment
for school policy decisions respecting the modes of coexistence
that might be promoted in schools. A raising of the phenomenon of public schooling into view will precede the discussion of
one item illustrative of how policy might be considered if
schooling were to respond to the moral problems raised into
orbit with Sputnik I.

The phenomenon of public schooling consists of elementary,
junior and senior high schools, community junior colleges, and
tax-supported universities in Alabama and Alberta, Harlem and
Highland Park, Toronto and Tanganyika, Peking and Buenos
Aires, Moscow and Minnesota, and so on and so on, by definition of what free, public, universal, compulsory schooling is, regardless of certain factual considerations to the contrary. Schooling can exist as public only if it is free, compulsory, and universal. The basic criterion that any consideration of policy has to
meet in order to be relevant to schools that are public is that it
has to be equally applicable to all public schools, wherever, even
where they have not yet been brought into being. Otherwise it
lacks scope, comprehensiveness, and adequacy. It lacks applica-

bility to public schools because its application changes them into something else. It lacks adequate consideration of the moral dimension of schooling because it overlooks respect for the possibilities of the children in the various places not taken into account, especially if the places are under- or over-privileged. This criterion (of applicability to all public schools) is not a proclamation of a vague, humanitarian sentiment because it is precisely opposed to the humanitarianism that can degenerate to the "white man's burden" or "Yankee imperialism." It is not ideological because it is the *only* means available to assist in the derivation from the phenomenon of public schooling of that which may assist in preventing parochialism or provincialism, ideological bias or prejudice, ethnocentricism or cultural relativism. It is desirable to avoid these by transcending them because they constitute alienation and contribute to further alienation from other people. Public is public, arbitrary boundaries to the tax-bases of school financing notwithstanding.

From the view of what public schooling is, it appears that the preliminary step in the reduction of the alienation of men from each other is the establishment of a common schooling system: a common curriculum on a world-wide basis. Any policy that could not be instituted universally contributes to alienation because it arrogates to some children that which is thereby denied to other children. This is almost but not quite a version of the Kantian categorical imperative to act such that all one's actions are capable of being legislated universally because it is not an imperative, an ought, at all. It merely indicates how one would recognize policy that showed partiality and privateness, that failed to recognize the responsibility involved in the publicness of schooling and in what schooling signifies. It is not an ought because it has not been said that schooling should "function" to alleviate contemporary problems. It is merely descriptive of what public schooling is and perhaps indicative of what the outlines of a response to Sputnik I might resemble were anyone to decide to take it seriously.

Prior to the existence of common schooling, mere attendance forces the child to live immorally in an unjust world. It lets and encourages him to arrogate to himself possibilities that are not accorded to other children. He must and ought to attend, yet for him his actions are not universalizable. He grows up immorally, alienated from others, and guilty.

Public schooling, moreover, exists perforce as mass schooling. Although this feature has been raised into prominence by the growth of population and the development of mass communication and mass transportation, that public schooling is compulsory and universal makes it inherently mass schooling. It occurs in the realm of anonymity. Teachers and pupils are anonymous. Anyone who is prepared can teach. Anyone can go to school. Schooling is average, everyday human existence, especially when it pretends explicitly to oppose the anonymity of everydayness through encouraging "individuality" through various well-known devices. Self-conscious attempts to achieve "individuality," in school as elsewhere, are express recognition that one is not individualized. In the assumption that people are different the basic alienation is to be found, for before they can be said to differ they have to be compared on some impersonal dimension or isolated "property." That people are either different or the same is not understandable. Each person is simply himself, nameable only by his proper name, e.g., "Bernice."

If individuation is a modification of the temporal structure of human being, if it is basically a matter of how one projects forward into his own possibilities, in his achieving a "self-constancy" through concrete tasks, then whatever is done in schooling cannot contribute to individuation directly because of what childhood and adolescence are in any society that has compulsory schooling. The existence of public schooling constitutes a *de facto* assertion that the child or youth cannot project into his concrete possibilities, that he cannot be himself, that he is not ready to choose his own possibilities, that he can choose his own future for himself only on condition that it includes schooling along the way: public schooling is mass schooling perforce. It not only constitutes itself in the realm of anonymity but is the "instrument" of "society," i.e., of anonymous everydayness, for it is the deliberate attempt to perpetuate "society" in its averageness (so-called cultural transmission). Concern with general policy, finally, is concern with the mass aspects of schooling, with precisely the average dimensions of the everyday enterprise that is schooling by definition of what the phenomenon of *policy* is: that which stretches across all teachers and within which concrete, pedagogical decisions occur. There is no possibility of pulling up one's skirts, so to speak, through attempting to avoid the "mass" aspects of schooling at the level of general policy, for they are wedded to each other. The average everydayness of schooling is its facticity, its "that-it-is," such that to try to avoid it is to avoid the existence of the public school itself. All departures from the mass aspects are departures from how public schooling constitutes itself and all have to fail when instituted because they have to become the "new" form of everydayness by being instituted.

An examination of one such "departure" will serve to illustrate how policy might be decided if one were to accept the facticity of the publicness of schooling as universal and compulsory education. One item will suffice to indicate a way to grapple with the relation of educational problems to societal problems, to indicate the kinds of policy decisions that could be made if one wished to promote the educational development of the kinds of persons who might be able to solve or alleviate the problems of the post-Sputnik world. "Ability grouping" will be discussed as paradigmatic of the "innovations" that have been widely advertised to "cure" whatever it was that ailed public schooling. The treatment will focus on the moral dimension of the problem.

Very often the decision to group or not to group is made on political or empirical grounds: to suit the majority or most powerful interest groups within a community or to increase the acquisition of knowledge as allegedly indicated by empirical studies. The latter can be discounted because the necessary information is not forthcoming. It is beyond the range of empirical research. An adequate study of the effects of various instructional groupings would require:

(1) Perfectly matched instructional groups, individual for individual and classroom interaction for classroom interaction. Two people who are perfectly matched on all the objectively attainable data including Rorschach and T.A.T. findings may not be matched at all on the subjective data. They would still have differing projects of being, differing "having beens," differing temporal structures, or, in empirical language, differing

motivations and experiential backgrounds, and face their own future in differing ways. They have differing home lives during experimentation and different people sit across the aisle from them during experimentation. They cannot be matched. To rest content with statistically matched groups or random sampling does two philosophically arbitrary things, the first of which is to remain within very gross, abstract preconceptions of what it is that is examined in inquiry. The second is the postulation of a metaphysical thesis as soon as the findings are used for something other than the direction and redirection of further inquiry. When "empirical findings" are taken to represent the real, a very non-empirical system of natural law is postulated in the best rationalistic, realistic, metaphysical manner. The findings have to be presumed as embodying generalizable laws of human conduct that exist in the world as soon as existential, experiential decisions of policy are based on them. The scientific inquirer himself does not have to make this assumption that his findings are of general value or that they correspond to anything apart from his context and method of inquiry. He will not make it if he is cognizant of the limitations of his inquiry. He cannot make it without leaving the area of his specialization and entering the area of philosophy.

(2) Perfectly matched teachers. An adequate study would necessitate teaching all groups in an experiment the same way: same teaching style, same personality, same method, same classroom atmosphere and mood, same competence of the teacher in the subject matter, etc., so that all pupils in all classes within both heterogeneous and homogeneous groupings and within both experimental and control groups, including both "fast" and "slow" groups within "homogeneous" groups, are taught in the same way. They would have to be taught in the same way in the most minute of detail in order to insure the stability of the variable under inquiry and to make a common achievement test possible. If they were taught differently, or if any other of a multitude of variables were not held constant, the achievement test would not be a common test and there would be no way of making it common. There is absolutely no way of knowing whether one has all the variables under control or not, except by assertion. All this means is that there could be no way of

knowing what happened within the experiment because there is no way of insuring that exactly the same thing happened except for the variable being examined, the grouping itself.

(3) Continuous study "habits." It would have to assume that all students in all groupings worked equally efficiently from day to day, always at the "same" rate according to their "capacities." This would seem to involve a very atypical teaching situation, if not a teaching utopia. To assume that day-to-day differences were statistically negligible or perfectly correlated but unresponsive to the groupings tested is rather bold, convenient, and question-begging. To ignore the issue is to retreat to a very gross level of experience.

(4) Equivalence of fact and values. Assuming the "empirical" information were at hand, it would still require a value judgment to go from the proposition, "Students, by and large, learn most when X-grouped," to the proposition, "Schools ought to have X-grouping." It would require a great many other considerations as well. That schools are a place for learning is still an open question despite the declaration of some ideologies to the contrary. What "learning" means is still an open question because it presupposes an idea of what knowledge is. What "knowledge" is is still an open question despite the declarations of ideologies to the contrary, because current arguments for "revelation" and "intuition" make as much sense and have as much appeal and exert as strong an influence among philosophers, among first-rate philosophers, as various forms of, say, positivism. Besides suggesting that experimentation of instructional groupings could not be carried out unless a *decision* were made concerning the nature of knowledge, which might mean that any findings were limited to groupings within the conception of knowledge that was accepted by commitment, the crucial issue here is that even if it were accepted that the implication of Sputnik I (and similar events) for schooling is the maximal diffusion of knowledge, the second proposition does not follow from the first. One has to know which groupings promote which kinds of learnings, which students learn more, how much more of which kinds of learnings are learned by whom over the entire span of schooling, and if sufficiently more of some kinds of learnings is enough to warrant priority over other kinds of

learnings and other considerations. Because "maximal diffusion" is two words, the maximal acquisition of knowledge is not necessarily the maximal diffusion of knowledge. This would be so even if it were clear as to what knowledge is. From neither the world situation nor the college preparation situation, then, neither the maximal acquisition nor the maximal diffusion of knowledge follows directly. It is neither clear as to which should follow nor if either should follow, except to some ideologies.

The value, or moral, dimension of this item of policy, in other words, is the *decisive* issue. It is that which makes a decision possible. It is the decisive issue particularly when it may sound as though one is referring to facts, for it is *precisely* then that the value issues dominate because they are mostly submerged, like an iceberg. From the moral point of view, "ability" grouping contributes to the alienation of men from each other and from themselves because it institutionalizes differences and qualities that are unrealizable in personal experience. One cannot "feel" or "see" or experience in any way various "levels of intelligence" in oneself or in others. That is why they made tests. People who think they can experience "levels of intelligence" in themselves or others are living their decision to approach living situations in a stereotyped and preconceived manner, their perception obstructed and the flux of human experience objectified in such a way that a living encounter with other people is prohibited. The *being* of levels of intelligence and intellectual achievement lies out there in the world in a more (or less) finely articulated, more (or less) coherently interrelated contexture of meanings that become possibilities of action through projecting into them: differences between apparently slow and bright pupils are differences in the structures, fluidities, depths, and possibilities of their worlds, out there in front of them. The institutionalization of "ability" grouping suggests to them that the differences are over here, inside the skin, as properties one already has. This promotes alienation because it (1) considers human being with categories appropriate to non-human entities, (2) places "societal expectations" on pupils not with respect to who they are but with respect to what they are, (3) structures the worlds of pupils in such a way that it makes subsequent authentic coexistence impossible, and (4) is the institutionalization of the desires of dominant social groups, who collectively constitute an oppressing class. These will be discussed in some detail in turn.

(1) Because "ability" groupings define the predominant structure of the school, they suggest that the decisive aspect of human being in respect to schooling is "intelligence" or "intellectual capacity" or "academic achievement." Because the child's horizons are opened up in their way, they suggest to the child that the most important aspect of human existence in general, in social life and in the cosmos, is the same as that by which he is grouped in school. This is necessarily so because he is "learning" all these at once regardless of attempts to isolate the school from its social and cosmological context because these attempts do not isolate but define a different relation to the "outside" world. The point, furthermore, is not that "intelligence," etc., are unimportant to schooling but lies in their reification and in the concomitant reification of the pupils. "Intelligence," "intellectual capacity," "academic achievement," or whatever, do not exist except in action, yet the atmosphere of the school under "ability" grouping not only reifies them but reifies them as the most *significant* "attribute" that the school is concerned with. More important than the value hierarchy (hence ideology) that is thereby implied is the fact that the major criterion for making room for the pupil within the school is an unrealizable. He cannot make room for himself in the same space that room is made for him without undergoing alienation from his own world, which includes the other children that he finds within it. He cannot be conscious of this "thing" by which he is grouped, nor can he go to the world, making room for himself, by what he can be conscious of.

Although no one else can be conscious of the reified "thing" by which "ability" grouping is instituted either, the practice nevertheless implies that "ability" is something one already has; it becomes a metaphysical, unknowable *Ding an sich.* Whereas the traditional conception of the superiority of "character" to "intellect" may have underestimated "intelligence," particularly in respect to its place in the attainment of "character," it does seem correct to say that if the honors student does not contribute significantly five or ten or twenty years after schooling is completed and if the "B" student does, then the significance of the latter's *schooling* achievement is greater than the former's. Although it may be correct to predict greater achievement from the former, schooling achievements are in some respects irrelevant to who one is, especially when human being as a totality is considered. They may be irrelevant to future achievement (i.e., low correlation). Predicting future achievement, moreover, may be irrelevant to the tasks of schooling. Then advocating schooling policy on the basis of a future promise may overestimate the importance of schooling to authentic achievement, committing what Aiken has called the "educator's fallacy," and it may overlook the possibilities of the present for the sake of a nonexistent future. What are needed, if one wants "empirical" information, are tremendously comprehensive and extensive longitudinal studies, more precise and controlled than Terman's or the Eight Year Study. It might be interesting to find out, for example, what becomes of National Merit Scholarship winners in the United States in order to see if the expense, annual disruption of school life in almost every school in the country, and distortion of curriculum entailed is actually worth while. Perhaps the money involved merely to administer the tests might be as well spent if it were donated to any college selected at random. How would one know? What kind of social contribution might one expect from "winners" to make the examinations worth the time? What percentage of "winners" might make wholesale administration of the tests worthwhile?

In general, that is, there has been little awareness of long range effects of recent "innovations," including "ability" grouping, and little attempt to examine thoroughly those things that sound good. The absence of longitudinal examination of the "innovations" such as "ability" grouping, that is, the absence of significant estimates of their value, accompanied by wide acceptance, can only make one wonder why they are considered desirable. At least part of the phenomena of being a good student has been a "capacity" to "learn" more from any schooling experience than "average" pupils, and at least part of the phenomena of "giftedness" has been doing whatever is assigned and finding more on one's own, i.e., until recently part of what was meant by "academic talent" was *less* need for teachers and schools. *Less.* Conceptions of good students or academic talent that do not focus on "self-motivation" as revealed in action are based on a belief in "magic": "talent" or "giftedness" is an entity that resides within the person that he already has and that is separable from that he does. To think that someone can do something because he has a "talent" or "gift" or "ability" for doing it rests upon a mode of reasoning from effect to cause whose paradigm is magic: to explain something is to name its "cause" even though there is no assurance that what is named actually exists. Then invocation of the name is supposed to produce the effect. It is also reminiscent of faculty psychology: "talent" or "ability" or "giftedness" can be improved through special exercises of the faculties that "ability" groupings are supposed to enable. They are either supposed to accelerate the acquisition of information or develop "abilities" (i.e., faculties). Because there is nothing holding any "talented" or "gifted" pupil back in any heterogeneously grouped class, and because faculty psychology is at least indefensible if not completely outmoded, one can only wonder why homogeneous groupings are deemed desirable in the absence of clues as to their worth.

If there are any students who need *no* innovations on their behalf, it would be good students, the *academically talented.* All that the words *academically talented* could possibly mean is doing well in school. Then "innovations" in schooling to help those who do well in school are rather redundant. One can only wonder how redundant items of policy become taken to be a response to societal problems. One can only wonder at the motivations of people who advocate redundant items. It is not appropriate to question the sincerity of persons advocating, teaching, or enrolled in "fast" classes: (a) such questioning would be *ad hominem* to which only an *ad hominem* reply would be appropriate, which would end all chances for dialogue; (b) consideration of policy has to suppose a context wherein the decision is open to decision, i.e., a specific school system that is contemplating institutionalizing "ability" grouping. This supposing can be purely imaginative, for imagining what might be is sufficient to free thinking from the bonds of previous decisions. Then, in imagination, one can question motivations, for in concrete situations motivations are as relevant to the outcome of deliberative proceedings as evidence and logical argument are. From the viewpoint of any depth psychology they may be more decisive. If so, then one can legitimately question why "talented" or "gifted" pupils would want "ability" grouping: to relieve the anguish of not being able to be conscious of one's own "talent"? To avoid later trial by concrete action? To achieve one's being at a stroke? To achieve merit once and for all as if it were not the kind of thing that had to be earned anew in each situation? To avoid the risk of schooling with the "average"? Why would parents want it for their children? To insure a "head start" in later life "competition," i.e., to put their child's being out of question? Why would teachers want it?

The item takes on new dimensions if one asks *why* rather than *whether*. If the pupil's way of existing in school is related to his later way of existing in social life, then the most relevant question concerns his desire to enroll in "fast" classes and the sanction given his reason through permitting him to do so. Some of the reasons might be related to (a) unwillingness to accept the responsibility of relying on merit alone, that is, on action alone, without the aid of special privilege, which is failure to live up to the human condition of having to be responsible for one's actions; (b) anxiety, when it is motivated by accepting societal "values," i.e., later vocational success, before having the experience that could make "accepting" them a responsible choice of concrete alternatives; (c) alienation from others, for it arrogates to oneself an assurance of later societal success that is concomitantly and in inverse proportion actively denied to other students, the "average" ones, who can only return the hate later when they sense the fraud perpetrated at their expense; and (d) alienation from oneself, when it is prestige or success or power that is desired, for these depend upon the admiration and compliance of the unsuccessful in order to constitute themselves as "prestige" or "success" or "power," which is to place one's being into the hands of others. This inexhaustive analysis suffices to suggest possible concomitant effects of groupings based on unrealizable, non-human categories: alienation from one's self and from others is promoted.

(2) When "ability" grouping is advocated as part of an

attempt to develop human resources, particularly when it is part of an attempt to discover, motivate, and develop "talent" for ends that are *a priori* as far as the "talented" pupils themselves are concerned, the overt suggestion is that the "talented" child or youth has no right to solve the problem of existing for himself as best as he can, that he has no right to dirt farm, paint, write poetry or novels, wash dishes, or any number of things to which schooling is not necessarily a help. It might not be tragic if a "gifted" youth, say, drops out of school: it could only seem to be when viewed through someone else's "values" when those "values" are projected on to him trying to dominate him, as if someone else knew what the youth's future should be, or what his best future could be. Advocating the discovering and motivating of "talented" children, in other words, is arrogant, deficient solicitude. It presupposes that "gifted" children can and should be "helped" by schooling. A great variety of questions concerning the "motivation" of "giftedness," of which very little is known, thrust themselves forward. What if the greatest possible motivation for the greatest possible contribution to society stemmed from and only from total neglect and indifference on the part of the school? What if it came from imaginative wanderings during dull classes? Or from rebellion and impatience with unimaginative teaching or with the "duly constituted" social order? Or from compassion developed through insight into the problems of quite ordinary classmates? What if premature recognition ruins "talent" or its "motivation"? What if long periods of solitary, undisturbed, and unrecognized periods of gestation are the *sine qua non* of solid creative accomplishment? How would one recognize a "talented" person such that "investment" would be properly directed? What if societal recognition or "success" ruins "talent" at least sometimes? Or what if Sartre was at least partly right when, after his existential psychoanalysis of Genet, he said, "Genius is not a gift but the way out that one invents in desperate cases"? Might it not make as much sense to institutionalize the conditions conducive to the happening of desperate cases as to institutionalize the conditions that might tend to prevent them? Who would try *that* experiment?

The foregoing questions are not the kinds of questions that can be investigated "empirically": if something is once tried, it is not possible to tell what might have happened had it not been tried or had something else been tried, except with different people. The teaching profession, moreover, unlike the medical or legal professions, never sees its own failures. Teaching and schooling failures are all mixed up with pupils' failures during school years. Apparent school "successes" may manifest themselves as "failures" ten or twenty years hence in another town, or they may be "failures" that never manifest themselves as such at all. That is, if "potential talent" is ruined by schooling either through being channeled through accelerated classes, through failure to be channeled through accelerated classes with other students of more discernible "talent" or through a myriad of other possible ways, it does not and cannot show. What might have been never shows. The "positive" results of ability grouping can be ascertained, but only to some degree because results in any case might have been better for all anyone can know. Negative results simply do not show.

The questions are not empirical in another sense. Even if they were amenable to research the application of the results is not an "empirical" question. Because any application involves children's lives, application falls *ipso facto* within the area of normative anthropology guided by existential concern for better or for worse. How life should be lived is a question of normative anthropology no matter who does it under whatever label. How other people's lives should be lived is guided by existential concern no matter how lucidly.

(3) Under "ability" grouping the structure of the life of the school structures the world of the pupil, both in school and afterwards. Because human temporality is not a continuous progression, a remembrance of school days years later brings the social structure of the "past" right into the present world. If vividly enough, the "past" remembered can be closer and more relevant to the present situation than incidents of the same day. Later remembrance of "ability" grouping prohibits authentically human relations because of the "earlier" inauthentic relations. "Ability" grouping is being there in school inauthentically with others because the grouping is based on ontic grounds: it has no foundation in human being and cannot be based on ontological differences between people. The "inequalities" it is based on are

"real," within the assumption of certain methodological procedures that make them real, but they have no being apart from
the bracketing of a particular method of inquiry. Groupings on
ontical properties prevent the formation or development of an
underlying "we are in it together" that is necessary for corporate
action, i.e., authentic human relations. If Sputnik I demonstrated that there is only one world, and if the educational
development of pupils is assumed to promote the kinds of
persons who are capable of overcoming societal difficulties, then
"ability" grouping runs counter to the main pedagogical intent.
That children can come to "accept" or "adjust to" "ability"
grouping when it is introduced early enough, then, is not a
mitigating but a damning factor, precisely where tragedy may
lie. Explication of this will lead to the final point.

In his criticism of "American culturalism," Sartre suggested
that its mechanistic approach treated societal roles as essentially
things *past,* removed from the temporality of a living perspective, but that "everything changes if one considers that society is
presented to each man as *a perspective of the future* and that
this future penetrates to the heart of each one as a real motivation for his behavior . . ." [1] because the societal possibilities are
his possibles. To understand a society, therefore, it is necessary
to study the structures of the future that are presented to
children. How are the structures available in the future presented in schools that have "ability" grouping? How are they
presented to pupils within *their* temporal structures? As each
person is "defined" by his societal possibilities, each is "defined"
negatively by the societal possibles that are impossible for him;
for the underprivileged each societal enrichment is one more
impoverishment, one more societal possible that is impossible
for them. Each schooling possibility that is added for only some
children becomes another impossible for other children, another
impoverishment, because it increases the number of routes forward that are closed to them. It increases the number of doors
marked "No admittance." Whether "average" groups are col-
lege-bound or "college material" or not, "ability" grouping cuts

[1] Jean-Paul Sartre, *Search for a Method,* trans. Hazel E. Barnes
(New York, Knopf, 1963), p. 96. (Italics Sartre's.)

off their future by institutionally (i.e., legally) negatively defining it. This is necessarily premature because it murders hope. Separate facilities are once again inherently unequal.

"Homogeneous" groupings provide segregated schooling that is necessarily unequal in the humane dimensions. The ontic property on which "ability" grouping is based is as irrelevant to schooling as the ontic properties of skin color or hair texture if schooling has anything to do with opening up future possibilities of being to children and youth. It is very difficult to see it doing anything else. Then the institutional elevation of some people on ontic differences is inherently immoral because it alienates pupils from future possibilities, i.e., from themselves, as well as alienating them from each other in their major institutional deliverance to the broader society.

(4) In light of the preceding, there is no "explanation" for the existence of "ability" grouping in any system other than the reinforcement of the dominant group by filtering off "talent" for its preservation (except for unawareness of the ramifications). This constitutes oppression of those who are not "acceptable." To define other people negatively by defining their impossibles for them is oppression. Any other term would be descriptively inadequate. A few facts help. The trend since Sputnik I has been a return to traditionalism: renewed emphasis on college preparation, acceleration, "ability" grouping, and the return to "standards" and "hard subjects" in the "new" suburban curriculums, as well as team teaching and educational television, not to mention "machines," have all been part of the Thermidorean reaction to progressive education. The recipients of these "advances," of these "conservative innovations," have not yet reached the labor market, but there still seem to be major difficulties abroad in the world that are *not* caused by shortages of trained scientists and technologists, and there is less assurance today that solutions can be found simply through having greater supplies of trained personnel available. The schooling response, in other words, has been out of proportion because it has been a response to the demands of some and only some organized interest groups who collectively constitute a dominant or oppressing class in respect to schooling because their impact has in fact dominated and tended to negatively define children

and youth by negatively defining their futures for them. It also constitutes exploitation of the rest of the public insofar as it is the utilization of public facilities for private interests, so that wherever there is "ability" grouping, there is oppression in the strictest Marxian sense. That this may have been accomplished without awareness of the consequences does not change the consequences.

Concerning the item selected for analysis to indicate how educational policy might be reflected on within a normative concern: if one begins with the phenomenon of world-wide, compulsory, free schooling and attempts to reflect on the arrangement that admits of the educational development of the kinds of persons capable of resolving or alleviating contemporary societal problems, one finds that it is so-called heterogeneous grouping. Other items of policy could be examined in a similar manner if it were decided that the basic educational issue raised by Sputnik I were in fact that of how to live together and that this issue were to guide policy decisions. All that would need to be done to escape ideological justifications would be to keep the phenomenon of the publicness of schooling in view.

CURRICULUM SELECTION AND ORGANIZATION

As with the nature and aim of education, theory of knowledge is relevant to the problems of the design and validation of the curriculum (1) methodologically, (2) substantively, (3) contextually.

(1) The selection, sequencing, and organization of curricular content is related to the aim of education and to the educative process: How does the curriculum achieve the aim? If content is selected to achieve some highly specific objectives or to prepare the pupil for the next course (and so on to college), rather than to promote some general aim, there nevertheless remains some purpose behind curriculum selection. Whatever the purpose and however stated, the attempt to relate the content to the purpose to be achieved involves epistemological considerations. In fact, there is reason to believe that some attempts to evade this kind of epistemological inquiry through using lists of objectives for the guidance of the selection and organization of curricular content, or for restricting the aim to purely academic preparation in "subject matter," are based precisely upon epistemological grounds at the methodological level. How could one *know* if aims or objectives are being achieved unless they are *reduced* to what can be observationally and behaviorally tested? Or, how can one *know* that there is an "education" over and above the process of schooling (superficially) defined as vocational and college preparation? One can always ask, however, whether the achievement of a certain behaviorally defined objective is educative, or whether and to what extent particular studies are in fact vocational or college preparation and, if so, whether and to what extent they are also educative.

The methodological aspect of the epistemology of the selection and organization of curriculum, in other words, is concerned with the relations between curriculum and the aim and process of education. It is concerned with the relations between objectives at the level of abstraction and generality appropriate for curriculum selection and the wholistic, molar level of aims expressed in terms of life-outcomes, on one hand, and the highly specific, concrete actions of the teacher responding to unique personalities, situations, and events of the classroom on the other. Now, although some curriculum theorists have maintained that the entire curriculum could be ascertained empirically, the attempt to do so would *require* observational categories and definitions. This eliminates more general aims and more specific, intuitive procedures. If an empirical method cannot grasp the generality of aims or the specificity of the process without changing them into something else, it cannot measure the real "outcomes" in terms of the real "inputs," for no method can measure what it cannot grasp. This seems to require explicit statement in order to open up the methodological phase as an area of inquiry: How does one know what content is related to which aims and through which kind of teaching and learning procedures it is so related? Should curricular content be selected and organized ("structured") to serve the aim (Adler), policy (reconstructionism), the educative process (Dewey)? Which, if any, of the conclusions concerning aims, policy, or the educative process should become of paramount concern to content selection and organization? If curriculum becomes paramount, how and why should which kind of balance toward aims, policy, and process be maintained? Because answers to these questions should be cognitively adequate in order to guide particular methods and criteria of selection and organization so that they may be cognitively adequate, one phase of the epistemology of curriculum concerns the methodology of curriculum construction.

(2) More important, however, is the cognitive adequacy of the curriculum: What kinds of knowledge should constitute the curriculum and what arrangement of it is conducive to the pupil's knowing?

The phrase "kinds of knowledge" in the question includes any and every kind in order to avoid begging the prior question of whether or not there should be noncognitive components to the curriculum. We can say that the curriculum should exclude noncognitive components if cognition is initially conceived very broadly to avoid imposing preconceptions on the inquiry, if we ask for kinds of knowledge. Athletics, for example, depends upon various kinds of knowledge as exhibited in common sense statements, "He knows how to play football according to official regulations and in the finest spirit of sportsmanship," "He knows how to sink baskets from midcourt." If athletics did not involve cognition in some sense it could not be added to the curriculum either as "extra-" or "co-." If all this seems odd at first, it accents the significance of the philosophical question behind the educational question: What is knowing? What is the nature of knowledge? If one wishes to argue that sports do not contain forms of cognition or knowing the way we use those words when we talk about curriculum matters, he is well on his way into the substantive issues of the epistemology of the curriculum.

The phrase "what arrangement is conducive to the pupil's knowing" concerns the degree and kind of structuring at the curriculum level, rather than at the classroom level, that insures that the pupil's learning constitutes knowing. How much evidence of what kind should be included to support which kinds of generalizations or concepts so that the pupil not only learns the concept or generalization but also understands and knows it? How much of the process of inquiry and how much of the product of inquiry should structure the curriculum? The relevance of the theory of knowledge and its examination of the nature of inquiry, evidence, data, and the structure of the process and its product, to the educational questions is obvious. Which kinds of structuring of the curriculum are conducive to the pupil's knowing what he learns? Inductive, deductive, experiential, organic, dialectical, teleological, or some combination of some or all of these? Whose structuring of the curriculum is most educative? The expert's, the teacher's, or the pupil's? Which of these are questions of the educative process rather than of the curriculum? Are they curriculum problems from the microcosmic level of the individual lesson to the macrocosmic level of the entire program insofar as one is seeking general answers?

(3) If it is decided that some kinds of knowing or learning are not to be dignified by attributing a kind of cognition to them (if it is maintained that a distinction between the cognitive and noncognitive components of the curriculum is necessary and perhaps even worthwhile to make), then the contextual prob-

lems of the epistemology of the curriculum come into being. When something other than a contextual logic is used to structure the curriculum, then the logic that is used to supply the structuring omits parts of the context in which teaching and learning occurs: the pupil's experiental background, his interest, motivation, feelings, and purposes are omitted from the sphere of influence of the organized curriculum. Then how the whole body of organized knowledge making up the curriculum meshes in with the pupil's whole being is the problem of the contextual phase of the epistemology of the curriculum. It is the problem of integration.

The problem arises because the cognitive/noncognitive distinction is so frequently made in the substantive phase. The distinction obtains in schooling but not in reality. The consequent over-structuring of the curriculum calls forth doubts concerning its adequacy expressed in terms of the total context of learning and the apparent need for some integration of the whole program in terms of the pupil's experience of it. This is most appropriately seen as the relevance of taking the nature and aim of education and the educative process into account in the curriculum design, but it emerges as a curriculum problem when these other aspects are beyond the horizons of one's perspective. When all that can be held in conscious attention is the curriculum, then the contextual aspect of the epistemological dimension of curriculum design arises as the problem of integration of the program.

The selections that follow further explicate the relations between theory of knowing and knowledge and the curriculum. The first three are basically concerned with the methodological aspects, the next three with substantive aspects, and the last four selections with contextual aspects, although their concerns overlap considerably.

Gardner's paper, for example, utilizes Aristotle's metaphysics and epistemology to illustrate a point concerning the nature of science and knowledge and dealing quite substantively with the issues of the epistemology of the curriculum, but all this is only an illustration for his major point concerning the methodology of Tyler's rationale. Because Gardner seems to be right when he says that a different conception of science, i.e., valid knowledge, would lead to a different curriculum, Champlin's paper follows his. To investigate the idea of integration, Champlin employs a view of science that denies the Aristotelian "truth by correspondence." Because Champlin is essentially doing philosophy of science in what we take to be a Deweyan manner, his concern is likewise more methodological than substantive, although his denial of some of the previously suggested bases for integration is quite substantive. Miel's paper contains an adequate survey of recent work on structure in the curriculum in the context, however, of presenting "guidelines" for substantive and contextual inquiry.

Miel's final suggestion to have the curriculum structured "both ways," i.e., structured according to the nature of the educative process and according to the logic of the discipline, is the cue to the following selections by Dewey and Phenix. By comparing Dewey and Phenix, who illustrate each way in turn, one can come to some estimate of the actual difference between the two ways. A basic merit of the Phenix paper, in addition to the clear articulation and defense of "structure" as often recently conceived, is the explicit assertion of the correspondence of the structure of a discipline to reality in the closing paragraphs, for this puts the argument squarely on epistemological and metaphysical grounds. It would seem to make a vast difference in structuring the curriculum according to the structure of the disciplines if the latter corresponded to the structure of reality. If so, the structure of the knowledge of the expert would be one thing; if not, then another. The importance of the structure of the expert's body of knowledge for the curriculum would vary accordingly. We take it that this was Dewey's point, although Dewey was not a "nominalist." This point becomes clearer in contrasting Phenix's view with that of Stadt's paper, for Stadt's argument concerning the variety of models and categorical systems available to curriculum construction seems to rest upon a nominalism. Also seeming to rest upon a nominalism is McClellan's paper. McClellan raises some very significant, nominalistic doubts about a number of attempts to structure the curriculum. His suggestion that propositional knowledge be arranged to promote the development of what he terms "cognitive action," which we would construe as "cognitively adequate action," is illustrated, perhaps, in the selections following his.

The last four items advocate some kind of epistemological pluralism in the curriculum, with the consequent loss of tight structure and organization (and its desirability). Taken as a whole, the four selections indicate how a considerable variety of theories of knowledge are relevant to structuring various parts of the curriculum. Their ordering in this volume is toward an increasing emphasis upon an ontological grounding of knowledge, although they never quite get to Phenix's realism, and toward an increasing emphasis upon integration of the curriculum through the contextual considerations. The variety of these last four selections is indicative of the complexity of the work that has to be done on the problem of the structure of knowledge in the curriculum before it is possible to speak of "structure" without the oversimplification that borders on nonsense.

A major attempt to grasp the structure of structure in an interdisciplinary way is the volume edited by Stanley Elam, *Education and the Structure of Knowledge* (Chicago, Rand McNally, 1964). Important and representative examples of principles for the total organization of the curriculum are Spencer's "What Knowledge Is of Most Worth?" in *Education,* Gentile's "The Ideal of Education" in *The Reform of Education,* Dewey's efforts in Chapters XV–XVII of *Democracy and Education,* and the work of Broudy *et al.,* excerpted from in Part One. For a critical view of Dewey, see Archambault's "The Philosophical Basis of the Experience Curriculum" in the *Harvard Educational Review,* 26 (Summer, 1956), pp. 263–75. Otherwise, see the resources listed by Miel and by the Henderson and McClellan papers in the Smith and Ennis volume, *Language and Concepts in Education.*

THE RELATION OF PHILOSOPHY TO CURRICULUM DEVELOPMENT *

Leonard Gardner

This inquiry may be viewed as a search for the educational problems which are capable of profitable treatment within the context of philosophic considerations. The answer and its justification will be presented within the framework of a critical evaluation of certain aspects of the curriculum theory of Professor Ralph W. Tyler.

A curriculum theory, particularly one so comprehensive as Professor Tyler's, must consider the primary problems of education; consequently, it is capable of serving as the nexus for a general consideration of the relation of philosophy and education.

Professor Tyler defines education as "a process of changing the behavior patterns of people." He views the educational process as a series of learning experiences aimed at the fulfillment of carefully considered educational objectives; consequently, it is the selection of objectives, goals or ends which is the determining factor in the construction of the curriculum.

The curriculum objectives are derived from considerations of the nature of (a) the student, (b) the social context within which the school is located, and (c) the subject matter. The objectives once derived are screened through a theory of learning psychology and a philosophy of education.

Professor Tyler writes, in *The Basic Principles of Curriculum and Instruction:*

> To select a group of a few highly important, consistent objectives, it is necessary to screen the heterogeneous collection of objectives thus far obtained so as to eliminate the unimportant and the contradictory ones. The educational and social philosophy to which the school is committed can serve as the first screen. The original list of objectives can be culled by identifying those that stand high in terms of values stated or implied in the school's philosophy.

* Reprinted from "The Relation of Philosophy to Education," *Educational Theory,* 4(January, 1954), 54–57, 64–68. By permission of the author and the editor of *Educational Theory.*

There is a second screen, through which the suggested objectives should be passed and that is the criteria for objectives implied by what is known about the psychology of learning. Educational objectives are educational ends, they are results to be achieved from learning. Unless these ends are in conformity with conditions intrinsic in learning they are worthless as educational goals.

The foregoing constitutes a somewhat abbreviated account of the theoretical framework by which the first of the "four fundamental questions" of Tyler's curriculum rationale may be answered. The questions are:

1. What educational purposes should the school seek to attain?

2. What educational experiences can be provided that are likely to attain these purposes?

3. How can these educational experiences be effectively organized?

4. How can we determine whether these purposes are being attained?

It should be apparent that the first question has more than a superficial primacy in the curriculum schema, that in actual fact, the answers to the first question, i.e., the educational objectives *per se, constitute the basic determinants of the curriculum.* If this theory of curriculum construction is to be evaluated with respect to its efficacy in determining the outcome of a practical educational problem, then it is necessary to examine the techniques by which educational goals are themselves determined.

Essentially, Professor Tyler is saying, "Consider the nature of the student, the society, and the subject matter," but he very deliberately refrains from dictating the manner in which these areas are to be viewed. In so doing, he denies the validity of educational theories which reduce the curriculum to purely psychological or social or informational considerations, but he allows complete freedom in choosing *between conceptions* of the nature of personality, or society and of the subject-matter. It should be obvious that the educational goals derived by a thoroughgoing behaviorist would be considerably different from those of a Freudian, that John Dewey's conception of personality is crucially different from Mortimer J. Adler's. Consequently, any curriculum constructed in terms of this rationale will be determined almost completely by the way in which these three fundamental areas are perceived.

It would seem that a theory which has been constructed for the purpose of solving practical problems should operate to reject certain alternatives and espouse others. The complaint registered here is that Tyler's theory allows far too much freedom, hence is indeterminate with respect to the problem. The solution which will be proposed lies within a conception of educational philosophy markedly different from that of Professor Tyler.

The position which we shall advocate rests on the assertion that most of the traditionally important commitments about the nature of reality, *viz.,* theories of personality, the state, and of knowledge, have derived from (and consequently may be reduced to) distinctions which are essentially philosophic in kind. Consequently, the terms in which a comprehensive philosophy is conceived serve to determine the conceptions which define the fundamental areas of the Tyler curriculum. These terms may be metaphysical, epistemological, or some third class, depending upon the philosophy; however they may be conceived, it is only by a prior commitment to a particular set of terms that a curriculum can be predetermined in an explicit and consistent manner. Clearly, this perspective serves to move philosophy in the Tyler rationale from the position of a "screen" to that of direct involvement in the search for objectives.

The following discussion will be concerned with the clarification of the role of educational philosophy which was asserted here. Our presentation will be concerned with conceptions of personality, society and subject-matter, the conceptions themselves considered as *consequent* upon the metaphysical distinctions of a major philosophy and as *suggestive* of a set of curriculum goals. The selection of the Aristotelian philosophy for this purpose is mainly due to the fact that much of traditional educational thought, as well as "common sense" views of all sorts, are Aristotelian in origin.[1] The purpose here is neither

---

[1] A glance at Chapters 4 and 5 of John Dewey's *Logic* will serve to substantiate the argument that "common sense" and Aristotelian views have much in common. In Chapter 5 Dewey lists four conceptions of

to describe the philosophy completely nor to develop fully a curriculum based upon it. It is our concern to present adequately the relation of philosophic terms to the concepts involved in the universe of investigation and to display the relation of such concepts to educational objectives.

Metaphysics referred originally to that section of Aristotle's writings which followed immediately after the *Physics*. The word is used here to mean the ultimate distinctions upon which are based the conceptions of reality or of Nature. Since such terms are the most general in import and are consequently ingredient in more specific statements, their prior definitions will serve as an aid in later considerations of greater specificity.

For the purposes of this paper, it is possible to restrict the consideration of Aristotle's metaphysics. Of prime importance is his conception of the four causes. Any thing or event is capable of being known as a separately existing entity, by searching out the answers to Aristotle's four famous questions:

1. What is the material cause? The material cause of a shoe is leather, of a man, tissues and organs.

2. What is the formal cause? The formal cause of a shoe is the principle of organization by which its material is arranged, such that a (leather) shoe may be recognized as such, and is clearly distinct from, say, a (leather) hat. Similarly, the form of a man consists in the arrangement of the materials in the characteristically man-like way.

3. What is the efficient cause? By what agency does leather become a shoe, sperm and ovum become tissues and finally man? The principle by which leather changes into shoe lies in the shoemaker and his art. But a child becomes a man (or protoplasm becomes tissue) by virtue of an internal necessity for change.

4. What is the final cause? What is the "that for the sake of which a thing is"? A shoemaker makes a shoe so that it will serve as footwear; a man exists for his own sake.

Several of the important relations between the four causes

---

major importance in both views: (1) the category of substance; (2) the category of fixed species; (3) teleological conceptions; (4) hierarchical organization in the world of things and of social relations.

may be best described by the following quotation from Aristotle's *Metaphysics:*

. . . those who define a house as stones, bricks, and timbers are speaking of the potential house, for these are the matter, but those who propose "a receptacle to shelter chattels and living beings" or something of the sort, speak of the actuality. Those who combine both of these speak of the third kind of substance, which is composed of matter and form. . . . It is obvious then, from what has been said, what sensible substance is and how it exists—one kind of it as matter, another as form or actuality, while the third kind is that which is composed of these two.

This quotation serves to define the material and formal causes in terms of the relation of *potential* to *actual;* in addition it introduces the conception of matter and form as constituents in a third thing, which Aristotle often refers to as the *composite entity.* It is the composite entities with which men deal directly, and it is the material and formal causes (as well as final and efficient causes, in another sense) which become the objects of inquiry.

In the discussion of the four causes, another distinction becomes obvious: that of natural and artificial objects. A shoe is a thing of art: the efficient cause of its being lies in the maker or artist. A man is a natural object just because the efficient cause of his being lies within him. This distinction will be elaborated upon in greater detail in a later discussion. It is important here because it provides the basis for a conception of two main types of inquiry, hence the two types of possible knowledge.

The distinction is that of inquiry into natural objects, which yields necessary and certain knowledge, and that of inquiry into artificial objects, resulting in knowledge which can only be contingent. Aristotle refers to the first kind of knowledge as *theoretic,* the second as practical. In the inquiries into the student, the society, and the subject matter, which follow, this distinction will be of considerable importance. . . .

Aristotle writes: ". . . the citizens must not lead the life of mechanics or tradesmen, for such a life is ignoble, and inimical to virtue. Neither must they be husbandmen, since leisure is necessary both for the development of virtue and the performance of political duties." It may be argued that it is possible, in a modern, industrialized culture, to be both a mechanic and a citizen; the brute fact for education is, however, that education for citizenship in Aristotle's ideal state is clearly different from that for a vocation. Further, and more important, is the fact that for such a state, education specifically for citizenship is crucially necessary, and that such an education does not consist in a course in "civics" or "Athenian government" but rather in an extensive program calculated to develop fully the essentially human potentialities. In modern terms, the choice lies between an educational program conceived as *liberal education* as against a curriculum which has as its end professional or vocational training.

The primary consideration of Aristotle's theory of personality was of the nature and development of the emotional faculties with respect to the formation of good moral character. In these terms, it would seem reasonable to expect that the subject-matter components of the Aristotelian curriculum would constitute those pedagogical elements most directly concerned with the development of the intellectual faculties.

If this is the case, if the subject-matter is a cause of the development of the intellectual faculties, then a spelling out of the nature of those faculties should provide at least a part of the answer to the question, "What is the proper subject-matter of the curriculum?" But "subject-matter" is only a kind of short-hand symbol used by educators, and refers ultimately to some prior conception of the nature of the store-house of knowledge possessed by the culture. However, what knowledge is, and what kinds of knowledge are possible, are questions whose answers constitute a crucial part of any philosophy.

Knowledge, for Aristotle, is knowledge of the four causes of a thing or event. Two kinds of knowledge are possible, theoretic and practical, the latter being further divided into the knowledge requisite for prudent action in the conduct of life, and that required in the execution of the arts.

The three kinds of knowledge, hence, kinds of inquiry, may be distinguished from each other and defined in terms of the causes.

With respect to the material cause, the theoretical sciences are inquiries into "natural" phenomena, while prudence and art are concerned with matters which are "artificial." This distinction between natural and artificial is itself grounded upon a classification of things in terms of efficient cause. This is made quite clear in the first chapter of Aristotle's *Physics:*

> "By nature" the animals and their parts exist, and the plants and the simple bodies (earth, fire, air, water)—for we say that these and the like exist "by nature."
>
> All the things mentioned present a feature in which they differ from things which are *not* constituted by nature. Each of them has *within* itself a principle of motion and of stationariness (in respect of place, or of growth and decrease, or by way of alteration). On the other hand, a bed and a coat and anything else of that sort, qua receiving these designations—i.e., insofar as they are products of art—have no innate impulse to change.

As regards the final cause, theoretic knowledge is desired for the sake of the attainment of truth; prudence as a guide to the right action of men, either as individuals faced with the problem of moral choice, or as members of social groups, encountering the problems of the household and the state; and artistic knowledge for the purpose of the production of art or of artifacts.

The formal cause of scientific knowledge consists in its essential quality of logical necessity; whereas, the knowledge of the practical sciences can never be more than probable. This point will be considered in greater detail in a subsequent discussion.

The efficient cause of knowledge, i.e., the agency by which knowledge is attained, is the intellectual faculties.

The foregoing account constitutes the initial basis for the discrimination of the various species of knowledge; prior to the derivation of educational implications—some of which are now quite obvious—it is necessary to clarify this position with respect to its metaphysical basis. In particular, the distinctions between theoretical and practical knowledge with respect to their material and formal causes, stand in need of further amplification.

In the sense that knowledge consists of knowledge of the four causes, inquiry is centered upon entitative particles, i.e., things, or composite entities. Composite entities, as has been asserted, contain formal and material constituents. The distinction between "natural composites" and "artificial composites" is based, in one sense, upon the locus of the efficient cause; in another, upon the character of a "natural" matter as potentially capable of realizing a single form and of "natural" forms as actualizing a specific matter. This is a characteristic not shared by artificial objects; bricks are potentially houses, fireplaces, doorstops, weapons, etc., and houses are actualized bricks, wood, mud, or reeds, while man is composed of distinctly *human materials,* and human materials, while they may fail to result in rational animals, can never result in dogs or cats. Further, while it is undeniable that the members of a species of a "thing of nature" are not identical, i.e., that no two men are exactly the same, it is asserted that the form, or essence of man is eternal and unchanging. And it is by virtue of the existence of eternal, unchanging forms that eternal, unchanging knowledge—logically necessary statements of universal import—is made possible in the theoretical sciences.

A basis for the initial discrimination of the subject-matter has been made: studies may be organized with regard to their contributions to theoretical or practical knowledge, the latter being conceived in its dual meaning. (It is necessary to recall here that the final selection of subject-matter involved psychological and social considerations; the problem of this discussion consists in the definition and description of the kinds of subject-matter made possible by this theory of knowledge.)

Theoretical knowledge is, for Aristotle, in every respect, the most desirable, and by its nature, most specifically an appropriate educational objective. Accordingly, the remainder of the discussion will focus upon the nature of such knowledge.

The theoretical sciences, as distinguished on the basis of their subject-matter are physics, mathematics, and metaphysics. The physicist studies the natural composite entity, while the mathematician is concerned with the abstractions from existents of the qualities of number and form or shape. The metaphysician is concerned with the ultimate distinctions of the four causes, of form, matter and composite, and their relation to knowledge.

The distinctions within the theoretical sciences raise questions which are often taken for granted: this is particularly the case for metaphysical considerations, or a consideration of "first philosophy" as Aristotle called it. If most of the major academic subjects have ingredient within them assertions about the world which refer to such entities and processes as atoms and molecules, force and energy, ego, superego and id, evolution and genetic mechanism, marginal value, balance of power and, particularly, scientific method, then the question arises, shall these entities and processes be considered as existent or as standing in some relation to existents. If the latter alternative is accepted, it then becomes necessary to provide, within the curriculum, opportunity for consideration of the basis of the relation—not merely in the respect of its conformity with empirical data or with respect to its logical validity, since these are proper considerations within the subject of sciences, but rather with respect to the ultimate irreducible terms which have served to mediate between the observer and the raw data of his observation. The consideration of such terms and their relevance to the knowledge which is a product of the sciences would constitute a metaphysical inquiry.

If theoretical inquiries have as their goal universal truths, then the method of the sciences must involve considerations of logical necessity. That is to say, scientific knowledge is demonstrable, and the training of the faculties by which theoretical wisdom is attained, consists of training in syllogistic logic. But purely formal syllogisms do not convey information: it is necessary to know the premises of a science as well as the logical forms by which valid conclusions may be reached. (This defines the scientific syllogism as not merely valid, but true as well.)

For a premise to be true requires, in at least one sense, that there exist some correspondence between the verbal assertion and the nature of things. The final question of this paper is, then, "What kind of statements about mathematical or physical objects are made by Aristotelian science?" These statements will constitute the subject-matter (in the narrowest sense of the term) of the curriculum.

Mathematical objects are for Aristotle abstractions from physical entities. While they may be treated as the subject of a single, separate science, they have no separate existence in nature; but they are none the less "natural," hence existential. On this basis, the alternative postulational systems of modern mathematicians would be inconceivable: there can be only, for Aristotle, a "Euclidean" geometry, never a Riemannian alternative. And it is the case that, in most secondary school geometry classes, the subject is treated as "natural" and with an appeal to an intuition of postulates, rather than as one of a number of alternative postulate systems.

Aristotle's physics (which includes such studies as chemistry, biology, and the like) is characterized by the qualitative distinctions made between the objects of inquiry. This excludes any possibility of a reduction to material causes or to investigation conceived as the relation of variables, studied mathematically. Also, a natural object may be studied independently of other objects, since such objects have an eternal, unchanging nature, the knowledge of which is attainable and unaffected by the methods of the investigator.[2] A notable consequence of this position is the rejection of the Darwinian theory of evolution by "modern" Aristotelians.

This paper represents an attempt to face the problem of the relation of philosophic inquiry to the educational enterprise. In the development of the Aristotelian curriculum on the model of the Tyler rationale, the relation of the concepts of the sciences (of psychology, sociology, and those sciences which are considered as subject-matter) to the terms within which these sciences were conceived was emphasized.

That a given conception of science leads to a curriculum of one sort, and a different conception of science leads to quite a different kind of curriculum should be clear. Consider, for example, the Aristotelian conception of natural science which has been discussed: such knowledge consists in apprehension of fixed qualities of immutable objects. Theoretical science thus conceived is divorced from considerations of practical problems, in the degree that particular individuals differ markedly from the essence of the species. Such scientific knowledge which is made possible on this basis has only limited extrinsic value, and is, therefore, desired simply for its own sake. The curriculum which is consistent with this position is one in which the subject-matter is literally desirable for its own sake.

---

[2] See footnote above. The Aristotelian conception of science, as indicated here, can hardly be appreciated if it is not viewed in contrast with the radically different nature of modern science, as perceived by Dewey.

In contrast is the Deweyan conception of scientific knowledge as apprehension of the relations between objects and as fore-knowledge of future consequences of present actions. In this context, knowledge may be valued for its own sake, but is viewed primarily as arising from past problematic situations and directed toward the settlement of present and future problems. Further, no sharp distinction can be maintained between the theoretical and practical, with the consequence that the student is confronted, not with deduced qualities of ideal entities, but rather with problematic situations requiring settlement.

It would indeed appear that the manner in which science is conceived makes for a considerable difference in the nature of the curriculum.

What are the implications of this argument for Professor Tyler's rationale? Our discussion here argues for the fact that some of the most significant differences discernible between curricula lie in the conceptions of reality, inquiry, knowledge, and practice upon which they are based. Since the Tyler rationale makes no provision within itself for the selection of the conceptions basic to the formation of the curriculum, it is necessary to conclude that the rationale *per se* is inadequate with respect to the problem. Whether, on the other hand, the rationale can be employed effectively in conjunction with a prior formulation of a philosophy is still a question which must be answered. I do not think that Tyler-cum-Aristotle yields a curriculum which is in any sense different from Aristotle alone. The rationale can, however, offer an organizational device for committee work of considerable value. Faculties which have employed Professor Tyler's rationale as a device for inquiry into their existing curricular practices have undoubtedly been forced to re-examine many hitherto uncritically accepted assumptions. The rationale has been particularly valuable in challenging the position of educational extremists, who, in their reaction to the traditional over-emphasis on *subject-matter,* ignore the latter in order to over-emphasize the *student* as the primary, if not exclusive, locus of educational problems.

To resume, Professor Tyler's position can be considered as an appeal to science for knowledge of reality. But within the sciences there exist sharp disagreements on the answers to the very problems with which education is most concerned: the nature of man, of society, and of knowledge. In inquiries such as these, where the basic terms of the investigation have often been chosen for purely heuristic reasons, it is particularly important to understand those terms and their role in delimiting the inquiry. In short, it is necessary to perform the operations of philosophic analysis *in order to appeal to science.*

CONCERNING INTEGRATION *

Nathaniel L. Champlin

From the time of Plato down to the present, men have attempted to effect integration in their lives. According to one theory that has come down to us both art and science are finite, partial or fragmentary approaches to a reality, divine or other, which provides, in the form of unity, the guide and goal for art, science and, indeed, all human endeavor. Called "Platonic" ("idealism" for some), it was imported into the theoretical architecture of Christianity. It profoundly influenced Emerson, and it gained major educational expression in Froebel. It has moved men to deplore fragmentation and to seek integration in their most significant institution—education. It still operates as a court of appeal for educators throughout the contemporary scene.

In the recent past, integration and unity became an object of concern for analytic philosophy directed to the sciences. A "unified science" movement took form.[4] Contributed to by some of the finest scientific methodologists of our time it achieved a respectability of inquiry not enjoyed by the more mystical, metaphysical or religious concerns. This inquiry attempted to locate an alleged inter-relatedness of the various sciences and to formulate principles of integration. . . .

However, the movement has failed to locate any unifying principles or any trans-science generalizations except those principles of inference and empirical investigation which permit us to locate the various sciences *as sciences* in the first place. The different sciences simply do not contribute to, nor do they rest on the assumption of, a "total" reality, unity or integration. It is

* Reprinted from "Value Inquiry and the Philosophy of Education," *Educational Leadership*, Vol. 13, No. 8 (May, 1956), 468–73. By permission of the Association for Supervision and Curriculum Development and Nathaniel Champlin. Copyright © 1956 by the Association for Supervision and Curriculum Development.

4 Rudolf Carnap *et al., Encyclopedia and Unified Science,* Vol. 1, No. 1 of *International Encyclopedia of Unified Science,* ed. Otto Neurath, Rudolf Carnap, and Charles Morris (2 vols., 20 monographs; Chicago, University of Chicago Press, 1938–1952).

impossible to "add" the theorems of physics, for example, to the concepts of biology, economics, and/or sociology. Rather than different "parts," the sciences provide us with different theoretical contexts within which we find knowledge claims, predictions and hypotheses. The different sciences *are* these different and non-additive contexts of control, prediction and inquiry. Neither are they "copies," duplications, or exhibitions of the objects or subject matters to which their concepts refer, nor are they "abstractions" *from* these objects or subject matters.

The quest for a conception of a whole, unified or integrated person (or personality) suffers in the same way. Chemistry, physiology, psychology, biology, anthropology, and artistic descriptions—empirically based—provide non-additive, non-correlated, and unrelated meanings. They cannot, without breaching the canons of scientific methodology, presuppose or contribute to a conception of a total, unified or integrated person.[5]

Some current theories of an integrated person commit one of two methodological fallacies: the *teleological fallacy* in which a describable consequence of an object or event is converted into a causal constituent of that object or event, and the *symbolic fallacy* in which a *term* having stipulated usage in one theory is used in another and different theory with the tacit assumption that its precision still holds.

Teleology, the practice of claiming a purpose behind, above or other than that purpose or those purposes distinctive as *human* goals and anticipations is something most of us are familiar with in religion. More technically we find it in theology and those metaphysics which proceed on the assumption of a reality ordered by, or in the service of goals, ends, objectives, purposes and/or first or final causes. However, one will find the presence of teleological explanations also in what sometimes passes for scientific formulation.[6] In biological language, for

[5] One resort is to return to the mysticism of an Emerson or Rousseau, holding that the child has the unity and that adults, not having it, vitiate it as they "impose" their "wills" on the child. This, of course, is itself a view imposed not only on the child but on those educators who prefer to stick to the usual standards of scientific intelligibility.

[6] Ernest Nagel, "Teleological Explanation and Teleological Systems," *Vision and Action: Essays in Honor of Horace Kallen on His 70th Birth-*

example, one may find it in the first of each pair of the following statements:

1. The purpose of gastric juices is to help break down food matter for other and related bodily functions.

2. Food breakdown is a consequence of, among other necessary conditions, the presence of gastric juices.

Another example in the same order:

1. The infant is crying because it wants (or needs) food in order to satisfy its hunger.

2. The infant's cry is a consequence of, among other necessary conditions, a state of the digestive system alternative to the state subsequent to the introduction of food.

The first statement in each pair of illustrations erects describable consequences of bodily relations into *causes* for themselves while the second statement conveys the *scientific content* without resort to teleological luggage. "Instincts," "wants," "needs" (a major metaphysical prop) or "drives" are other terms illustrative of the teleological fallacy. They, too, function to impute goals and purposes which are *not available as ends-in-view of those objects and relations to which they are assigned*. In order to assign goals to gastric juices or to infants we must gain *representatives of the future*—symbols which represent. In the case of the infant the cry must be connected to the food or to the "tummy" by more symbols or by a simple pointing supplied *by the infant*. However, it is usually the mother's symbolizations (her thinking) or the reified dialectic of an "inquirer" that we find to be the case.

Now it is properly scientific to assert that food is a necessary condition for crying to cease or, for that matter, for the infant to live. But to say the infant *needs* or *wants* food is to hide a value judgment. To say that the infant *should* have food, or that the infant *ought* to live is more correct, for it points us away from the descriptive-predictive domain of scientific inquiry and to the normative-prescriptive domain of value theory. Otherwise we face the age old riddle of how the *ought* is derived from the *is* and *is possible*.

---

day, ed. Sidney Ratner (New Brunswick, Rutgers University Press, 1953), pp. 192–222.

One operation of the *symbolic fallacy* may be found in the rather fashionable practice of borrowing terms from the context of the physical sciences in which they have gained precision, and using them *as though they retained* that precision in other contexts of symbols.[7] Thus, for example, in physical theory, "force," "tension" and/or "energy" make reference to relations of qualitied structures and thereby gain status as "short hand" symbols fashioned to explain the relations. Yet, as theoretical symbols, they become converted into mysterious *agents* lurking behind those relations and, therefore, candidates for fancy metaphysical explanations. Now, instead of being used *to explain* they *must be explained.* Furthermore they are pressed into psychological and sociological service as a means of gaining scientific *sounding* explanations for human conduct. Without re-defined rules of usage for these terms we find ourselves *sounding* scientific as we speak of "the force of personality," "the release of subconscious tension," "adjustment mechanisms," "levels of learning" and "the intellectual energy of the group." But, failing at being scientific, we produce little more than the aesthetic or poetic character of science and, more unfavorably, we cloak a materialistic metaphysics—a particular philosophic bias—in the guise of scientific profundity as we press it in the schools.

Symbolic fallacies yield, oftentimes, a curious case in which a mode of description—a theoretical discipline—itself is erected into a cause for what is explained or described. For example, one may find reference to food as being a *biological need* or to love as being a *psychological need* of the infant.

Now it has been demonstrated that we smuggle in a philosophic outlook or we bootleg a value theory when we impute wants, needs, drives, inherent potentialities or innate faculties to infant behavior. But when we elaborate this obvious teleology with the qualifying term of *biological* and *psychological* we do more. We assert that the infant is a biologist and/or a psychologist; for *biology* (coined in the early part of the nineteenth

---

[7] Ernest Nagel, "Some Reflections on the Use of Language in the Natural Sciences," *The Journal of Philosophy,* Vol. 42, No. 23 (November 8, 1945), 617–30.

century), *psychology, physiology, economics* and *anthropology* refer to theoretical disciplines which attempt to be *sciences.* A biological "need" is nothing more than a necessary condition for biology to proceed, just as an astronomical "need" is nothing more than a necessary condition for astronomy to proceed. A live food consuming creature is *needed* for scientific *and* non-scientific purposes to be achieved. Plainly, the infant has neither these purposes nor the conceptual facility required to have a most basic *biological need*—at once the principles of logic and the conceptual techniques of biology.

It is most certainly scientific to say that *planetary motions,* a concept found in astronomy, makes reference to empirically discernible relations of heavenly bodies which were around *prior* to the appearance of astronomy. It is equally scientific to say that *organism* is a concept, defined in biology, making reference to an inter-related, inter-influencing set of bodily functions which graced the planet *prior* to the appearance of biology. But, scientifically, it is as much nonsense to *call* or *label* the inter-related, inter-influencing set of bodily functions *biology* or *the biological* as it is to call or label the heavenly bodies *astronomy* or *the astronomical.*

It is not a matter of "mere semantic" flippancy to state that only biologists, or those whose *purposes* require knowledge provided by biology, have biological "needs." And it is not "verbal gymnastics" to state that only psychologists have psychological problems—that only economists have economic problems. It is simply a matter for the same precision of inquiry that yielded the different sciences and their varying degrees of precision in the first place. Only as inquiry has *rid itself* of teleological and symbolic fallacies has precision in the several sciences been gained. To carve up, dialectically, the human creature, or "reality," and to label the alleged parts with the terms which distinguish *only* different universes of discourse or theoretical disciplines is to block the advance of science and to make a mockery of education, the institution upon which all science depends. Indeed, the theoretical foundations of the educational profession are at stake in this matter.

If education is to become a profession with its distinctive discipline, then efforts to formulate an "integrated" program

must come to grips with three significant philosophic-methodo-
logical questions:

1. What *is* integrated?
2. What *does* the integrating? and
3. With what standards or criteria do we determine whether
or not integration has been achieved?

Proposed and instituted programs which are advanced as
"integrated" or "core" on the strength of "needs of the child,"
"interest of the student," or "teach children and not subject
matters" are camouflaging these questions as well as the value
preferences of those advancing the programs. Until "integration" finds a methodologically defensible meaning, it must go
the way of all metaphysical doctrines.

Some educators, working out of Dewey's thought, have recognized the dilemma yielded by inner, outer, personal or cosmic
theories of integration and have shifted attention to *problems* as
an organizing category. Only as we locate a problem, the theory
goes, can we institute relatedness in personal and/or social
experience or in the curricular structure of our schools.

Such a theory constitutes a significant alternative to the traditional view of integration. However, if problems establish relatedness and integration, and there are many problems, then it
would follow that there are *many* relatednesses and integrations
possible. Thus the problem of *significant* problems appears. The
problem of establishing *categories* for locating, fashioning and
organizing problems for purposes of curricular programs becomes the most significant philosophic problem of education for
this view.

Whatever view or views educators may have, it is to their
methodological and value assumptions they must turn. A responsible and intellectually sophisticated framework for conceiving an educational program will come only as the tools and
concepts of philosophy of education, the most *practical* resources available, are put to work upon these assumptions.

A tragic twist appears, however, when we note the variety of
ways in which the philosophy of education, as a discipline, is
circumvented at those points in educational theorizing where its
tools and concepts are singularly appropriate. Among these
ways we find: the conception of integration ambiguously used

(the humanities movement, integrated science movement, "total" child movement); the conception of "needs" floating independently of purpose, significant or insignificant ("needs" whether of the child, organism, group, community, society, mankind or cosmos); the conception of problem solving *method* minus a formulation of the *principles* of method entailed; the conception that statistical and other *descriptions* (levels of learning, "reading readiness," "normal-abnormal," "adjusted-maladjusted," "mental-physical age," "healthy-neurotic") are cases of *normatives* or *prescriptions* for the educative process.

Another way in which philosophic inquiry is circumvented is via the assumption that *everyone* has a philosophy already and that by *collecting* individuals representative of different departments or subject matters we have a condition in which the "give and take" of opinions will produce the value decisions.[8] Called "democratic" by some, and "watered down Hegelianism" by Dewey,[9] this view finds contemporary expression in the group-dynamic-workshop movement. This movement has failed to give us criteria for establishing common meaning, common procedures for testing, and other bases for building critically forged social agreements. Its appeal to "give and take" is an appeal to teleology; and, in consequence, the movement is fraught with the danger of benevolent indoctrination.[10] Needless to say it provides the critics of education with an excellent target.

This should not serve to suggest that philosophers of education occupy the Platonic realm of law givers. Rather it is intended to underline *philosophic competence* as a necessary competence for anyone caught up with the problem of reaching

---

[8] These euphoric decisions would be what Rousseau called the *Volonté Générale,* the "consensus" arrived at from the play of *Volonté De-Tous* or "the will of all." "But take away from these same wills," he writes, "the pluses and minuses that cancel one another, and the general will remains as the sum of the differences" [*Social Contract,* quoted in Robert Ulich, *History of Educational Thought* (New York, American Book Co., 1950), pp. 215–16].

[9] John Dewey, *Liberalism and Social Action* (New York, G. P. Putnam's Sons, 1935), p. 71.

[10] Fred N. Kerlinger, "The Authoritarianism on Group Dynamics," *Progressive Education* (April, 1954).

value decisions in education. The view that everyone has this competence in consequence of "experience" (unspecified) permits one to avoid the "pangs" which oftentimes attend the inquiry required to build it. This permits one to assume that philosophy is identified with *values* rather than with a demanding methodologically oriented inquiry into value *criteria*. It permits one to smear over the distinction between a Plato and a Willie Sutton, a John Dewey and Bob Hope.

SOME GUIDELINES *

Alice Miel

What knowledge to select and how to package this knowledge for the instruction of the young have been a concern of educators for as long as education has been conceived as a deliberate process. Today, for a variety of complex and interrelated reasons, there is unusual and widespread concern with the problem of organizing knowledge for teaching. Most notable is the attention being given to the matter by representatives of the scholarly disciplines. Not only are they examining the nature of knowledge in their fields but they are preparing outlines of content and materials for use in elementary and secondary schools. A disciplines seminar, convened at the NEA Center in June 1961, is called unique in that "it caught the ground swell of spreading interest in the disciplines. . . ." [15] A political scientist at the seminar is quoted as saying that political science must now join mathematics, science and geography as a contender in the elementary school program.[16] He failed to note that economics and physics also are strong contenders for space in the same program.

Just one year before the disciplines seminar, Bruner published an immensely readable and deceptively simple book in which he emphasizes the importance of producing understanding of the structure of a subject. "To learn structure . . . is to learn how things are related," he states in explanation.[17] He makes other references to structure when he writes of broadening and deepening knowledge in the form of "basic and general ideas" and mentions the "basic or underlying principles of

---

* Reprinted from "Knowledge and the Curriculum," *New Insights and the Curriculum,* 1963 Yearbook. Alexander Frazier (ed.) (Washington, D. C., Association for Supervision and Curriculum Development, 1963), pp. 79–87. By permission of the Association for Supervision and Curriculum Development and Alice Miel. Copyright © 1963 by the Association for Supervision and Curriculum Development.

[15] National Education Association, *The Scholars Look at the Schools* (Washington, D. C., The Association, 1962), p. 1.

[16] *Ibid.,* p. 42.

[17] Jerome S. Bruner, *The Process of Education* (Cambridge, Mass., Harvard University Press, 1960), p. 7.

various fields of inquiry." [18] There is no doubt that this book has contributed to the deepening interest in the place of the disciplines in the curriculum.

McLuhan gives credit to Bruner for an "account of the structural approach as one involving depth awareness of a simultaneous field of relations." It is clear, however, that Bruner is referring to the structure of a subject and may well have been suggesting mere categorizing and restructuring that subject by more complex lineal arrangements. If so, there is a real difference between his views of structure and those of McLuhan, who sees the possibility in this postliterate world that the "unity of human culture and experience [may] become manifest as a single spectrum" with subjects disappearing from the curriculum.

In any case, in considering proposals with respect to the disciplines, it is advisable to keep certain guidelines in mind.[19]

1. There is no general agreement on what a discipline is. Phenix defines it as "knowledge organized for instruction," which would seem to equate a discipline with a school or college subject.[20] Others use the term to signify field of inquiry or creativity. (This is the view taken in the final section in this chapter.) A third view includes applied fields like medicine and journalism.

There is a still greater problem when it comes to deciding what disciplines shall be included in the school curriculum. The disciplines seminar, to which reference has already been made, was organized to deal with the following areas: in the humanities—art, music, English, foreign languages, philosophy, and religion; in the physical and biological sciences and mathematics —mathematics, chemistry, physics, and biology; in the social sciences—sociology, communications, geography, economics, history, political science, and psychology. This list will bother some for what it includes as disciplines. Other areas were

---

[18] *Ibid.*, pp. 17–18.

[19] The suggestions of Arno A. Bellack and Arthur W. Foshay of Teachers College, Columbia University, have been especially helpful in this connection.

[20] Philip H. Phenix, "The Disciplines as Curriculum Content," *Curriculum Crossroads*, A. Harry Passow, ed. (New York, Bureau of Publications, Teachers College, Columbia University, 1962), p. 58.

omitted because invited representatives were unable to attend.

2. It is idle to assume that the scholars in a field like physics or biology can easily agree on one structure for their field. Furthermore, ways of structuring a natural science are not likely to be suitable for the arts and the humanities or even the behavioral sciences. Schwab points out the existence of at least three great genera of disciplines: the investigative (natural sciences), the appreciative (arts), and the decisive (social sciences).[21]

Broudy arrives at five groupings of disciplines by classifying them with respect to the role played in the totality of knowledge:

(a.) Bodies of knowledge that serve as symbolic tools of thinking, communication, and learning. These include the language of ordinary discourse, of logic, of quantity, and of art.

(b.) Bodies of knowledge that systematize basic facts and their relations. These disciplines [the basic sciences] give us a way of speaking and thinking about the world and everything in it; a way structured by the conceptual system that characterizes each discipline.

(c.) Bodies of knowledge that organize information along the routes of cultural development. History, biography, and evolutionary studies served this purpose by giving some kind of order to the past.

(d.) Bodies of knowledge that project future problems and attempt to regulate the activities of the social order. Tykociner [to whom Broudy gives credit for this way of classifying the disciplines] cites agriculture, medicine, technology, and national defense as examples of the former, and political science, jurisprudence, economics, and management as examples of the latter. We have also developed sciences to guide dissemination of knowledge, e.g., education, mass communication, journalism, library science, custodianship of records and relics.

One may also mention here what Tykociner called "zetetics," the science of research, or better, the sciences that sustain and promote research.

(e.) Finally, there are integrative and inspirational disciplines which create syntheses or value schema in the form of philosophies, theologies, and works of art.[22]

[21] Joseph J. Schwab's remarks are summarized in *The Scholars Look at the Schools,* p. 3.

[22] Harry S. Broudy, "To Regain Educational Leadership," *Studies in Philosophy and Education,* 11(Spring, 1962), 152–54.

For the fifth category Broudy recommends the "exemplar approach: a careful study of a small number of examples of great books, great works of art, and systems of ideas." This approach, as he points out, is considerably different from the structural, developmental, and thematic (or problem) approaches which would be employed in relation to the foregoing groups (b), (c) and (d), respectively. The purpose of his suggested classification is to exhibit "the enormous range and complexity of human knowledge" and to show "the futility of trying to find an adequate sample of it that can be studied structurally as separate subjects in Grades 7–12."

The report of the disciplines seminar at which Schwab spoke represents the attempt of individual academicians to give brief characterizations of the essential nature of their respective fields. Work done by economists through the Joint Council on Economic Education for the past ten years in delineating their domain has put the field of economics far ahead of other disciplines in that respect.[23] It will probably be some time before such carefully distilled key concepts will be available for most other disciplines.

3. Knowledge of structure, conceived as a set of interrelated principles in current good standing in a discipline, is abstract and static knowledge. While such knowledge, even though static, is preferable to isolated bits of information lacking any system of organization, it stops considerably short of being the essence of a field of knowledge. The *dynamics* of a field, which would constitute the means of continuing inquiry, is to be found in the key questions of concern to scholars in that field, in the methods or rules according to which data are sought and handled, and in the language and other symbolic tools employed. According to Foshay,[24] any discipline also has a history, or a tradition, which enters into decisions on the domain and the rules. Learning the structure of a discipline, while useful, is not

[23] See the report of the National Task Force on Economic Education, *Economic Education in the Schools* (New York, Committee for Economic Development, 1961).

[24] Arthur W. Foshay, "Discipline-Centered Curriculum," *Curriculum Crossroads,* A. Harry Passow, ed. (New York, Bureau of Publications, Teachers College, Columbia University, 1962), p. 68.

enough; it stops with learning the results of someone's work without having the basis for understanding changes already in the making. The central question for the student is, rather, how was this structured knowledge arrived at—what was the structure of inquiry?

4. Even though a structure may be agreed upon for a discipline, it is not likely to persist unchanged. Schwab makes a useful comment on this point.[25] As digested in the seminar report, his argument runs as follows: It is to identify the durable aspects—durable from the standpoint of imparting both knowledge and skills—that we must examine the structures of the various disciplines. The durable aspects undoubtedly constitute the warp and woof of "education that frees the mind." They constitute also a paradox in that, verities though they are, they are characterized by constant shift and change.

Schwab is then directly quoted as follows: ". . . the logical forms, the conceptual structures . . . [of] the disciplines are themselves corrected continuously by a reflexive examination of the very knowledge, decision, or art work they produce; that is, they lay the ground for their own demise and replace themselves."

5. He who reads Bruner on the run may miss all the cautions introduced in the chapter on "Readiness for Learning." [26] When used as a noun, the word *structure* may easily be thought of as a thing, stripped bare of facts, that can be packaged and handed to someone else. We can no more deliver to a young person a ready-made and full-blown structure of a discipline than we can hand him directly any other type of conceptualization.

Vygotsky realizes the complexity of the learning called for:

At any age, a concept embodied in a word represents an act of generalization. But word meanings evolve. When a new word has been learned by the child, its development is barely starting; the word at first is a generalization of the most primitive type; as the child's intellect develops, it is replaced by generalizations of a higher and higher type—a process that leads in the end to the formation of true concepts. The development of concepts, or word meanings [or *structures,* we might well insert] presupposes the de-

[25] National Education Association, *op. cit.,* pp. 3–4.
[26] Jerome S. Bruner, *op. cit.,* Chapter 3.

velopment of many intellectual functions: deliberate attention, logical memory, abstraction, the ability to compare and to differentiate. These complex psychological processes cannot be mastered through the initial learning alone.[27]

Vygotsky adds that a teacher who tries direct teaching of concepts usually accomplishes nothing but empty verbalism, "simulating a knowledge of the corresponding concepts but actually covering up a vacuum."

Oversimplification of the process of concept formation is perhaps what Schwab has in mind when he refers to "romantic notions" held by some scholars in the disciplines today,[28] about the intellect and what can be done for it.

It is more accurate to think in terms of structure-finding as one activity in the process of education. It may be even better to express this idea by the words *ordering* and *patterning* as part of what Randall calls a search for intelligibility.[29] Educators will be on safe ground with respect to "teaching the structure of a subject" only if they help pupils to arrive at the structure of various disciplines and the interrelationships among them through a gradual buildup over time.

6. Another caution has to do with the level of sophistication to be aimed at in education with respect to the disciplines. Programs for the preparation of specialists in various fields differ from those designed to educate nonspecialists with respect to those same fields. Broudy suggests that the various domains of knowledge be regarded as several kinds of maps. With respect to general education for "political wisdom," he writes: "Now clearly the citizen, unlike the specialist, cannot utilize a highly detailed map written in a complex code. . . . Nevertheless, a map can be accurate and helpful even if much of the detail is omitted. For the citizen, therefore, the kind of knowledge needed is like that afforded by clear, large, outline maps on which a social problem can be plotted and its essentials put

[27] L. S. Vygotsky, *Thought and Language,* ed. and trans. by Eugenia Hanfmann and Gertrude Vakar (New York and London, Massachusetts Institute of Technology Press and John Wiley and Sons, 1962), p. 83.

[28] National Education Association, *op. cit.,* p. 3.

[29] John Herman Randall, Jr., *Nature and Historical Experience* (New York, Columbia University Press, 1958).

into focus. This sort of knowledge we derive from 'general studies.' " [30]

At another point Broudy contrasts knowledge of and knowledge about a field. Both kinds of knowledge are the responsibility of organized education. The former type of knowledge, appropriate for the specialist, is secured from teaching a young person to "think like an historian" or "think like a sociologist." Knowledge about a field appropriate for the nonspecialist comes from a type of general education that uses various means of helping students to grasp the basic conceptual schemes of a discipline and to come to understand how the field has developed and where it is going. Toward this end, some experience in the rediscovery (or perchance discovery) of knowledge, using the methods and tools of the scholar in a particular field, is useful as one way of building an understanding of how such a specialist thinks.

It is impossible for an individual to go deeply into many disciplines, but general education can at least help people in different fields to be able to talk with one another.

7. Becoming enamored of the idea of teaching the structure of a subject may lead to emphasizing the fields most easily structured, mathematics and science. This, in turn, often leads to an emphasis on education relating to production of knowledge and a neglect of education for knowledge consumption, for it is the mark of a science that it is knowledge producing but not concerned with any use of the knowledge produced except for continued exploration in the field. After we have the best information we can get from a scientist as to the likely consequences of this or that course of action, social policy questions remain. What course of action should be taken? We need a disciplined way of dealing with social policy questions, where values must be applied and strategies worked out, but no such discipline exists. [31]

---

[30] Harry S. Broudy, *op. cit.*, p. 143.

[31] Feeling this lack, which philosophy does not quite manage to fill, a group of educational philosophers some 20 years ago propounded a "discipline of practical judgment." See: R. Bruce Raup et al., *The Discipline of Practical Judgment in a Democratic Society* (Chicago, University of Chicago Press, 1942). Harry S. Broudy also addresses himself to this problem, *op. cit.*, pp. 137–48.

Two difficulties arise from failure to consider the problem of knowledge "consumption," as contrasted with knowledge production. The first is a problem of motivation. The assumption appears to be that the excitement of learning more about a field is motivation enough, and so it may be for some students. It is true that "competence motivation" and an "intrinsic need to deal with the environment" have not been counted upon sufficiently by even the proponents of a subject-centered curriculum.[32] They have frequently failed, therefore, to make pursuit of a subject exciting in its own right. As Foshay notes, "The difficulty with the old subject-centered school was that the subjects were not conceived as having intellectual merit, but only as preparation for some later period in life when intellectuality was to be pursued on its own terms."[33]

The pursuit of intellectuality on its own terms is of course to be provided for through organized education. However, it is unrealistic to rely at all times and for all students upon sheer interest in a discipline to make the effort of working with it seem worthwhile. Much of the time for most students it will be important that the discipline have patent and early usefulness. This was the point underlying the whole progressive education movement, but which had been stated even earlier by Dewey: "That education which does not occur through forms of life, forms that are worth living for their own sake, is always a poor substitute for genuine reality, and tends to cramp and to deaden."[34]

Forty-one years later Dewey still held to this principle that students must be able to see the relevance of what they are studying: "Anything which can be called a study, whether arithmetic, history, geography, or one of the natural sciences, must be derived from materials which at the outset fall within the scope of ordinary life-experience."[35]

[32] R. W. White, "Motivation Reconsidered: The Concept of Competence," *Psychological Review*, 66(1959), 317–18.

[33] Arthur W. Foshay, *op. cit.*, p. 71.

[34] John Dewey, "My Pedagogic Creed," *The School Journal*, 54 (1897), 77–80.

[35] John Dewey, *Experience and Education* (New York, Macmillan Company, 1938), pp. 86–87. Printed by permission of Kappa Delta Pi, owners of the copyright.

It is this line of reasoning which has accounted for the wide appeal of the idea of a problem-centered curriculum, through which a need to consult different fields of knowledge emerges.

A problem-centered curriculum has promise in relation to the second difficulty relating to education for knowledge consumption. This difficulty is that skill in using or applying knowledge does not come automatically with acquisition of knowledge. As Broudy puts it:

> In addition to familiarity with the terrain of the major disciplines, the political thinker also requires the art of adjusting perspective. By this I mean the art of ascertaining the import of particular events for the human enterprise as a whole. In the mature human being, the reference frame for such judgments is a hierachical value set together with principles and rules that allow him to make a logical connection among values, policies, and proposals for action.
>
> Finally, the grids of knowledge and maps of value have to be combined by the processes of deliberation, decision, and commitment. . . .[36]

With these words, Broudy spells out [a version of] the "discipline of practical judgment" mentioned earlier. Development of such a set of skills is something to be attended to as deliberately as the development of knowledge itself.

8. How best to organize the curriculum has long been a moot point. Those who today advocate teaching the logical structures of the disciplines have not discovered any new magic. While Dewey throughout his career insisted on "materials which at the outset fall within the scope of ordinary life-experience," he consistently urged "progressive organization of subject matter": ". . . the organized subject-matter of the adult and the specialist cannot provide the starting point. Nevertheless, it represents the goal toward which education should continuously move." [37]

Bode also made a plea for beginning with a "psychological order" of subject matter but ending with a "logical order." [38]

Lucy Sprague Mitchell, while advocating a laboratory approach to discovery of relationships in the field of geography,

---

[36] Harry S. Broudy, *op. cit.*, p. 144.

[37] John Dewey, *Experience and Education*, p. 103.

[38] Boyd Bode, *Modern Educational Theories* (New York, Macmillan Company, 1927), p. 65.

nevertheless made a clear delineation of the essential nature of that field.[39]

Somehow it has always been easier for the mature adult who knows the logical structure of a subject to begin with that structure in trying to educate the young, and none of these writers minimized the difficulty of psychological or laboratory approaches. Today's interest in teaching the structure of the disciplines does not necessarily mean a return to teaching the subject in a "logical" order without regard to the student, but the temptation to do so will persist.

9. Bruner does not propose in his *Process of Education* any attention to interrelationships among disciplines, and he does not address himself to the question of the structure of the curriculum as a whole within which the fields of knowledge are to find their place. In speaking of the structure of philosophy, Phenix stresses the skill of synthesis, the ability to combine relevant parts of various fields of knowledge.[40] He suggests that another dimension be added to the learning process, a dimension covering the integrative aspects of knowing. While integration is far from a new term in education, it is becoming increasingly clear that the profession must take a new look at that concept along with new attempts to deal with separateness in fields of knowledge.

As Goldberg writes, "What the profession needs are lively and persistent enquiries, on the level of conceptualization related to wholes, wholeness, and the making of wholeness. . . ." [41]

Foshay has a proposal for integration of the curriculum which he gives after his comment on the difficulty of the older subject-centered school already quoted:

The difficulty with a problem-centered approach used as the only approach to the selection of curriculum content is that the problems as they come are not disciplined, nor do they ordinarily lead us to an understanding of the disciplines through which hu-

[39] Lucy Sprague Mitchell, *Young Geographers* (New York, John Day Company, 1934).

[40] National Education Association, *op. cit.,* p. 16.

[41] Maxwell H. Goldberg, "General Education and the Explosion of Knowledge," *College and University Bulletin,* 14(February 15, 1962), 4.

man truth is developed or discovered. An approach through one discipline at a time alone would not be adequate, since practice in problem solving is also necessary. We have to have it both ways—both problem-centered and discipline-centered, if you please—if we are to produce students who, at the same time that they think, are fully aware of the intellectual processes that they themselves are using.[42]

How to "have it both ways" may be analogous to the dilemma posed earlier—how to maintain the advantages of the lineal approach of a print culture without being incapacitated for coping with the simultaneity of a postliterate world.

Is there a possibility of abandoning "either-or" approaches to curriculum organization? Can we approach the curriculum as being *both* problem-centered and discipline-centered? If so, what is a promising line of solution? Dewey and Bode would have had it both ways by starting with one type of organization and ending with another, presumably within each major segment of experience. Many others have adopted the easy solution of assuming that the elementary school would employ in general a psychological approach while the secondary school would deal primarily in logically organized subject matter. Foshay seems to suggest carrying along two approaches at the same time, but he has left the details undeveloped. Clearly some rather specific proposals are needed.

[42] Arthur W. Foshay, *op. cit.*, p. 71.

THE LOGICAL AND PSYCHOLOGICAL ASPECTS OF EXPERIENCE*

John Dewey

It may be of use to distinguish and to relate to each other the logical and the psychological aspects of experience—the former standing for subject-matter in itself, the latter for it in relation to the child. A psychological statement of experience follows its actual growth; it is historic; it notes steps actually taken, the uncertain and tortuous, as well as the efficient and successful. The logical point of view, on the other hand, assumes that the development has reached a certain positive stage of fulfilment. It neglects the process and considers the outcome. It summarizes and arranges, and thus separates the achieved results from the actual steps by which they were forthcoming in the first instance. We may compare the difference between the logical and the psychological to the difference between the notes which an explorer makes in a new country, blazing a trail and finding his way along as best he may, and the finished map that is constructed after the country has been thoroughly explored. The two are mutually dependent. Without the more or less accidental and devious paths traced by the explorer there would be no facts which could be utilized in the making of the complete and related chart. But no one would get the benefit of the explorer's trip if it was not compared and checked up with similar wanderings undertaken by others; unless the new geographical facts learned, the streams crossed, the mountains climbed, etc., were viewed, not as mere incidents in the journey of the particular traveler, but (quite apart from the individual explorer's life) in relation to other similar facts already known. The map orders individual experiences, connecting them with one another irre-

* Reprinted from *The Child and the Curriculum*, Phoenix Books edition (Chicago, University of Chicago Press, 1956), pp. 19–24. By permission of The University of Chicago Press. © University of Chicago Press, 1902.

spective of the local and temporal circumstances and accidents of their original discovery.

Of what use is this formulated statement of experience? Of what use is the map?

Well, we may first tell what the map is not. The map is not a substitute for a personal experience. The map does not take the place of an actual journey. The logically formulated material of a science or branch of learning, of a study, is no substitute for the having of individual experiences. The mathematical formula for a falling body does not take the place of personal contact and immediate individual experience with the falling thing. But the map, a summary, an arranged and orderly view of previous experiences, serves as a guide to future experience; it gives direction; it facilitates control; it economizes effort, preventing useless wandering, and pointing out the paths which lead most quickly and most certainly to a desired result. Through the map every new traveler may get for his own journey the benefits of the results of others' explorations without the waste of energy and loss of time involved in their wanderings—wanderings which he himself would be obliged to repeat were it not for just the assistance of the objective and generalized record of their performances. That which we call a science or study puts the net product of past experience in the form which makes it most available for the future. It represents a capitalization which may at once be turned to interest. It economizes the workings of the mind in every way. Memory is less taxed because the facts are grouped together about some common principle, instead of being connected solely with the varying incidents of their original discovery. Observation is assisted; we know what to look for and where to look. It is the difference between looking for a needle in a haystack, and searching for a given paper in a well-arranged cabinet. Reasoning is directed, because there is a certain general path or line laid out along which ideas naturally march, instead of moving from one chance association to another.

There is, then, nothing final about a logical rendering of experience. Its value is not contained in itself; its significance is that of standpoint, outlook, method. It intervenes between the more casual, tentative, and roundabout experiences of the past, and more controlled and orderly experiences of the future. It gives past experience in that net form which renders it most available and most significant, most fecund for future experience. The abstractions, generalizations, and classifications which it introduces all have prospective meaning.

The formulated result is then not to be opposed to the process of growth. The logical is not set over against the psychological. The surveyed and arranged result occupies a critical position in the process of growth. It marks a turning-point. It shows how we may get the benefit of past effort in controlling future endeavor. In the largest sense the logical standpoint is itself psychological; it has its meaning as a point in the development of experience, and its justification is in its functioning in the future growth which it insures.

Hence the need of reinstating into experience the subject-matter of the studies, or branches of learning. It must be restored to the experience from which it has been abstracted. It needs to be *psychologized;* turned over, translated into the immediate and individual experiencing within which it has its origin and significance.

Every study or subject thus has two aspects: one for the scientist as a scientist; the other for the teacher as a teacher. These two aspects are in no sense opposed or conflicting. But neither are they immediately identical. For the scientist, the subject-matter represents simply a given body of truth to be employed in locating new problems, instituting new researches, and carrying them through to a verified outcome. To him the subject-matter of the science is self-contained. He refers various portions of it to each other; he connects new facts with it. He is not, as a scientist, called upon to travel outside its particular bounds; if he does, it is only to get more facts of the same general sort. The problem of the teacher is a different one. As a teacher he is not concerned with adding new facts to the science he teaches; in propounding new hypotheses or in verifying them. He is concerned with the subject-matter of the science as *representing a given stage and phase of the development of experience.* His problem is that of inducing a vital and personal experiencing. Hence, what concerns him, as teacher, is the ways in which that subject may become a part of experience; what there is in the child's present that is usable with reference to it; how such elements are to be used; how his own knowledge of the subject-matter may assist in interpreting the child's needs and doings, and determine the medium in which the child should be placed in order that his growth may be properly directed. He is concerned, not with the subject-matter as such, but with the subject-matter as a related factor in a total and growing experience. Thus to see it is to psychologize it.

It is the failure to keep in mind the double aspect of subject-matter which causes the curriculum and child to be set over against each other as described. . . . The subject-matter, just as it is for the scientist, has no direct relationship to the child's present experience. It stands outside of it. The danger here is not a merely theoretical one. We are practically threatened on all sides. Textbook and teacher vie with each other in presenting to the child the subject-matter as it stands to the specialist. Such modification and revision as it undergoes are a mere elimination of certain scientific difficulties, and the general reduction to a lower intellectual level. The material is not translated into life-terms, but is directly offered as a substitute for, or an external annex to, the child's present life.

THE DISCIPLINES AS CURRICULUM CONTENT *

Philip H. Phenix

In 1956 I published a paper entitled "Key Concepts and the Crisis in Learning," in which I developed the thesis that economy and efficiency in learning, in a time of vast proliferation of knowledge, can best be achieved by attending to the "key concepts" in the several fields of learning. Since that time many important developments in curriculum studies have taken place along somewhat similar lines.

In recent years various study commissions have been at work reorganizing the subject matter of some of the major fields of learning, the T.E.P.S. commissions have worked for rapprochement between academic scholars and specialists in education, and leading investigators like Jerome Bruner have dealt with the importance of structure for the mastery of knowledge. The present paper seeks to develop some of these same themes, with special reference to the idea of the disciplines.

My thesis, briefly, is that *all* curriculum content should be drawn from the disciplines, or, to put it another way, that *only* knowledge contained in the disciplines is appropriate to the curriculum.

Exposition of this position requires first that we consider what is meant by a "discipline." The word "discipline" is derived from the Latin word *discipulus,* which means a disciple, that is, originally, one who receives instruction from another. *Discipulus* in turn stems from the verb *discere,* to learn. Etymologically, then, a discipline may be construed as knowledge, the special property of which is its appropriateness for teaching and its availability for learning. A discipline is knowledge organized for instruction.

Basic to my theme is this affirmation: the distinguishing mark

* Reprinted from "The Uses of the Disciplines as Curriculum Content," *Educational Forum,* 26(March, 1962), 273–80. By permission of Kappa Delta Pi, an Honor Society in Education, owners of the copyright.

of any discipline is that the knowledge which comprises it is instructive—that it is peculiarly suited for teaching and learning. Implicit in this assertion is the recognition that there are kinds of knowledge which are not found within a discipline. Such non-disciplined knowledge is unsuitable for teaching and learning. It is not instructive. Given this understanding of what a discipline is, it follows at once that all teaching should be disciplined, that it is undesirable to have any instruction in matters which fall beyond the disciplines. This means that psychological needs, social problems, and any of a variety of patterns of material based on other than discipline content are not appropriate to the determination of what is taught—though obviously such non-disciplinary considerations *are* essential to decision about the *distribution* of discipline knowledge within the curriculum as a whole.

I hardly need to remind you that the position here taken is quite at odds with the one taken by many people both in the field of education and in the several disciplines. The common assumption of these people is that the disciplines are in the realm of pure knowledge—of specialized professional scholarship and research—and that ordinary education is quite a different sort of enterprise. The disciplines have a life of their own, it is held, and knowledge in them is not directly available for the purposes of instruction, but to be suitable for education must be translated and transformed so as to become useful and meaningful to ordinary learners. Thus, the argument goes, for the curriculum we should draw upon life situations, problems, projects, and the like, for the primary *content* of instruction, using the knowledge supplied by the disciplines as auxiliary material to be employed as required by the basic instructional process. The person is supposed to learn primarily from experience as it comes naturally and not as it is artificaly conceptualized and organized in the academic fields. . . .

The characteristic feature of disciplined intelligence is that difficulties and confusions are overcome and understanding of the subject is thereby facilitated. In short, the test for quality in knowledge is its communicability. Knowledge which is hard to teach is for that reason inferior. Knowledge which readily enlightens the learner's understanding is superior.

Now what is it that makes knowledge instructive? How does undisciplined differ from disciplined understanding? There are three fundamental features, all of which contribute to the availability of knowledge for instruction and thus provide measures for degree and quality of discipline. These three are (1) analytic simplification, (2) synthetic coordination and (3) dynamism. Let us consider each criterion in turn.

First, analytic simplification. The primal essential for effective teaching is simplification. All intelligibility rests upon a radical reduction in the multiplicity of impressions which impinge upon the senses and the imagination. The infant begins life with the booming, buzzing confusion of which James spoke, and his learning consists in the growing ability to sort and select, that is, to simplify. The lower animals have built-in simplifiers in the instinctive mechanisms. Human beings have a much more interesting and powerful apparatus of simplification, through intelligence. The index of intelligence is of course, the power of symbolization. Symbols—preeminently but not exclusively those of language—are means of marking out useful and memorable features of experience for special notice. All significant words are such markers. . . .

This simplification of experience through the use of symbols may be called analytic. The sorting out of classes of things is the process of analysis. It proceeds by the discrimination of similarities and differences, whereby entities may be divided and arranged in orderly fashion. Analysis is possible only because the human mind is able to *abstract,* that is, to discern properties, qualities, or forms of things. Every concept is an abstraction—a drawing out of certain features of a class of things for purposes of generalization and grouping. The function of abstraction is to simplify—to reduce the complexity of unanalyzed experience by selecting certain shared properties of kinds of things and neglecting their other features.

It is commonly assumed that abstract thinking is difficult and complicated. This assumption betrays a misunderstanding of what abstraction is. Analytic abstraction is a way of thinking which aims at ease of comprehension and reduction of complexity. For this reason all learning—all growth in understanding—

takes place through the use of simplifying concepts. It is the key to effectiveness of instruction.

All of this bears directly on the question of the place of the disciplines in teaching and learning. A discipline is essentially nothing more than an extension of ordinary conceptualization. It is a conceptual system whose office is to gather a large group of cognitive elements into a common framework of ideas. That is, its goal is the simplification of understanding. This is the function of the techniques, models, and theories which are characteristic of any discipline. They economize thought by showing how diverse and apparently disparate elements of experience can be subsumed under common interpretive and explanatory schemes.

Thus, contrary to the popular assumption, knowledge does not become more and more complicated as one goes deeper into a discipline. If it is a real discipline and not merely a field for the display of erudition, the further one goes in it the more pervasive are the simplicities which analysis reveals. For example, how grand and liberating is the simplicity afforded by the atomic theory of matter as one seeks to comprehend the endless complexity of the world of material substances! Again, how much simpler Copernicus made the understanding of the apparent motions of the stars and planets, and how much easier Darwin made the comprehension of the varieties of living things!

The test of a good discipline is whether or not it simplifies understanding. When a field of study only adds new burdens and multiplies complexities, it is not properly called a discipline. Likewise, when a real discipline in certain directions begins to spawn concepts and theories which on balance are a burden and hindrance to insight, in those areas it degenerates into undisciplined thinking. . . .

Let us now turn, more briefly, to the second feature of a discipline which makes knowledge in it instructive, namely, synthetic coordination. A discipline is a conceptual structure whose function is not only to simplify understanding but also to reveal significant patterns and relationships. Analysis is not an end in itself; it is the basis of synthesis. By synthesis is meant the construction of new wholes, the coordination of elements into significant coherent structures. Disciplined thinking is *organized* thinking. Differences and distinctions are recognized within an ordered framework which permits synoptic vision.

Such synthetic coordination is not opposed in tendency to analytic simplifications; both are aspects of a common process of intelligible ordering. The perception of meaningful differences is possible only against some common measure. Thus, the notion of parts within an ordered whole involves both the differentiation which is presupposed by the idea of parts and the unity which is implied by the idea of a whole. A discipline is a synthetic structure of concepts made possible by the discrimination of similarities through analysis. It is a hierarchy of ideas ordered as a unity-in-difference.

It is only in this sense that disciplined knowledge can be called complex. The simplifications of abstraction make possible the construction of cognitive complexes—i.e., the weaving together of ideas into coherent wholes. Concepts are no longer entertained in isolation, but are seen in their interconnections and relationships.

What occurs in disciplined thinking is a reconstruction of experience. The brute multiplicity of primordial experience is simplified by conceptual abstraction, and these abstractions are then synthesized into more and more comprehensive patterns of coordination. In this way naive experience is transformed from a meaningless hodge-podge of impressions into a relatively meaningful pattern of understanding.

Herein lies the great pedagogical virtue of a discipline. Whatever is taught within a discipline framework draws strength and interest from its membership within a family of ideas. Each new idea is illuminated by ideas previously acquired. A discipline is a community of concepts. Just as human beings cannot thrive in isolation, but require the support of other persons in mutual association, so do isolated ideas wither and die, while ideas comprehended within the unity of a discipline tend to remain vivid and powerful within the understanding.

The third quality of knowledge in a discipline I have called its dynamism. By this is meant the power of leading on to further understanding. A discipline is a *living* body of knowledge, containing within itself a principle of growth. Its concepts do not merely simplify and coordinate; they also invite further analysis and synthesis. A discipline contains a *lure to discovery*. Its ideas excite the imagination to further exploration. Its concepts suggest new constructs which provide larger generalizations and re-constituted modes of coordination.

James B. Conant has pointed to this dynamism as a distinguishing feature of scientific knowledge. Science is an enterprise in which fruitfulness is the mark of a good conceptual scheme. Theories which merely coordinate and organize a given body of data but do not stimulate further experimentation and inquiry are scientifically unimportant. This principle may also be taken as definitive for any discipline. Instructiveness is proportionate to fruitfulness. Knowledge which only organizes the data of experience but does not excite further questions and inquiries is relatively undisciplined knowledge. Disciplined ideas not only constitute families of concepts, but these families beget progeny. They have generative power. This is why they are instructive. They lead on and out: they educate.

There is, of course, no sharp dividing line between disciplined and non-disciplined knowledge. There are on the one extreme isolated bits of information which are not within any organized discipline, and on the other extreme there are precisely articulated theoretical structures which are readily recognized as disciplined according to the meaning developed above. In between are bodies of knowledge which have all degrees of discipline. Perhaps it would be well also to speak of weak disciplines and strong disciplines, the difference being in the degree to which their contents satisfy the three criteria for instructiveness earlier stated. Thus, mathematics, with powerful analytic tools and the dynamics for endless fruitful elaborations, by the present criteria would appear to be a stronger discipline than most present-day political science, which (from my limited knowledge of it) seems to have relatively few unifying concepts and theoretical schemes permitting wide synthesis and creative expansion. . . .

A distinction may also be useful between a discipline and an area of study. Not all areas of study are disciplines, since not all of them display analytic, synthetic, and dynamic qualities. Thus, it seems to me that "education" is an area of study rather than a discipline. Within this area disciplined learning is possible. . . .

My theme has been that the curriculum should consist entirely of knowledge which comes from the disciplines, for the reason that the disciplines reveal knowledge in its teachable forms. We should not try to teach anything which has not been found actually instructive through the labors of hosts of dedicated inquirers. Education should be conceived as a *guided recapitulation of the processes of inquiry which gave rise to the fruitful bodies of organized knowledge comprising the established disciplines.*

In this brief analysis there has been no time to consider the problem of levels. I do not intend to suggest that the whole conceptual apparatus of a discipline should be brought to bear on teaching at every level of education. There are elementary and advanced stages of disciplined inquiry. The great simplicities, the comprehensive syntheses, and the powerful dynamisms usually belong to the more advanced stages. . . . Every discipline has in it beginning concepts and more developed concepts, all of which belong to the discipline authentically and properly. There is no place in the curriculum for ideas which are regarded as suitable for teaching because of the supposed nature, needs, and interests of the learner, but which do not belong within the regular structure of the disciplines, for the disciplines are in their essential nature bodies of knowledge organized for the most effective instruction.

This view asserts the identity of the psycho-logic of teaching and learning with the logic of the disciplines, contrary to many of the current theories of the teaching-learning process. Or, it might be more generally acceptable among educators to say that the view measures the logic (and the authenticity) of a discipline by its instructiveness. . . .

The priority and primacy of the disciplines in education are greatly buttressed by a realistic view of knowledge, as opposed to a nominalistic one. In realism it is asserted that concepts and theories disclose the real nature of things, while in nominalism it is affirmed that the structure of thought is a matter of human convention. Academic and educational nominalists believe that experience can be categorized and concepts organized in endless ways, according to the inclination and decision and for the convenience of individuals and societies. Furthermore, it is held, scholars can choose their own special ways of organizing knowledge and educators can choose other ways, the differences corresponding to the disparity in purposes in the two groups. Thus arise the supposed contrasts between the logic of the disciplines and the psychologic of the educative process.

Such nominalism is rejected in the realistic view here proposed. From a realistic standpoint nominalism is epistemologically impious and pedagogically disastrous, a source of internecine strife and intellectual estrangement. There is a logos of being which it is the office of reason to discover. The structure of things is revealed, not invented, and it is the business of inquiry to open that structure to general understanding through the formation of appropriate concepts and theories. Truth is rich and varied, but it is not arbitrary. The nature of things is *given,* not chosen, and if man is to gain insight he must employ the right concepts and methods. Only by obedience to the truth thus discovered can he learn or teach.

In short, authentic disciplines are at one and the same time approximations of the given orders of reality and disclosures of the paths by which persons may come to realize truth in their own being; which is simply to say that the disciplines are the sole proper source of the curriculum.

PROPOSITIONAL KNOWLEDGE AND COGNITIVE ACTION*

James E. McClellan

"Knowledge" is scarcely a common-sense word. The etymologists tell us that the abstract noun is itself derived from the more basic verbal usage; that *scio* came before *scientia, weis* before *wissenschaft*. But more important than etymological evidence is the logical primacy of the active, transitive verb form over the noun in curriculum theory. For curriculum construction always begins with the sociological datum that certain persons are said to know certain things that others do not know. Hence the task of a curriculum theory is to say what part of that which is known by some in the culture is to be taught to some or all of those who do not know it. This means that a logical beginning for analysis is not with "knowledge" but with what the plain man means when he says that certain people know certain things.

Looking to the language of the plain man, not for immediate answers to our normative problem of curriculum construction but rather for a possible clarification of the terms in which the problem might be posed, we can note several different contexts in which the word "know" occurs in its active, transitive sense. Four are chosen here as typical, not of all possible contexts but of those illustrating the big question of curriculum theory.

1. A knows how to build a house.
2. A knows that the orbit of Mars is elliptical.
3. A knows what he is doing (determinate situation).
4. A knows this building.

Is there any way of reducing this list so that we can use the form of one of the sentences to say what is said in another form in another sentence?

The easiest relation to identify is that between sentences 1 and 3. Sentence 1 is clearly the dispositional form of sentence 3.

---

* Reprinted from "Knowledge and the Curriculum," *Teachers College Record*, 57(March, 1956), 410–18. By permission of the author and the editor of *Teachers College Record*.

Hence, any time a sentence like form 1 appears, it may be translated to an indefinite series of sentences of form 3. Thus if one says that a particular farmer now plowing knows how to plow, this may be translated as saying that in this (and any other) situation of plowing, the farmer knows what he is doing. What the translation shows, and this is important for the rest of the discussion, is what form the know-how statements would take when applied to actual states of affairs. As far as the problems of logic are concerned, it is assumed here that there are no more difficulties in explaining the translation from the dispositional to the descriptive usage of "know" than are connected with other dispositional terms.

If the analysis above is correct, we can leave out sentences of form 1 in the further discussion. But this sense of knowing when we say that someone knows what he is doing (or, more colloquially, knows what he is about) is certainly one primary and irreducible meaning of common sense usage.

Now is it possible to translate sentence 2 as a form of sentence 3? One could, perhaps, make a good case for the translation where A is interpreted as a learned astronomer and the determinate situation one in which A is writing the sentence "The orbit of Mars is elliptical." But even here the correspondence is not exact. We do not mean literally that A knows something about penmanship when he writes the sentence. Rather we mean that he knows something about Mars, the solar system, and so forth. It would seem closer to common usage to regard sentence 2 as not translatable to the form of sentence 3.*

Sentence 4 has no very interesting properties. It is reducible to sentence 3 or to sentence 2 in common-sense usage. One alternative—that 4 is a way of expressing the ultimate sense of a mind–world relation—is a refined philosophical notion and makes no particular impression in common-sense language.

What conclusions are indicated by this brief linguistic analysis? The purpose of this analysis, it will be recalled, derives from the fact that curriculum construction begins with the state of affairs that some persons in a society know some things not

---

* Cf. the somewhat different conclusion reached by Gilbert Ryle in *The Concept of Mind* (New York, Barnes and Noble, 1949), Chapter 2.

known by the rest. We ask what this might mean. We can now answer: This may mean, on the one hand, that some persons know certain propositions or statements—roughly in the sense that they can state the proposition, define the terms of the proposition, perhaps ostensively, and, finally, can offer some reasoning for the belief that the proposition is true. It may mean, on the other hand, that certain persons exhibit a kind of behavior that might be characterized by efficiency in relating means to ends, by purposeful organization of various phases of an action, and the like.

While these two usages are relatively distinct in what they point to, they are related at least in this way: the actual behavior we would call "knowing what he is about" is a function in part of the kinds of propositions potentially available to the agent in the situation. Thus a farmer of a hundred years ago might be said to have known what he was doing in a situation of plowing when he plowed a fine straight furrow down the side of a mountain. Such action today would be quite the contrary of knowing what one is about in plowing. The difference is not in the behavior itself but, in part, in the propositional knowledge available as to the erosive effects of that kind of plowing. This relativity of the *meaning* of sentences like 3 to a whole complex of cultural resources in the form of sentences like 2 must be kept constantly in mind in the remainder of this discussion, for it is obviously of far-reaching import when knowledge in the curriculum is considered.

A precise description of what is meant by the two indicated usages cannot be given here. All that is necessary is recognition that there is a genuine difference between the two meanings. This difference is crucial; it sets the most fundamental task of curriculum theory.

The goals of any educational scheme, be they cognitive or otherwise, are behavioral. They are expressible in the form of sentence 3, uttered in the optative mood. What is pointed to in sentences of that form is called herein (somewhat infelicitously) "cognitive action."

If the goal of deliberate education is cognitive action, the available intellectual resources to be used in achieving this goal are in the form of knowledge, as in sentence 2. (In order to avoid the confusions that surround the words "symbolic" and "verbal," I call this kind of knowing "propositional knowledge.")

The curriculum problem can be restated thus: What is the best way to select, organize, and teach propositional knowledge in order to achieve goals expressed as kinds of cognitive action? To put it positively, we must select sentences for teaching on the basis of their contribution to cognitive action. But we cannot teach isolated sentences that will apply to every conceivable situation in which a person is expected to know what he is doing. Therefore, we must somehow teach sentences in such a way that the individual who learns them learns the organization of propositional knowledge rather than mere isolated sentences. Yet, this principle of organization, in turn, must be such as to lead to what is here called cognitive action. Any serious theory of curriculum must recognize this problem in the basic character of knowledge itself and must try to solve it directly. This is a persuasive definition of "serious" applied to curriculum theory, but it will serve to point up the three major curriculum theories I want to consider. Concerning each of them, one question must be asked: Does this theory account for what is open to inspection concerning the organization of propositional knowledge in the culture? At this point, attention is restricted to *propositional* knowledge, roughly, knowledge of statements which may be translated into the "if . . . , then" form. The assumption is that this form of statement includes at least the sciences, history, mathematics, and most common-sense descriptions of the world.

A. Knowledge of first principles as providing structure to the curriculum

The school of thought which holds that propositional knowledge is organized in accordance with first principles qualifies easily as a serious theory of curriculum. Its strength lies in giving theoretical justification to an intelligibly organized program.

According to this theory, knowledge in a propositional sense of first principles is the end, the final cause, for all education. The road to this end is difficult and rough, though not without its proximate joys. In order to attain to this knowledge, the learner must first master the linguistic media through which first principles are expressed. He develops his linguistic skills at every stage in his travel along the road to wisdom by using them on that portion of the scientific and literary tradition appropriate to his age and ability. He is recompensed emotionally for his efforts in the delight which comes from grasping new meanings and relations, in the noetic pleasures which are a genuine feature of the child's, as well as the adult's, world.

For those who can attain it, the end of this education is not only the delight of contemplation but also a deeper understanding of the basic principles underlying practical work and social life. The truly human person is one who not only can perform his task but also understands the foundational *reasons* for what he is doing. He knows that a certain action will have a certain effect; he also knows the basic principles of causality. He not only gets to work on time, as it were, he also knows what time is; he knows the distinctions between relative and absolute time, between perceived and public time. This is the highest form of knowledge in our culture—the kind that should be extended to everyone, or as many as can possibly grasp it. And the question of what proportion of all learners can actually attain this knowledge is properly seen as empirical. We do not know until we have tried it.

The question of knowledge in the curriculum apparently is answered. For in every situation in which an actor finds himself, certain first principles of knowledge are involved. If he knows the first principles, he can move by logical deduction to the more proximate propositional knowledge relevant to the particular situation.

Despite its obvious appeal, this theory is profoundly mistaken. It asserts that a certain kind of knowledge should be taught to learners, and that kind of knowledge is simply nonexistent in our culture.

The bluntness of that statement is deliberate. A theory emphasizing first principles is valid only if knowledge in the culture possesses certain features. The theory would require that all our knowledge involve ordered, regulated systems. Consider some examples. In our search to determine the good of a particular situation we could refer to more general conceptions of the good in situations like the present, conceptions which, in turn, are ultimately derivable from completely general and synthetic principles of the nature of good. To determine whether one event is the cause of another, we could refer ultimately again to the basic nature of causality. These basic principles would presumably be certifiable to pure reason, so that all who would discipline themselves sufficiently would agree upon the conclusions reached.

Now the argument I wish to make is in the nature of a sociological generalization and prediction. Propositional knowledge in our culture is *not* organized in this fashion, nor is it likely to be so organized in any foreseeable future.

The further we depart from sense experience, the greater is the disagreement found among equally competent scholars. Consider the principle of causality mentioned above. It is interesting to begin, say, with Hume's formulation of this problem and to trace the successive steps by which other philosophers have attempted to resolve the problem or to show that it is meaningless. One of the latest major contributions to the discussion is Tarski's semantic definition of cause; but this neither answers nor eliminates the question of the actual nature of the causal relation, in the sense required if we are to know fundamental synthetic principles. It is merely a way of stating what the scientist and the plain man have in mind when they use the word "cause." We know no more and no less about the nature of the causal relation in the world than we did. . . .

The same conclusion would be reached, I think, if we took such conceptions as the nature of good, of truth, of justice, or of beauty for consideration. Those who aim, then, for knowledge of fundamental principles as goals for education are aiming at the nonexistent.

Their proposals regarding method and content on the lower rungs in the educational ladder become rather obscure when this shining pinnacle is removed. If the lower steps are not the way to knowledge of general principles, by what justification are the linguistic disciplines and the scientific and literary traditions included in the curriculum? One must either hold that they are good in themselves, just as learned, or he must appeal to some further good they serve. The former, as we have seen, is no basis for a curriculum theory. To seek an answer to what further good they might serve, we turn now to a second theory, which also emphasizes the basic disciplines in curriculum construction.

B. The basic disciplines as ways of organizing propositional knowledge

The current believers in teaching academic disciplines have a quite sophisticated view. It runs something like this: knowledge in our culture is not, as the first position would have it, organized systematically as logically derivable from certain fundamental principles. It is, rather, organized around the particular kinds of questions which people put to their environment and the ways in which they certify their answers to these questions. In theory, the number of questions which may be asked of the environment is limitless, but in practice, people ask only a rather small number of really different questions.

In the course of time, or immediately if a person of genius addresses a new kind of question to his environment, conceptual systems are developed. These conceptual systems are, in essence, relations of meanings among those terms used in asking and answering questions of the world. The physical sciences and the conventional studies furnish the best immediate examples, but the trend is toward making ever more of our knowledge achieve this form. The terms or meanings in these disciplines lose their power to describe the multiplicity and emotional tone of a concrete situation, but they gain in their potentiality for systematic organization and in their power to guide reliable predictions about limited facets of concrete events.

Thus the student, for whatever purpose he may be educated, comes to appropriate in useful form the highest and best developed intellectual resources of his culture; that is to say, he comes to know more in *both* senses of the word "know" as he acquires the ability to understand and use the various disciplines of his culture.

In criticizing this theory, let us follow the figure suggested by the analysis above and posit an individual facing an environment more or less inimical to his wishes, more or less unknown in those features that bear upon his achievement of purposes. Let us imagine further that this individual has access to every proposition written in every book or spoken by every mouth, except for those sentences designed specifically for school-like instruction. Let us imagine, *per impossible,* that he understands fully the meaning of every sentence he reads or hears. What pattern of organization would he discover in attempting to move logically from the propositions he now knows to those he thinks would be useful in answering the questions forced on him by his environment?

This is not the kind of question that can be answered by a priori logical analysis; rather it is a question of the sociology of knowledge in its broad sense. It is conceivable that the propositional knowledge in a culture could be organized as interrelated, systematic sets of propositions answering directly the kinds of questions one would like to have answered in guiding his actions. But this is not the way propositions in the various sciences and in common sense are related to one another in our culture. Rather, it would appear that they are organized as more or less related theories, ranging on a whole series of intercrossing spectra from the less general to the more general, from the less well-grounded to the better established, from the vaguely connected to the highly systematized, and so on.†

The organization of propositions referred to by the expression "a discipline" is, in fact, only a more or less convenient way to group scientific theories and common-sense descriptions for pedagogic or administrative purposes. If that is the case, then obviously we cannot appeal to these particular ways of organizing propositions as a final answer to the question of how propositional knowledge should be organized for instruction.

The logical steps of this argument should be made explicit. It is assumed, both by the theory under consideration and by me, that there is some selection, organization, and method of instruction in propositional knowledge which will tend to bring about the particular cognitive actions defined as a goal of education.

Now the theory under discussion asserts that the so-called

---

† For a description of what is meant by theory, see J. J. C. Smart, "Theory Construction," A. G. N. Flew, ed., *Logic and Language,* Second Series (Oxford, Blackwell, 1953), p. 222.

disciplines, in their structure, represent the inherent organization of propositional knowledge itself in our culture. The theory asserts also that this organization will lead to the extension of cognitive action as a goal of instruction.

I am denying outright the first of these assertions. It is obvious that without this support the second assertion loses its plausibility as an answer to the curriculum question.

The argument given here hinges on the accuracy of the sociological description of the way propositions are intrinsically related to one another in our culture. In the final analysis, I can appeal only to your understanding of the structure of knowledge in the world in order to establish my point here. But I can possibly assist my case by pointing out one example of a discipline and showing how my contention applies to it. Consider the case of the conventional disciplines—rhetoric and grammar.

The practical question which these disciplines are designed to answer is this: How can I so word and express my ideas that they will carry the most appeal to my auditors? The sophists of classical Hellas developed a set of more or less related theories which could be applied in answering this question. They, especially Isocrates, developed also some pedagogical techniques for teaching these theories and their application. The combination of all this, including also ethical and political maxims relating to the use of this knowledge, became the disciplines of grammar and rhetoric. It is quite a simple matter now to analyze these disciplines and distinguish the essentially sociological theories of linguistic usage in a culture from the pedagogical and ethical theories which are traditionally included in them.

Each of the kinds of propositions included in these disciplines has some title to the appellation "knowledge." The force of the example is not in denying that a discipline is one way, and perhaps a very effective way, of pulling together different kinds of knowledge for instruction. It is rather in pointing out that *logically* the sociological theories of linguistic usage have a great deal more affinity with other sociological theories than with the other kinds of knowledge which are included in the so-called conventional disciplines. There is nothing inherent in this particular way of organizing propositions for instruction.

If the argument above is correct, its conclusion is clear:

Merely to advocate the teaching of the disciplines provides no
theoretically grounded answer to the question of knowledge in
the curriculum. For example, to assert that everyone should
learn the discipline of grammar is to assert that everyone should
learn the congeries of theoretical propositions from sociology,
certain common-sense prescriptions, and certain rather crude
ethical rules. Now it is certainly not self-evident that this will
yield a person who knows better what he is doing in using a
natural language. To decide whether these conclusions apply to
other so-called disciplines is left to the reader.

C. Cognitive action as a basis for curriculum construction

It would seem plausible to begin at the other end with cognitive
action itself rather than the intrinsic structure of propositional
knowledge as a basis for organizing the curriculum. Perhaps it is
possible to find out what kinds of action are most in need of
cognitive control and to teach that propositional knowledge
most relevant to action.

There are two distinct kinds of theory within this general
approach. I term them "empirical" and "epistemological."

1. If we are empiricists in curriculum theory, we ask in what
kinds of activities the participants of our culture are most likely
to engage throughout their lives; we then try to provide them
with whatever propositional knowledge (the meaning of which
must now be broadened to include all forms of symbolic materials) will be useful to them. "Useful" is defined as leading to
cognitive action, that is, leading to a condition in which individuals and groups of people know what they are doing in the
ordinary affairs of life.

Agreeing or disagreeing with their conclusions, we are forced
to admire the audacity of those who take this approach. The
members of our society do such a wide variety of things, and the
typical kinds of activities change so rapidly and basically, that
we would presume an initial impossibility for this enterprise.

And we actually find that those who so audaciously approach
the problem of knowledge in the curriculum from this standpoint lose their nerve at the last minute. They do not undertake
actually to survey the forms of action practiced in the society in
an attempt to find those most in need of cognitive control and

then to organize propositional knowledge in relation to those
activities. Rather, they select categories which already have
some fairly clear relation to propositional knowledge. For example, a category that might be designated as "leisure activities"
is chosen. This suggests, but certainly does not entail, the teaching of organized and related sets of propositions such as those
found in literary criticism, music appreciation, travel information, and the like.

In practice, then, this approach is just a way of dodging the
curriculum question without being aware of it.‡ It appears to be
a solution, but actually is not. It is not a theoretical solution
because it does not give an intelligible rationale for organizing
propositional knowledge to achieve aims of cognitive action. No
doubt the study of literature in a critical way will enrich the
leisure activities of many students. But why have we chosen to
enrich leisure activities and why in this particular way? The
correct answer is that the teaching of propositional knowledge
in schools has been *traditionally* organized to do both. What
purports to be a theory, then, is merely an apology, and an echo
of the traditional curriculum.

2. The limitations of the empirical approach to curriculum
theory are removed only by constructing a general theory of
what it means to be cognitive in action, of what it means to
know what one is about in action in general rather than in
specific acts. A curriculum program constructed on this basis
would try to provide those experiences leading to an increase in
general intelligence in the wide range of practical affairs found
in our culture. Such a theory would recognize the relativity of
intelligence to propositional knowledge potentially at the dis-
posal of the agent. Only in this way, I believe, can a genuine
resolution between propositional knowledge as the material of
instruction and cognitive behavior as the goal in instruction be
achieved. This is the epistemological approach to the curriculum.

‡ In theory, of course, it is logically impossible (*a*) to derive normative principles (how teaching should be organized) from these purely
descriptive premises (how people typically spend their time), and (*b*) to
determine the typical kinds of activities without some a priori categorization of the things to be looked for.

Certain rather obvious features of cognitive action point toward a theory of the kind suggested:

A. Knowing what one is doing is a way, a mode, a style of doing something. It is not doing *and* something else internal and unobservable. This observation has a double relevance for curriculum theory. Negatively, it indicates that the theory does not have to account for some alleged isomorphism between the internal and external world of the learner. Positively, it points toward a possibly generic characteristic of cognitive action in the style, stance, manner of the actor.

B. The manner or style of acting pointed to above is not mere bravado, mere posturing. It is doing things in a way that connects different phases of the action into a unified whole, a way that in some fields of activity, for example, mathematics, would be called critical thinking, in other fields, say painting, would be called creative process. Are there propositional materials in the culture particularly helpful in developing that kind of action? This is an empirical question and requires experimental evidence in warrant of any answer. Yet a prima-facie case can be made for hypothesizing the signal appropriateness of certain kinds of materials for making this change in learners.

C. Another generic characteristic of human action is that it is valuational. Knowing what one is doing, even in the most technical fields, is knowledge of the *fittingness* of means to ends in a context of competing ends. This suggests that the separation of moral training, for example, citizenship education, from the rest of the curriculum is scarcely justified. Any curriculum theory constructed on this model would *be* a theory of how to improve the ethical quality of action.

It is not necessary to proceed further. The reader immediately recognizes the appeal to return to the main stream of educational theory.

CATEGORICAL SYSTEMS AND CONTENT ORGANIZATION*

Ronald W. Stadt

If education is to facilitate intellectual development and intellectual development depends upon one's ability to categorize and integrate objects and events, one who would organize materials for instruction should understand the nature of categorical systems. Understanding the processes of categorization and integration is not enough. To assure that youngsters use these processes intelligently as they organize ideas in their minds and/or to organize instructional materials, educators must also understand the products of these processes, i.e., categorical systems themselves. . . .

Perhaps the most important characteristic of categorical systems is their multiplicity. Objects and events that occur with reasonable frequency can be classed in many ways. For example, major aspects of productive society, important segments of the world of work, can be categorized: (1) according to size of organization from the small, local firm which employs a limited number of workers to the large corporate enterprise which employs thousands of workers and operates at the international level; (2) according to degree of mechanization from the organization which produces custom goods or services to the organization which mass produces goods on continuous, highly automated production lines and seldom redesigns products; (3) according to type of institution, e.g., financial, governmental, religious, educational, recreational; (4) according to degree of vertical integration with reference to primary, secondary, and tertiary operations; (5) according to degree of horizontal integration with reference to diversity of goods and/or services produced; (6) according to major materials, e.g., rubber, metals, plastics; (7) according to major processes, e.g., mining, data processing, communication, casting, repair; (8) according to major products, e.g., automobiles, appliances, toys, missiles.

* Reprinted from "Intelligence, Categorical Systems, and Content Organization," *Educational Theory,* 15(April, 1965), 123–29. By permission of the author and the editor of *Educational Theory.*

These are only a few of the ways organizations that produce goods and services can be classified. One could easily devise several useful systems of classifying firms by location alone.

These and many other categorical systems, singly or in combination, are useful tools of analysis for the sundry purposes one might have in analyzing productive society. If one's purpose is general understanding, he will need to use categorical systems which have been established by specialists of many kinds. Some of the specialties which study productive society are: sociology, psychology, political science, economics, psychiatry, anthropology, philosophy, and theology. Each of these specialties has developed several or more methods of classifying segments of productive society. Most objects and events can be classified in several or more ways.

A second characteristic of categorical systems is their artificiality. Categorical systems can be said to be artificial simply because they are man made. It is difficult to identify dichotomies and other systems of discrete categories which occur in nature.[7] Dichotomies in particular have suffered severely at the hands of philosophers, e.g., John Dewey. Many theoreticians have submitted that one or another dualism is false. One of the most interesting attempts to win the point that categorical systems are artificial is an argument developed by Karl Pearson, prominent mathematician and early statistician. In developing formulae for the tetrachoric correlation coefficient, Pearson argued that many variables commonly thought to be dichotomous are actually continuous—even sex. He submitted that if one considers the totality of sex characteristics rather than simple physiological equipment—the physiological sex boundary has been crossed by a few individuals—one finds that most people display both masculine and feminine characteristics in nearly equal quantities, i.e., that most people fall near the midpoint of the composite sex variable, and further that only a few people are so extremely masculine or feminine that they fall several standard deviations from the midpoint. In other words, one finds that sex is a normally distributed variable.

[7] Many of the categorical systems used by statisticians consist of mutually exclusive and exhaustive categories. However, these are usually established by statisticians to facilitate investigation.

A related and very significant characteristic of categorical systems is their mutability. They do not always fit actual objects and events; [8] i.e., they are changeable. When, as is often the case, we are unable to classify certain things, we are forced to establish new categorical systems or to modify existing ones. For example, when we find it difficult to classify an object as either fruit or vegetable, we establish a "half and half" kind of category. We are often forced to recognize that our categorical systems do not suit natural occurrences.[9]

For the most part, fundamental classification of the animal, vegetable, or mineral order are well suited. However, lower-level classifications nearly always require finer distinctions and are thus more difficult. If birds are feathered vertebrates, we have one thing; but if we add the characteristic "flying," we make modifications to accommodate grounded species such as ostriches. The wealth of controversy regarding classifications in biology (and many other disciplines) is evidence of the artificiality and inevitable fallability of categorical systems. When the variety of forms is great, it is difficult to establish division points which do not make classification of certain new-found or man made forms difficult.

Classification above the animal, vegetable, mineral level is also often difficult. Some of mankind's most controversial issues are found in the discourse which deals with the nature of things. Whether ours is a world which was created by a supreme being or not, whether the universe was formed by explosive or other forces, whether the universe is an expanding one or not—these kinds of classifications and the kind which deal with the nature of things generally at the molecular and atomic levels; e.g., questions regarding the classification of particles in nuclei are very difficult. Generally accepted, well demonstrated categorical systems at these levels of understanding are few and very mutable.

In several very similar ways, then, we perfect knowledge by

[8] When categorical systems "fit" all objects and events, we will have exhausted the possibilities for intellectual growth, i.e., will have learned to categorize and integrate everything—an impossibility.

[9] Because of their greater variability, man made objects and events are often more difficult to classify than are natural objects and events.

modifying categorical systems. (a) We perfect knowledge when we arrange old ideas and constructs in new ways. (b) We perfect knowledge when we discover new phenomena, by modifying old categorical systems or devising totally new ones to accommodate the new material. (c) We perfect understanding when, having made many integrations between categories within a system, we no longer use that system. With prolonged use, we arrive at a point where the division points, the tools of analysis, are not necessary to the understanding of what we are analyzing. Of course, this situation is only temporary; new methods of analysis and new relationships cause us to examine what we "know" again and again.

Perhaps the paramount characteristic of categorical systems is their importance. Categorical systems are important insofar as their relationship to the processes of thought and the development of intelligence is as direct and universal as it was described in the first section of this article. Secondly, they are important insofar as they give organization or structure to, and thus facilitate understanding of, bodies of knowledge. It is for this reason that we value the organization which Euclid gave to geometry.[10] Similarly we value what Newton and his followers did for physics, Einstein's more fundamental and larger structure (of which Newtonian physics was just a part), and organizations in which Einstein's ideas share a similar relationship.

The search for larger and more meaningful systems of categorizing what we already know about the world and the results of contemporary investigations is of primary concern to scholars, creative artists, and theoreticians of all kinds. The search for sets of common denominators, i.e., logical categorical systems which give meaning to all that is known and all that is presently being discovered about kinds of phenomena, is very important.

The foregoing suggests no specific procedures for organizing and presenting units of content. How to sequence elements in given classroom or laboratory experiences has not been the concern of this article. However, several closely related, general implications for content organization are evident.

It follows from what has been said that the content of instruc-

[10] The existence of non-Euclidian geometries supports the idea that there are multiplicities of categorical systems.

tion cannot always be structured as it appears in organized disciplines. For general education purposes, content must be organized in several ways. Much of what is taught in schools, e.g., arithmetic and reading, does not come from organized disciplines. In the secondary school, it is obvious that units of content of sufficient size and duration cannot be presented from each of the specialties and/or disciplines with which youngsters should become familiar. Unless their understanding of the world, and of specialties themselves, is to be limited to a few fields, high school students cannot always study specialties and organized bodies of knowledge in the fashion people who hope to work in the respective fields study them. Purpose and time limitations suggest that so long as education is general, some content must be organized differently.

The nature of methods of organization has been of major concern to educationists. Renewed attempts should be made to resolve issues raised by the advocates of core, broad fields, activity, experience, social process, and life function approaches to content organization. Perhaps one day, the better of these methods will themselves fit into a larger and more generally applicable method of organizing content for general education purposes.

For purposes which are utilitarian in emphasis, much of the content should be organized as it is organized in the discipline or field for which the students are preparing.[11] (In many specialties, students must become familiar with the several ways prominent theoreticians organize the discipline.) Because all schools are somewhat alien to the working world, content organization in utilitarian education will depend upon pedagogical and administrative decisions and may thus differ from content as it exists in the discipline itself. However, unless these differences can be understandable and small, the preparation of specialists will be nominally effective.

It follows also that regardless of their purposes, students

[11] Except for the preparation of teachers, educationists have no special abilities to organize major units of content for preparing physicians, mechanics, or specialists of any kind. Pedagogues can assist people who organize content in utilitarian education, but decisions regarding the sequencing of large units of content are by definition the domain of specialists.

should be told why the content presented to them has been organized in a certain way and should furthermore be shown how it could be organized in other ways for immediate or future purposes. Students should learn the structure of the large and small units of content they are learning as Bruner, Ausubel and Herbart have suggested. This procedure expedites learning of a given body of content. When the procedure is extended, when students are shown other ways the material could be organized, broadened viewpoints, extensions, and related understandings in many dimensions are facilitated.

An example may clarify what is meant here. Suppose that the desire to develop a given understanding and certain practical limitations suggest that some content from economics, psychology and sociology should be presented. If the material is organized as it is found in sociology and what is said about the same issues in economics and psychology is tacked on, so to speak, students should be shown how the material might have appeared if economics or psychology had been used as the major thread and if material from other fields had been introduced.[12] The warp and woof of the cloth should always be made meaningful, and related materials that have been excluded because of time and other practical considerations should be made known to students to assure that learning can be continuous, i.e., that future learning is not restricted because of limitations placed on present learning. If people are not fully informed about the organization of what they learn in school, they get mistaken ideas, such as the attitude that they know all there is to know. Students should know where the material they are learning comes from, how it is valued by experts in fields that study similar phenomena, how it may fare in light of contemporary developments, etc. Textbooks and teachers should not give youngsters interpretations which are over-simplified or finalized in any way. . . .

Educators should not attempt to settle the controversy re-

---

[12] Perhaps as operations research, an approach whereby groups of experts from several or many specialties attack industrial problems, becomes more widespread in industry and elsewhere, more effort should be devoted to making the combined efforts of specialists meaningful to children and youth.

garding how we think and then organize and present materials in fashions compatible with *the* mode of thought; such procedures are beyond the capabilities of educational theorists and educational psychologists. This controversy should be treated just as other controversies should be. Youngsters in school should be exposed to the best viewpoints regarding how we think so that the quality and quantity of categorizations and integrations they may make is not limited by wrong analyses of the act of thought which educators might make.

Intelligence, categorical systems, and content organization are closely related. Insofar as the content of instruction creates awareness and understanding of multiplicities of important, mutable, and artificial categorical systems (including analyses of controversial issues such as how we think), intelligence will be maximized.

ORDERED PLURALISM – 1 *

George E. Barton, Jr.

How long has it been since anyone spoke of a cultured man as a "man of parts"? I want to use the old phrase in a new sense. One central business of teaching is disciplining men in "how to think." But if we think, not in one pattern of inquiry, but in four, then what? Then the educated man will have four parts.

Let us take all learnings as our universe. Let us take the relations which order them as our touchstone. When we classify by this principle, we discover four great kingdoms of the mind:

(1) Learnings ordered by *purposive* relations, to deal mainly with purposes and means;

(2) Learnings ordered by *internal* relations, to deal mainly with organs and organisms;

(3) Learnings ordered by *external* relations, to deal mainly with mechanisms and their parts; and

(4) Learnings ordered by *classificatory* relations, to deal mainly with genera and species.

But our image of kingdoms fails us, for the territories overlap. We cannot really draw boundaries, allocating some subject-matters to each; for each tries to take the whole intellectual world as its province. Each tries, but each partially fails; and so there are parts which—for a few centuries—appear really to belong to one or another. . . .

And so the educated man will have four parts—or four visions through four kinds of glasses. To develop him, the curriculum needs four parts. To teach it, the school needs four parts, from womb to tomb. Four functional parts, surely. Four corresponding structural parts, . . . well, maybe. But let us amuse ourselves by speaking concretely, as if we were revolutionizing the school.

* Reprinted from "Ordered Pluralism: A Philosophical Plan of Action for Teaching," *Educational Theory*, 13(October, 1963), 258–61. By permission of the author and the editor of *Educational Theory*.

1. The purposive vision of life

Let us promulgate a Division of Purposive Relations or Division of Purposes and Means, to discipline men to inquire skillfully into the purposive vision of the world. Let us invite all those to join who want to study or teach about purposes, and to explore how far it gets you to think in purposive terms. How far does it get one to try to understand how artists combine parts in works of art to achieve aesthetic purposes? how speakers combine parts in speeches to achieve rhetorical effects? how statesmen devise institutions to serve social goals? how scientists think and experiment to confirm scientific truths? how animals take effective steps to feed themselves? how God acts to attain His divine purposes? And so on.

The object of the Division is to inquire, not to dogmatize. This means that it must comprise all those who want to assess the values of the purposive view, pro or con. If somebody wants to talk about the purposes of animals or gods, he belongs here. If somebody else wants to argue that even men do not really have purposes—they only think they have—he also belongs here. But it would be my assumption that most people understand many aspects of life in terms of purpose, and that every student should get a chance to practice viewing the whole world through purposive spectacles, deciding for himself what he can see, and what he cannot usefully see, in purposive terms.

2. The organic vision of life

Let us promulgate a Division of Internal Relations or Division of Organs and Organisms, to discipline men to inquire skillfully into the organic vision of the world. Let us invite all those to join who want to study or teach about organisms and to explore how far it gets you to think in terms of internal relations. How far does it get you to try to understand how the parts of a painting function together organically to constitute an organic unity? how an institution grows, as if it were a living thing? how the organic structures of humans and animals function together while the humans and animals live? how men gain insights? how the pros and cons of issues get inextricably interwoven? how anyone could seriously say, "This world is a great animal"? And so on.

Again, the object of the Division is to inquire, not to dogmatize. This means that it must comprise those who push the organic view for all it is worth, and those who insist that it isn't worth much. But I would assume that most people understand many aspects of the world in terms of organism, and that every student should get a chance to become thoroughly competent in viewing anything in that mode which he finds it useful to observe in terms of internal relations.

3. The mechanistic vision of life

Let us promulgate a Division of External Relations or Division of Mechanisms and Parts, to discipline men to inquire skillfully into the mechanistic vision of the world. Let us invite all those to join who want to study or teach about mechanisms and to explore how far it gets you to think in terms of external relations. How far does it get you to try to understand how points in a pointillist painting add up to a picture? how individuals combine to constitute a democracy or a political "machine"? how a dog or a man is a machine, or like a machine? how learning is seen by connectionists? how simple tools combine to make mechanisms? mechanisms to make automobiles? or space capsules? And so on.

Always, the object is to inquire, not to dogmatize. Always, we let the proponents of mechanism push it as far as it will take them, and listen to those who think they push it too far. Since mechanism is one of the great modes for understanding many aspects of the world, the student will doubtless find its logic of external relations permanently useful in some realms.

4. The classificatory vision of life

Let us promulgate a Division of Classificatory Relations or Division of Genera and Species, to discipline men skillfully to use classificatory forms to get a classificatory vision of the world. Let us invite all those to join who want to study and teach about classifications and to explore how far it gets you to operate in classificatory terms. How far does it get you to classify in the arts? in the social studies? in the natural sciences?

in philosophy? And so on. I am sure I do not need to illustrate. I am sure I do not need once more to chant the litany about pushing classification as far as it will take you, but listening to those who warn against pushing it too far.

Instead, let me remark that there are some who would call "classificatory relations" a nonsense phrase. Perhaps there is no such thing as a complete "classificatory vision of the world." However this may be, classification is indispensable, if only to prepare the way for other approaches. After all, we are using it ourselves. We are suggesting that the kind of problem one is dealing with may determine whether one chooses to observe it as primarily purposive, organic, or mechanistic. If it is not one more perspective like the others, it may be even more useful, if it is the preliminary view that suggests which of the others may be most useful. The educated man should master it. The curriculum should teach it. The school should be structured to provide for it.

BETWEEN TWO CULTURES *

Dean W. O'Brien

Looking across the cultural gulf described by C. P. Snow, The Scientists seem to see The Literary Intellectuals as maddeningly ambiguous, blithely ignorant of social problems, and insupportably proud of the allegedly make-believe world they inhabit. Snow, looking in the other direction, sees The Scientists as precise, widely informed, and intellectually sound but lacking a bit in "imaginative understanding.". . .

Caught in the middle, the school is, on the institutional level, most strategically located to do something about the broken lines of communication between Snow's two cultures. And on the level of thought the existential temperament occupies a similar no-man's land.

Probably the educator and the existentialist will find it mutually embarrassing when they come to realize that they share common ground. But after the first blush has faded, the educator and the existentialist should find comfort in a natural alliance. They will get very little comfort elsewhere, except by giving up their exposed and necessary positions to give in to either the subjectivity of art or the objectivity of science, neither of which is the whole truth.

Existentialism is often mistaken for the subjectivity of the unscientific. Poets, painters, novelists, theologians, psychotherapists, and, of course, philosophers undeniably have represented existential thinking more than scientists have. Yet, most existentialists insist that it is a part of the nature of man to be in a situation, and today a good deal of that situation is composed of the products and abstractions of science. . . .

To an existentialist, the private, subjective world and the public, objective world are contingent upon one another, solitude being senseless . . . for anyone who has no human connections, and society being senseless . . . when it is not nourished by solitary individuals.

* Reprinted from "Between Two Cultures; An Existential View of Curriculum," *School and Society,* 89(November 18, 1961), 402–5. By permission of the editor of *School and Society.*

So it would seem existentially helpful to set up a dichotomous curriculum, to split the infinity, so to speak, and leave the student in the tension between the two halves. That is where he is anyhow, but he ought to know it.

One half would deal with the past, the public, the probable, the provisional, and the progressive. It would embrace the bulk of science, history concerned with "facticity," English concerned with the tried and approved techniques of language, mathematics and other rational systems that prevail, data on governments as they have been, and the like. There is nothing constant about this content; absolutes here are obsolete. Science continually junks its earlier work as almost ludicrously naive; new facts upset earlier notions of what actually happened in history; a statement written in another period or culture must be interpreted in the current vernacular; Euclidean geometry is almost moribund; and governments change.

The other half would lie in the precinct of the present, the personal, the possible, the permanent, and the perennial: the beauty, genius, and lucky coincidences of scientific discovery; history as human possibility (not here that Gandhi's life made no demonstrable difference in Indian independence, but that such an improbably fine human being could be); art and literature and philosophy in which one can hardly say that Picasso's work is somehow better than the prehistoric cave paintings or that Faulkner is a vast improvement over Sophocles or that logical positivism has invalidated Greek idealism; also here the utopian proposals that never will be adequately tested. The futility of publicly proving out these mysteries of Truth, Beauty, and Goodness should be no more depressing than the transience of solutions to problems in the objective half. . . .

Now nothing could be so existentially obnoxious as to tack on some explicit behavioral goals here. That is, the graduate would be expected to behave, but the definition of his action would be left to the individual, who is the only one both to know and decide what he is. The risk of such a position on the purposes of education is, of course, great, but human dignity and freedom require great risk. Furthermore, explicit behavioral goals would be existentially "inauthentic" in that they would have to be based on the somewhat arrogant assumption that one free and conscious human being (a curriculum planner, perhaps) can understand thoroughly another free and conscious human being (a student)—an impossibility without destroying the existential notion of being human. The educator, like any man, is morally responsible only for himself but has commitments . . . to both the pupil and the society. More specifically, an existential educator might be expected to have this set of commitments: to protect the pupil from external definitions of what he is; to show the pupil what a man can be; to protect the society from misconceptions of what it is; and to stimulate conceptions of what society could be.

To Protect the Pupil. It should be made clear to the pupil that psychological findings never can be definitive of what he is because, to be properly scientific, the findings must be repeatable and communicable, and human beings are neither entirely repeatable nor wholly communicable. . . . Such findings give more indication, in fact, of what society is in that they show how pupils are perceived by a specialized segment of society. They describe a mechanism that exists to permit social bodies, or institutions, to deal with, categorize, and otherwise apprehend their members for collective ends. Thus, only at the points where my private intent coincides with particular social purposes that someone else thinks he wants me to serve will my I.Q. have any bearing on my existential worth.

"Wherever two are together with a third thing, which takes both out of themselves, there is education," Ralph Harper says. The principle thing perceived by both teacher and pupil, then, ought to be the subject matter, not each other. . . .

To Show What a Man Can Be. This is the half of the existential curriculum described earlier as dealing with the present, personal, and perennial. It is a zone to be entered not as a problem, but, in Gabriel Marcel's expression, "as a mystery." And so such mysterious propositions as "Truth is Beauty," Sartre's "I am not, therefore I think," and many others would confront the pupil, but with no promise or expectation of intelligible solution. . . . But at least he might come to know that life and education are not matters so much of finding as of seeking.

To Protect the Society. Here is the transmission of the cultural heritage idea clothed, perhaps, in more existential language. The social past is, in fact, the only segment of time that can be transmitted at all, the present being private property that the individual cannot get rid of no matter how fluent he may be in translating his perceptions of experience into intelligible public idiom, and the future being existentially a matter of decision. This past is not unimportant. . . . Because it is dependent upon man-made naming systems like language and mathematics, it is abstract rather than concrete, made rather than born, intelligible rather than intelligent. Existentially, then, life must be lived forward but understood backward.

So that its past will not have been in vain, the society sponsors schools to pass the past on to pupils, the trespassers in a world that one day will be their own. And the pupils, on their side, ought to find the past useful in existentially working themselves out in their human situation.

Society ought to be curricular boss in this realm. The more bossy it is, the more directly . . . the pupil will be able to see the values of society at work. The only brakes on society's prerogative, and they are important ones, are the teacher's commitments to protect the child and to honor the whole of human society through the long span of history. The teacher's presumed sophistication as to what society really has been, in opposition to what society would like to think it has been, should qualify the teacher to fulfill this second commitment.

To Stimulate Social Conceptions. Leaving the pupil to his own decisions concerning his social action, this commitment would demand that the teacher rigorously criticize the inevitable flaws in ruling abstractions, in The Establishment, in The System. In today's world—where a critic is known not as a critic but as a "crank," where the individual tends too much to say that the world is a mess "but what can I do about it?," where open and sincere controversy is commonly considered "unsophisticated," where popular inclinations are so easily consolidated and perpetuated in the mass media, where professionals see their worlds as inaccessible to lay judgment, where eccentric behavior is called either psychotic or criminal and treated accordingly, where the unpredictable is seen as disturbing rather than as refreshing—in such a world, this fourth commitment of the teacher becomes the most important of all. Here is the modern tragedy, so well documented in the arts, of the individual's sense of anonymity, purposelessness, and helplessness. The culpable social condition might be called the rigged environment.

This condition can be perpetuated in the schools as handily as it is in the not-so-open society. It consists of one person, or group of persons (politicians, businessmen, teachers, or others), creating an environment in which it is not sane or decent for an individual to suggest that his personal worth in any important way could differ from what is expected of him, or to insist that he may have anything new or unanticipated to contribute to the environment. The result is that the individual feels compelled either to retreat into an abnormally subjective isolation and deny that he has some social relevance or else to join the adherents of communication (those who are for talking but against saying anything) and deny that he is an unprecedented human individual. . . .

Nor would the existentialist be happy with the tendency to think of teaching the skills in such areas as democratic process and scientific method or even in reading and arithmetic as significantly different from or superior to teaching "mere information." He would wonder if the teaching of a skill is really different in kind from reporting other sets of social agreements. If the pupil doesn't learn that such agreements are not so venerable as they are vulnerable, if he does not learn that the forms are actually dependent upon his alterations for vitality and meaning, then how will the pupil know that he can and must renew the otherwise inanimate social forms of language, mathematics, science, democracy? Like cliches, these forms are easily drained of meaning, but when that happens, the individual, despite his apparent fluency, is almost unable to say anything with his life.

It would be so simple to choose between science and art, or between the society and the individual, and then to dismiss the rejected hemisphere of the intellectual world as unreal or irrelevant. It would be simple, but not honest.

METAPHORIC LOGIC AND HUMAN INTEGRATION*

J. Donald Butler

. . . What remains is for me to try (1) to indicate some of the characteristics of the logic for which this paper may be a preface and (2) to suggest the nature of the bearing it might have on education.

1. The first and possibly chief characteristic of the logic I am proposing is that it will use words predominantly, if not always, as *symbols* or *metaphors* rather than *signs*. If, and as such, a logic can cope in any degree with ontology, its words will not comprise formulas which denote or point to that which they represent. They will rather function in such a way as to speak *in a kind* which is similar to the *kind* which the reality beyond verbal meanings has. This sentence I have just uttered is very faltering, but it is as adequate as I can make it. Of course, it goes without saying that what I am trying to get at by it is intangible and allusive if not evasive, and without direct equivalent in human discourse. This difficulty is my main problem; but I can highlight the focus of the difficulty by voicing another disagreement with Paul Tillich which is precisely relevant here. Tillich asserts that words so used as I have indicated *participate* in the reality of which they speak. It is not a quibble when I argue with this that the word *participate* is too strong. I can think of no human discourse, metaphorical or otherwise, which actually *participates* in reality. The closest that I can approximate Tillich's assertion is that *symbolic* or *metaphorical* interpretation may be used so as to be of a *kind* similar to the *kind* which the thing-in-itself is, all the while leaving the mystery of existence *qua* existence untouched.[19]

2. Another characteristic I believe such a logic would have is that its important reference will always be events—events public

* Reprinted from "Preface to a Logic," *Educational Theory,* 14(October, 1964), 247–53. By permission of the author and the editor of *Educational Theory.*

[19] Paul Tillich, *Dynamics of Faith* (New York, Harper and Brothers, 1957), p. 45.

to at least some community and certainly not the private subjective happenings of a solitary knower. The range of events relevant to such a logic will necessarily be unlimited. Events only observable by the sciences, however highly sophisticated, if sometimes virtually defying accurate reporting to the non-scientific world, I believe will be data for such a logic. Events of history, in the present and public to the entire world because of our mass media, as well as historic events the common knowledge of which is dependent upon careful research into the dim past, also comprise relevant data. Both of these examples represent the wide gamut within which all historical data will be pertinent. I am suggesting that no happenings of whatever sort, however discerned, and by whatever community interpreted will be irrelevant and can be ignored. Criteria of validity and degree of relevance may be needed, but none can be excluded because of their character or the source of the report concerning them.

3. This logic may also suggest that the significance of many events, if not all of them, can best be expressed in metaphor. If growth in the universe so-called can be accurately reported by the sciences as a happening by which man has always been confronted, although only detected by him in recent times, what meaning does this have in human terms? Can the significance of this best be expressed for man in a formula of words or signs? Or, can it better be expressed in a poetic pattern of some kind which "gives the feel," for lack of a better idiom, of what it is like to be in relation to an existence one of the phenomenalist aspects of which is continual expansion?

4. It may be, therefore, that literary and artistic forms may be most hospitably received by such a logic. Although it would be difficult to predict what it would do with them.

I have long been aware that philosophers for the most part write poor literature, although you know of the notable exceptions as well as I do. I have also been aware for years that there are some men of letters who, consciously or not, have proposed to set themselves up as philosophers. They have assumed the role—and here the trite and over-used figure of "the role" is appropriate—of unerring guides in all matters of importance in living. These two phenomena have forced upon me awareness of the epistemological issue occasionally drawn between philosophy and literature. Is the systematizing mind, aware of all of the problems of philosophy and their interrelationships, the more to be trusted with the important issues of life? Or, is the literary man more trustworthy in these matters because of his occasional insights of sharp penetration, although he might not recognize a fully articulated idea were he to trip over it?

My loyalty has long been with the philosopher, to the extent that I have correctly understood this issue. And I believe that is where my loyalty still lies. Yet there is much to be said for the aesthetic artform as a vehicle of the most significant meanings. Further, the logic of which I am thinking has a central place for them. If there is existence *qua* existence, I am inclined to the position that poetic expression, whether in narrative, painting, drama, or any of the other aesthetic forms, can communicate to us that which is *of a kind* with it more than formula can. And if the so-called thing-in-itself has initiative and speaks to man with his wonderful yet meagre equipment, I think the best vehicle of such revelation is the poetic one of narrative or drama in history and event, far superior to formula, even theological formula.

5. While it may repeat some of what has already been said, it should be emphasized that this logic will also necessarily be humane. This may have two meanings, one more intended than the other but the secondary meaning not fully excluded. Such a logic should speak in human terms, that is, in ways which are in the same key as human living. It might also be said specifically, as implied by this, that it should come as close to being understood by all men as possible. But this requirement is not directed so much at actuality as it is at potentiality. What such a logic may say in a given instance may not be readily understood, but it should be so much of a piece with the life of man as he lives it, that it lends itself to understanding whether ever fully understood or not.

It is generally appreciated that $E = MC^2$ commonly denotes the theory of relativity. But this formula, precise as I am sure it is in its own way, is so disparate with human living that I dare say few of us in this Society can say what it means in more humane terms. One of John Dewey's hopes for his version of the scientific method was that it would serve so well as a communicative device shared both by laboratory and market

place, that it would have almost unprecedented unifying power
in human life. While the almost complete disappointment of this
hope is not altogether the failure of its author, I wonder if
Dewey's scientific method has the humane potentialities he attributed to it. Of course, it was not sufficiently sophisticated or
specialized for many researchers, so they say. But even if most
men think according to the pattern by which Dewey analyzed
their thinking for them, are they able to recognize this pattern in
the abstract form which he gave to it?

By contrast, Ernest Hemingway's *The Old Man and the
Sea* [20] is concrete in the way human living is concrete, yet what
it says is abstract. I don't know what Hemingway meant to say
in it, nor would I presume to depict the intention which was on
his side of this particular creation. But when I read it, it is like
looking in a mirror. I know then that all of my struggles to do a
job of importance, or live a life, are to me like landing the
biggest fish in the sea! But I also know that when my peers and
the world look at what is my big fish, all they see are the bare
bones of a skeleton.

Tennessee William's *Twenty-Seven Wagons Full of Cotton* [21]
is a very painful mirror for me. It is not the sexual dalliance in it
which hurts because it laughs at my Puritan upbringing. This
can be almost amusing, it is so crude. But what is full of anguish
for me in this particular mirror is the desolate landscape. It
seems that I have been there so many times, suffering every time
in the midst of completely sapless surroundings, that I never
want to go back again. Yet this little play, later enlarged into
Baby Doll, [22] makes me do it.

I do not understand all that this same playwright has said in
Suddenly Last Summer. [23] Superficially there is beautiful balance, I'm convinced only aesthetic, between the clouds of birds
in the beginning of the play feasting on the newly hatched
turtles and the cannibalism at the play's end in which the central
character loses his life. For the most part the symbolism of the
entire work is too allusive for me; but yet it is in and of human

[20] New York, Charles Scribner's Sons, 1952.
[21] New York, New Directions, 1953.
[22] New York, New Directions, 1956.
[23] New York, New Directions, 1958.

living. While it may not be understood, it nevertheless lends itself to understanding.

Similarly, Picasso uttered a great message to his fellowmen in his *Guernica*. As far as I know, he has never interpreted the meaning of this painting although we have not been without pseudo-Picassos, some of whom have given us an entire vocabulary of *signs* for translating it into allegedly understandable language. *Guernica* is not pleasing to contemplate. For me it is full of suffering and anguish. I am sure it is a man protesting with all the power of all of his emotions against man's inhumanity to man. Beyond this I would not attempt to say more. I value the painting even though I do not fully understand it. And although not understood, it lends itself to being understood.

The prophet Hosea has this same humaneness mixed with a perplexing invitation to listen, in his autobiography or moving story, whichever it may be. What could be more unexpected and more confusing yet so human?

The Lord said . . . "Go, take to yourself a wife of harlotry and have children of harlotry." . . . and she conceived and bore him a son. And the Lord said . . . "Call his name Jezreel . . . . and I will punish the house of Jehu for the blood of Jezreel." . . . She conceived again and bore a daughter. And the Lord said . . . "Call her name Not Pitied, for I will no more have pity on the house of Israel." . . . When she had weaned Not Pitied, she conceived and bore a son. And the Lord said, "Call his name Not My People, for you are not my people and I am not your God." . . . And the Lord said, "Go again, love a woman who is . . . an adultress." . . . So I bought her for fifteen shekels of silver . . . And I said to her, "You must dwell as mine for many days; you shall not play the harlot, or belong to any other man; so will I also be to you." [24]

The same can be said of this composite of selections from Hosea as of the other examples given preceding it. Hosea may not be understood, but what he has written lends itself to understanding. It is of human living, not removed from it or disparate with it.

I am sure that I do not need to say that in this requirement of humanness I am not disparaging the relativity formula, nor the value of the kind of precision found in mathematics, symbolic logic, or language analysis. What I am saying is that none of

[24] Hosea I:2–III:3, a mosaic of selections; some of the capitalization is mine.

these lend themselves to the kind of understanding that a logic of poetry or metaphor do, because they are not of a piece with human life as it is lived. Neither formula-logic nor metaphor-logic may be understood in any given instance. But metaphor lends itself to understanding where formula-logic does not. And what is even more important, if there is any reality beyond verbal knowledge, it can be given expression, or better still, can give itself expression in metaphor-logic; whereas, formula-logic asks for precision where precision is either not to be found or not to be given to us.

Having prefaced a possible new logic and having ventured some guesses as to what its nature might be, I assume that all of us are most especially concerned to consider in addition what difference, if any, such a logic would make in education. . . .

It would be premature, and possibly not eventually very fruitful even, to attempt a direct transposition of supposed characteristics of this logic, for example, into their alleged counterparts in educational motifs. One thing I believe can be quite clearly predicted now, however, and that is that this logic will not yield any systematized five steps for learning, *a la* Dewey or Herbart.

. . . This particular set of formulas is directed more especially to that aspect of curricular theory from which general graduation requirements may be derived. Any bearing upon concentrations and electives is no more than implicit. There are nine presuppositions and they are as follows:

1. Education, at all levels and especially in the college and university, must proceed in the spirit and perspective of *universality* rather than parochialism, regionalism, or nationalism.

General graduation requirements should, therefore, be such as to help enlarge the student's perspective, correcting the likely parochialism of family, institutional, and community loyalties in the midst of which he has lived prior to college.

2. The tradition of liberal education has been too narrowly identified with the humanities. In essence liberal education needs to be redefined in our day; this is also a pragmatic necessity because of the rapid growth of knowledge and extension of the sciences. There is no magic nor mystique about the particular subjects of study by which a man may be liberated, as

long as they are not narrowly vocational nor woodenly stereotyped.

There is, therefore, no particular discipline or subject-matter
area which in itself is a necessary part of general graduation
requirements. There is much room for variation in the make-up
of general graduation requirements for each student, as long as
distortion is avoided and representativeness is achieved.

3. It is impossible for any man to be exposed to all knowledge; among many other ways of interdependence, men are
interdependent in being under the necessity of trusting the
knowledge of each other in some very real measure. Easy
examples which may be cited are the dependence most of us
need to have upon the physician and the airline pilot.

General graduation requirements should not, therefore, attempt to yield for the student an encyclopedia of knowledge,
except possibly in the barest outline, if at all. A part of being
educated today is knowing that we must depend upon others for
much of our knowledge as well as where to turn for particular
knowledges when they are needed.

4. Whereas comprehension and totality of knowledge are
impossible, the curricular structure and the guidance paralleling
the curriculum should approximate for the student some representativeness of the scope of knowledge.

Therefore, general graduation requirements should be structured, and also fully effective guidance of the student provided,
so that the student's selection of courses constituting his particular set of graduation requirements will be representative of the
scope and variety of knowledge.

5. One aspect of the meaning of a liberal education is freedom and responsibility for the student in determining his own
program of study.

Therefore, general graduation requirements should not be so
completely specified that the student has no choice among them
and is responsible for no decision regarding them. Under guidance he should be faced with the necessity of responsible selection of courses in this area, as well as in his concentration and
among his electives.

6. The curriculum must be paralleled by effectual guidance

by which the student is guided *into* his program of study by counseling, as well as guided *within* it by teaching.

General graduation requirements will not be adequately determined for each and every student, therefore, either by free election or by curricular structures, if the student is not provided guidance. There must be effective academic counseling, without control or direction, paralleling any curricular structure if that structure is to be effective and fruitful.

7. Any tendency toward a closed society must be avoided; e.g., emphasis upon concepts, understandings, or values which an in-group holds in common at the same time that it disregards the alien and the enemy.

Therefore, we must be cautious in seeing to it that any plan adopted for determining general graduation requirements moves toward the vista of an open and viable society, rather than a closed society in which *"our"* values are emphasized to the exclusion of others.

8. The correction of specialization and fragmentation in society is not to be found in some fund of knowledge held in common; the bases of community and social inter-relationship are existential rather than cognitive or conceptual.

There is, therefore, no conception of general graduation requirements which in actuality is causally connected with unity in society and correction of fragmentation. It is the spirit, perspective, personal relationships and such, permeating the climate of learning which bear more direct connection causally to unity and inter-relatedness in society.

9. Integration or the establishment of inter-relationships in knowledge is a function of the self and is not the result of alleged structures existing in knowledge itself.

Achieving integration for the student, therefore, will be accomplished by the kind of curriculum and teaching which guides the student in making his own integration. That any set of general graduation requirements will provide the student with a corpus of objectively integrated knowledge is an illusion.

TEACHING AND LEARNING

Theory of knowledge is relevant to teaching and learning methodologically insofar as the matter of knowing anything about
teaching and/or learning is an open question. The empirical
methods of educational psychology and sociology may be the
best ways of really knowing anything about them, but this very
statement stands outside the province of either in the realm of
epistemology and its truth probably ought not be taken for
granted. These methods of inquiring into the phenomena of
teaching and learning presuppose a theory of knowing in a
second and more important way. Actual teaching and learning
are of some kind of knowledge. The kind of knowledge constituting the content of instruction has to be decided upon *before*
any empirical inquiry can begin to investigate teaching and
learning phenomena, or there would be no phenomena to inquire into. If the empirical study results in explanations as to
what occurred, the explanations are valid to the extent that they
actually grasp what did occur and to the extent that the independence of the phenomena explained is maintained. Whether
the events thus explained can be subsequently guided by the
explanations in any normative way is open to question. It would
all depend upon the selection of the normative case in the
beginning, but if that selection of an occasion of "good" teaching or "good" learning were possible, its empirical study would
be mostly redundant. Be this as it may, any recommendations
for teaching and learning stemming from their empirical study
remain within the conception of knowledge operative before the
inquiry and presupposed by the inquiry. This is true by logical
necessity.

Theory of knowledge is relevant to the problems of teaching
and learning substantively in the development of various procedures to be instituted within the educative process to assure the
pupil that what he learns is true so that his learning constitutes
knowing. In educative learning the pupil not only learns things
but obtains the warrant for believing that what he learns is what
he is entitled to know. To insure that the pupil has evidential
grounds for the beliefs he acquires, various kinds of evidence,
their nature, and their relation to various kinds of beliefs are

investigated in the epistemological consideration of teaching and learning, and procedures based on the findings are instituted.

Theory of knowledge is relevant to the problems of teaching and learning contextually in respect to the phenomena of concomitant learnings and creativity.

Because we have discussed these three aspects of the epistemological dimension of education in respect to aims and curriculum at some length in this volume and in respect to teaching and learning in another volume in this series, these remarks will suffice.

The clearest way of pointing to the epistemology of teaching and learning, however, is to indicate that it takes into account the epistemology of aims, policy, and curriculum. In spite of the "chicken or the egg" problem, the epistemological investigation of teaching and learning differs markedly from other methods of inquiring into them. It is perforce related to considerations of curriculum and aims whereas other approaches to their study take these for granted. If the nature of the epistemology of aims, policy, and curriculum is clear, then this dimension of teaching and learning ought to be clear in a preliminary way: If one thinks linearly rather than contextually, the epistemology of teaching and learning deals with the "implications" of the epistemology of aims, policy, and curriculum for the actual teaching and learning process. Differences in their levels of generality forbid linear thinking, i.e., strict logical deduction of these implications, but there is heuristic value in seeing the readings that follow as extensions of previous parts of the volume, for print is linear at any rate.

The following chart reveals how the various authors have marched through the gateposts and how the readings that follow are related to those that have gone before:

Aims	DEWEY..ADLER			
		Brett-schneider	Donohue Peters	Broudy *et al.*
Policy	Clayton	Howie Vandenberg	Crittenden	Dupuis
Curriculum	Dewey Champlin	McClellan Miel	Stadt Barton O'Brien Butler	Aristotle Phenix
Teaching-Learning	Schwab Newbury	Gowin Weir	Wegener Barton	Plochmann

To obtain a whole educational theory from an anthology organized according to Deweyan principles of pedagogy on problems but on an Aristotelian frame, one can read through the four problem areas of education by the authors listed in one of the columns, at least in one of the outside columns. The next most consistent column is the center one, where most of the authors advocate some sort of epistemological and educational pluralism, which on one hand includes both extremes and on the other hand results in a traditional, moderately conservative educational theory. The readings in the second and fourth columns are least consistent with each other, for what they share is a denial of the validity of one extreme without full confirmation of the other. For example, Brettschneider, Howie (i.e., Mannheim), Vandenberg, etc., deny the Aristotelian truth by correspondence to antecedent reality; whereas Broudy *et al.,* and Dupuis deny the Deweyan truth by contextuality.

These qualifications having been made, we can return to the point. If one sees how Dewey's view of teaching and learning as indicated by Schwab and Newbury is related to what he said about aims and curriculum and to a lesser extent to what Clayton said about policy; and if one sees how what Plochmann says about teaching and learning is related to what Adler and Aristotle said about aims and curriculum and to a lesser extent to what Phenix said about curriculum; then he can readily see the relevance of theory of knowing to teaching and learning, for the epistemology of education results in a kind of talk about learning that is quite different from any other kind of talk about it. A distinguishing characteristic is its wholistic concern.

For the same reason that we have chosen to point to the realm of the epistemology of teaching and learning in an indirect way, we have ordered the selections as they are. After Wegener's paper which suggests that perhaps the dominance of a truncated empiricism in the study of education has diminished our conceptions of the process of education to the exclusion of appropriate concern for rationality, we have placed Plochmann's paper which argues for a full-blown and completely articulated rationalistic manner of teaching and learning. Then come two expository papers on Dewey's thought to show the contrast with Plochmann's view. There is no doubt that it is views similar to Plochmann's that Dewey vigorously and enthusiastically opposed. This should become clear in Schwab's paper particularly. Never was that view, however, so excellently and rigorously expressed as by Plochmann. The quality of Plochmann's paper, in our judgment, is matched by Schwab and Newbury on Dewey. The ordering, then, permits the issue to be squarely joined without the presence of the customary straw men around to practice jousting with in lieu of the real thing.

The remaining selections intend to represent a variety of cognitively adequate (given the epistemology involved) teaching and learning styles, each with its own valid point to make concerning the kinds of evidence that the pupil should have available so that his learning can also be a coming to know, so that his learning is educative.

Gowin begins with some features of Dewey's view, but by his emphasis he attempts to indicate how teaching and learning can be united, thus causing his view, in some respects, to swing away from Dewey back towards Plochmann's. At the same time, however, he allows for the presence of kinds of meaning (i.e., evidence) within the teaching and learning process that neither Plochmann nor Dewey would regard as cognitively valid. Weir in turn places central significance upon the pupil's subjective appropriation of knowledge, which Gowin seems to merely allude to. To balance this emphasis upon the personal realization of meaning and its consequent loss of rigor, there follows Barton's pluralism, which suggests how differing kinds of knowing not only can coexist in the events of teaching and learning but ought to be there so that the pupil's learning constitutes knowing in the broadest sense.

For the methodological aspect of the epistemology of teaching and learning, see B. Othanel Smith's "Logic, Thinking, and Teaching" in *Educational Theory,* 7(October, 1957), pp. 225–33; * Henle's "Philosophy of Knowledge and Theory of Learning" in the same journal, 8(October, 1958), pp. 193–99; Maccia's "Epistemological Considerations in Relation to the Use of Teaching Machines" in the same journal, 12(October, 1962), pp. 234–40 f.; and Komisar's paper on "The Non-

---

* Available in the *Professional Reprints in Education* Series (Columbus, Charles E. Merrill Books), No. 8012.

science of Learning" in *The School Review,* 74(Autumn, 1966), pp. 249–64. For the substantive issues, see Dewey's *Democracy and Education,* Chapters XI and XII, and its basis in Chapter V of *Knowing and the Known.* The soundest critical article in education on Dewey may be Broudy's "Dewey's Analysis of the Act of Thought" in the *Bulletin,* School of Education, Indiana University, 36(January, 1960), pp. 15–26. For a superior treatment in completely modern terms of a Neo-Thomistic exposition of learning in general and as applied to the classroom, see Tad Guzie's *The Analogy of Learning* (New York, Sheed and Ward, 1960), especially pp. 174–84, 192–99.

PERCEPTION AND CONCEPTION IN EDUCATION*

Frank C. Wegener

Immanuel Kant said that percepts without concepts are blind and that concepts without percepts are empty. The implications of this statement are very important for a well-balanced philosophy of education. In recent times there has been a steady development of the empirical point of view in modern thought and modern education. From the time of John Locke's enunciation of the "tabula rasa" theory and his denunciation of the doctrine of innate ideas, empiricism has exerted a tremendous influence on our thinking. The many diverse ramifications which followed British empiricism in terms of schools of thought need not be outlined here. But it should be noted that much of the educational theory dominant today tacitly assumes the Lockean rejection of a priori or innate ideas. Or putting it more positively Dr. Meiklejohn has suggested that "Down with the a priori!" has become one of the war cries of modern pragmatism. Educationally such an assumption places all of our educational theory and practice upon a strictly empirical base. The assumption begs one of the most challenging issues ever faced by man in philosophy—the question of how we know. It castigates the rational theory of knowledge without examination or consideration. In effect it places almost the entire emphasis of educational procedure upon a perceptual type of education. This observation brings us back to the statement made by Kant concerning the relative importance of percepts and concepts.

The consideration of the meaning of this statement implies that educators should be cognizant of the implications of epistemology, or the study of theories of knowledge. . . . They must, for example, consider the arguments both for and against empiricism and rationalism, rather than accept either blindly.

As a case in point let us consider some of the implications

* Reprinted from "Perception and Conception in Education," *School and Society,* 70(July 16, 1949), 37–39. By permission of the editor of *School and Society.*

which might be contained in Kant's observation concerning percepts and concepts. In the first place, Kant himself did not accept either empiricism or rationalism wholeheartedly. He is well known in the history of philosophy for his noble attempt to reconcile or integrate the long conflict between the arguments for empiricism and those for rationalism. In his monumental work, "The Critique of Pure Reason," Kant addressed himself to the problem of relating synthetic judgments of reason to the empirical data of sense. It was Kant who certainly asserted the subjective existence of the a priori and the categories of human thought. The chaotic world of sense data receives its meaning and orderly relationship from the conceiving mind which is equipped with the a priori categories and makes intelligible experience possible.

Educationally speaking, the historical emphasis upon perceptual or conceptual learning leads inevitably to error. Conceptual education without the substance of perception degenerates into a mere verbalism, if one is not careful. Perceptual education without arriving at conceptual judgments fails to utilize that which is most important in human capacity. Perceptual learning is that awareness of the external existence of objects such as chairs, trees, persons, houses, and the phenomenal world about us. Perceptions may vary from the extreme of animal awareness of a "something" which exists to a human apprehension or recognition that it is this or that. Perception is to be distinguished from the higher aspects of ideational thinking such as imagination, judgments, remembrance, and conception. One may function on an animal level of perception without any very great degree of conceptual insight. One may be perceptually aware of "water" as desirable without the rational conception of H_2O. The teaching of the abstract symbols representing chemical formulae without the perceptions of sense data would no doubt be very sterile and unprofitable. Such a process might well approach the memorization of nonsensical letter arrangements. On the other hand, mere dabbling with particular chemicals without formal identification and representation in terms of proportions and relationships might be almost equally unprofitable.

What are the educational implications? Foremost, teachers

should not slight either the empirical or the rational aspects of the learning process. Every unit of study should have its essential concepts and percepts. In other words, every unit must be seen in the light of the generalizations, principles, and concepts which are to be abstracted from the learning experiences and are rooted in firsthand observations, vicarious learnings, audio-visual experiences with aids, and particular experiences. The teacher who slights either one of these phases does a poor job. Of course, it is to be expected that students will vary considerably in their ability to generalize and achieve conceptual understanding. But the principle still remains the same as to a proper proportion of the perceptual and the conceptual.

Still more important is the implication that we should not overlook the all-important place of *form* in education. Learning certainly involves structuring and seeing relationships. This matter of "seeing" relationships may properly be taken in both the physical and mental sense. One may be able to "see" a right triangle in his mind's eye as an image, and he may also be able to "see" the right triangle mentally inasmuch as he understands the geometric principles involved in any right triangle. Thus *forms* in the learning process have both a sensible and a rational meaning. Both are essential.

Form is more evident in some subjects such as mathematics, logic, grammar, and the sciences and the arts. Realistically, these forms are in a sense external to the learner. These same forms have been discovered by the experiences and thinking of mankind. They represent the symbolic representations of relationships which are meant to facilitate human thought and action. As represented in mathematics, logic, science, and grammar, these forms are not merely the arbitrary expressions of man; they are the necessary manifestations of inherent real relationships.

Unfortunately, it appears that the strictly formal relationships have been stressed by formalists in education. They have too often neglected the material and sensible aspects of reality. Now we must not err on the side of being overly engrossed in the sensible and the material. Rather in the structuring of human thinking and understanding it is important that we attach adequate emphasis to both the material and formal aspects of the content of learning. . . .

In our enthusiasm to make schools "lifelike" and "purposive" and "real" have we not neglected the essential *forms* of understanding? In our conservative schools have we not neglected "activity," "participation," "firsthand learning experiences," in our desire to give youngsters the essential forms and principles of learning?

ON THE ORGANIC LOGIC OF TEACHING AND LEARNING*

G. K. Plochmann

One finds, upon reading many of the great philosophers, that they are wont to stress the links between logic and the theory of teaching. Plato, Aristotle, St. Augustine, Descartes, Spinoza, Kant, Dewey, and many others all indicate that teaching has foundations in logic, that there would be no teaching whatever if knowledge were without a logical structure. Yet the progress of psychology since the days of Immanuel Kant has impressed many of the leading philosophers with the importance of the conative, the emotive, and the circumstantial in their bearings upon teaching and learning. Not one of the older philosophers is content with the notion, so often found in our moderns, that teaching is primarily a question of motivation, stimulation, and appeal. One associates the name of John Dewey with this view, and, although this is not quite right, still the doctrine has gained such currency attached to his name, and the practice of teaching as permissive and environmental has become so widespread, that the hour seems ripe when, in the name of logic and epistemology, we should attack the theory and the practice.

In the logic of instruction—"instruction" being the word I shall take to comprise both the teacher's role and the learner's role in the process—in this logic we are not particularly interested in whether the student sees or hears or whether he is confronted with words or symbols, diagrams or objects. Nor does the logic of instruction deal with the question of personal dogma: one may teach something in which one does not personally believe or hold as an article of faith, though it is true that one must be epistemically content with it and know that it fits with other propositions capable of being known or at least believed by *someone*. But if speaking or writing, believing or disbelieving, are not quite germane, there is still a host of

* Reprinted from "On the Organic Logic of Teaching and Learning," *Journal of General Education*, 12(April, 1959), 119–24. By permission of the editor of the *Journal of General Education*.

considerations interesting to the logician, and these also lie at the bottom of every analysis of knowledge, no matter how one eventually becomes committed to possible answers to the questions. The logic of teaching is therefore not talk about the devices of teaching merely: it is the theory of teaching and learning knowledge; it is the theory of the transmissibility of knowledge.

This being so, the differences between instruction on the lower levels of mental development and the higher are not differences in the dilution or enrichment of logic but rather differences in the means by which the logic of the subject matter can be immediately made clear and, of course, differences in the choice of the subject matter itself. There is implicit in the teaching of the unprepared mind precisely the same structure of knowledge as there is in the most sophisticated; and in consequence every teacher, insofar as he is a teacher, possesses logic. If it be true that each subject matter occupies two places at once in the teaching-learning situation—the absolute or epistemic position and the relative or pedagogic one—then it is the latter that varies, not the former. Whatever the devices by which one mind undertakes to instruct another, the knowledge transmitted undergoes no alteration with the adding of protest, cajolery, etc. Pedagogy dictates whether a teacher should turn syllogisms into enthymemes, whether to use a progressive or a regressive method of exposition, whether to use symbols or words; whereas the epistemic considerations take one to the basic questions of logic—what a universal concept is, whether all judging is the same as conceiving, whether a *modus ponens* is a genuine inference, whether all science starts from arbitrary hypotheses. But I cannot allow that, if you had merely satisfied yourself upon these difficult questions, you would thereby have divested yourself of all responsibility to make an additional examination of teaching and learning in the light of your plural satisfactions. There is more to it, something over and above the confines of orthodox logical theory and something which may, paradoxically, reflect a small, thin ray of light back upon the doctrines of logicians, whichever they may be.

An old word for teacher was "magister," and this stood as well for "master"—"master" in the sense of someone who has mastered every significant part of his subject matter. There is some little difference between the two functions, for the master may not be an effective teacher and the teacher may instruct in important branches of the subject without having mastered the balance of it. Let us say that the master should be characterized, in the breadth of his grasp, by a superlative, the teacher by a comparative. If the teacher is a master as well, so much the better; but it is surely foolish to assume that one must know virtually all mathematics or politics in order to be able to transmit anything. My distinction also helps us with the fact that, even though the teacher when teaching is not learning, strictly, nevertheless the teacher can and generally does learn most while he is at the same time teaching—a well-recognized fact; but if he were to learn what he already knew or teach what he did not already know, the awkward paradoxes of the *Meno* and *Euthydemus* would result. But this is not to introduce a hierarchy, with the master leading the teacher, the teacher leading the learner; a dog-leg course takes us from the first to the third.

Let us reflect upon the equality of the preparation of the minds in an instructional situation. In this there are two possibilities to be considered: one where the two parties are unequal and one where they are equal in point of knowledge. Instruction takes place between unequals; discussion between equals. The terms "equal" and "unequal" do not refer to grasp of knowledge in different fields but to grasp within the same field. Equality of this kind is not often found, and what really takes place most frequently, even among experts, is instruction of a rather fragmentary sort. I say "fragmentary" because experts almost never permit themselves to enjoy the methodical co-operative study of subject matters found in a common university course—a bare minimum, almost. At any rate, the teacher endeavors, with respect to his subject matter, to bring the understanding of the learner to equality with his own understanding. This adequation is the fundamental idea of all teaching, all learning, and it implies much more than ordinary harmony or adjustment. The adequation of teacher and learner exists when there is common grasp of terms, propositions, arguments, sciences, and, finally, systems. The rest of my paper will explore this contention.

The ultimate end of teaching—the last goal—is the teaching of "system." This is the communication of knowledge in which many representative sciences are interlinked, in which there is a parceling-out of principles—some regnant over all the sciences, some over one or a few—and in which knowledge is expanded consistently to the fullest limit possible to the knowing mind. Properly, this enlarges the learner's mind, to use Conrad's phrase, and is desirable for its own sake; but, incidentally, it may do great damage where the learner is unable to go beyond this instruction to the exploring of new problems of his own discovery. However, putting this aside, I think we should agree that the teaching and the learning are for this final purpose. Step by dialectical step, this consists of three preliminary phases: first, the grasp of concepts or terms, universals, is for the sake of knowing whether propositions are true; second, the decision regarding each proposition is required for the sake of determining the validity of an argument relating supposedly true premises and conclusions; third, this determination in turn throws light upon the identification of warranties in the sciences, warranties which are true axioms or perspicuous definitions, and the selection of the most valuable consecutants of these warranties. As such, the teacher cannot teach isolated terms, random sentences (whether they be true or false), and disconnected arguments. I will allow that he *can* teach individual sciences; indeed, in view of limitations of human mastery, it is well that he should confine himself to such teaching, but in the main he should teach also with the aim of showing the co-ordination of sciences. . . .

We might say, then, that what is teachable per se is the science, or, better still, the system, and what is personally easier to communicate is pieces of the science, the subordinate elements, of which the science is the integral unity. The whole is inherently the most teachable thing, because in a system and to a lesser extent in a science the terms are more certain of receiving univocal meanings, the propositions are ultimately provided with standards by which they may be judged determinately true, and the arguments receive their validity not from the constitutive rules of syllogistic figure or of hypothetical inference but rather by epistemic tests of the analytic and synthetic truth of their premises. Meaning is not a function of the whole, truth is not a function of anything higher in complexity than the proposition, and validity refers exclusively to argument; nevertheless, these are all rendered explicit and final when the whole is presented. For instance, I do not know how to make the word "man" univocal except by using other words with it, say, "woman," "living," "animal," "species," or the like, although it is still the sense of "man" that is at issue; but to fix upon one definition for the word "man" would involve making univocal all the adjacent words, and this ultimately builds into a science and a system. The same remarks apply with equal force to propositions and arguments, only here the difficulty of being sure that the student comprehends is increased by the fact that, although he can perceive almost immediately whether he understands words as terms, the truth of a statement requires many checks upon it, and the settling of the validity of an argument is often a fairly technical matter. But, in spite of this, the three are on the same logical footing. The teacher is the person whose meanings (assigned to the words he uses) determine the meanings of the learner. At the juncture when there is common understanding—that is, when the words at last become unambiguous terms—transmission of knowledge in the form of propositions, arguments, and science is rendered possible. Univocation, of course, applies primarily to the fact that the meaning given within the mind of one person is proper, precise, and relates one term with one kind of thing only, not with several kinds; but secondarily it signifies as well that two persons can understand the same thing by a single term. Strictly speaking, then, if a teacher has assigned one unambiguous meaning for a term and the learner has (perhaps unwittingly) tried to assign another, then instruction-wise there is no univocation at all, and the discourse must be readjusted until agreement is reached. This implies, too, that the utterance by the teacher of terms intended to be univocal does not of itself constitute all of teaching. A teacher who on the logical level is misunderstood, even if it be the hearer's fault, is not acting as a teacher in the fullest sense of the term. There are riders to this remark, but this rough approximation will do here. Knowledge is not induced per se by the *chance* of agreement between two minds, although it is true, of course, that propositions which throw light upon other propositions—terms that illuminate the meanings of other terms—are heard by chance even when a teacher's main drift is misapprehended or ignored.

You may object here that I have used science and the elements of science, not the arts, as the chief instances of the instructional process; and this I have done, for the teaching of science is the primary type of teaching because of its inner logical structure—the truth being that the structure of science can be fully actualized and *all* of science rendered explicit, statable, communicable. Some of the effect of art is based upon the suppression of parts, and much of its creation is based upon native taste and feeling. But I do allow that, insofar as art can be made statable, insofar as its rules can be brought, so to speak, to the surface, my remarks about teaching apply to it as well as to science. I really intend my remarks to be general, then, in their scope. But I insist that they be taken as referring only to the structure of that which is taught, for otherwise they are frivolous and wrong. Thus, while the temporal orders of speaking and of hearing are the same and move in parallel straight lines, the temporal order of understanding what a teacher is trying to communicate is less simple, and the learner's coming to know univocal terms from the discourse of the teacher is contrapuntal.

You may also object that to teach a system or even a science is biologically impossible—it would take infinite time. We do not wish to teach the whole, you say; we teach the pupil to *make* this totality by his own efforts. This I grant, but you must allow that the teacher teaches the parts in the most nearly integrated form at his command, with the suggestion not only *that* there is a totality but *what* that totality is at every stage of his instruction. The good teacher has a system which is full of blank spaces, at best; but this is because of his common human weakness, not because he is unprepared, whereas, of course, the learner's faintly outlined system has lacunae potentially remediable by reference to the more complete knowledge of the teacher. For this reason, teaching is at once the most human and the least human of occupations: the able teacher develops and enlarges the mentality of another human soul, but he also keeps the learner's opinions, his talents, and his deficiencies well in the background—I am talking logic now, not the pedagogy which must be allowed, as occasion requires, to supersede the logical considerations—because it is the whole science and system constituting the subject matter to which he owes his greatest debt.

Properly, then, the central and peripheral in what is taught should be the same as the central and peripheral in what is learned, although teaching and learning can go on, in a reduced way, when these do not exactly coincide. The teacher reasons from premises, and the terms of these almost certainly mean something to the learner because of chance associations of ideas in his mind, i.e., former experiences. His associations being different; his reasoning processes taking rise from these will be divergent from those of the teacher, unless the latter can in some fashion cut through the chance associations based upon this or that experience and memory and force a selection to take place in the learner's mind which will bring the remaining associations into line with the meaning he intends. In the order of time, experience and memory are prior to a common grasp of univocal terms; in the order of understanding, experiences and memories are merely raw materials out of which the able teacher fashions scientific knowledge. The teacher uses experience as a way of reaching the intellectual levels of the learner's mind. Experience is not a teacher, because experience, with its randomness of impressions, is limitless and is therefore peculiar to one mind—the mind of the teacher or that of the learner. What has infinite variety cannot be reproduced because it does not receive a form, cannot be made to pass from mind to mind. Science is teachable only insofar as it is ordered, limited, and restricted. The form is what is common.

However, it seems true that thinking can be prepared *out of* experiences and, furthermore, that thinking is a predisposition, almost as surely as a precondition, *for* experiences. But this is equivocating, of course, on the idea of sequence in these two cases: thinking is not the raw matter of experience but the informing light of experience, and, while it predisposes us to *seek* further experience, perhaps in order to verify some thought not yet determinately true in our system, still it does nothing more than that. . . .

To sum up this point, then, associated ideas which have only a material and accidental relation to each other and not a strictly logical relation are sorted out, and those allowed to remain as relevant are elucidated and rendered as universals in the mind of the learner. Thus proper teaching involves the suggesting, by visual devices, experiments, or verbal examples, of the individuals falling under the universals to be communicated, in case the experience of the learner is lacking in familiarity with such individuals. Only in unusual cases have the experiences of the teacher and the learner antecedently been the same, and hence these autoptic devices are necessary. But if the teacher is able and the learner acute, then the teacher can *e*duce generic concepts and principles out of his own experience and transmit them to the learner in substantially the same form, and this process is the *in*ducing of knowledge. It is not *produced;* indeed, it would mean nothing to say that knowledge transmitted is at the same time produced. It is *induced,* and this carries with it the notion of rational inference in both parties. Both teacher and learner are active, though in different ways, and the learner is passive with respect to the teacher alone, as the beloved is with respect to the lover. But, indeed, the learner, like the beloved, must bring every resource to bear. If instruction proceeded by mere association of ideas or if it were wholly intellectual, that is, if the inference had a constitutive aspect only, then my present analysis would be unnecessary, and I dare say that teachers would be out of their jobs.

Because we enjoy activity, as learners we enjoy most, all other things being equal, those instructional situations in which we are made most nearly active by the teacher. The moment of learning is the moment of becoming clear about the connections within our experiences and the connections between the concepts which are made to grow out of them. The implications of the multitudinous consecutants of the principles which can be stated when universal terms are joined are what we find most fruitful. Hence good teaching is a balance between filling implicative gaps in the learner's reasoning and creating gaps, not by removing knowledge already present but by transmitting suggestive fragments of new knowledge. The fragments are, however, as I have already indicated at length, not random ones, any more than the skeleton, while but a part of the human body, is an unordered collection. So we often say that good teaching may not furnish this or that particular principle, because it may not be concerned with the parts of the subject matter at hand; but teaching exhibits the *method* by which the subject matter should be surveyed. This is a half-truth, because the concepts and terms must go hand in hand with the method and are, in fact, only analytically separable from the method.

The teacher, then, brings to the learner's attention either connections of concepts or the need for these connections. If they coincide with what the learner has formerly vaguely thought, the concepts appear to be the learner's own; and, in this sense, any artist or scientist or man of wide experience and understanding with whom the learner is in accord is a teacher, although by no means a deliberate and habitual one. If the concepts are not like those heretofore entertained by the learner, then the teacher seems instead to have introduced knowledge to the learner. But, in actual truth, this is a very trifling distinction; what is more significant is that the teacher brings to actuality the knowledge latent in the learner and, in so doing, actualizes the learner as well. For, without the teacher, the learner is more completely passive, and without activity— the characteristic activity of learning—the learner is something else—a refractory adolescent, perhaps, or a charming young girl, or a muddled businessman, or another teacher on a holiday.

We have spoken of knowledge and its transmission, which is like the ingestion of proteins: one can be fed them whole but they must be broken down and resynthesized in order to be transformed into assimilable materials, and even then not all the original material is used, although the new flesh is as completely organized as the old. To say that we teach the whole is, when taken without qualification, just as untrue as to say we cannot possibly teach the whole. This transmission is made possible because, although knowledge has a structure, a very distinct form, nevertheless that structure is not utterly destroyed by being dismantled and then reassembled. Understandably, if one of the parts of a science is not rebuilt by the learner, the knowledge eventually readjusts itself so that the gap is filled; and presently, any false newcomer into the science is altered, by the process of *elenchus,* until it comes to have the function of the old. Logic shows that knowledge is transmissible, not to this or that mind, but to any mind in general, and this it does by showing that the *elements* of knowledge are transmissible insofar as they can be verbalized or symbolized. Terms and propositions and arguments can be made to retain single definite meanings as they pass from one person to another. Also, logic asserts the transmissibility of knowledge when it says that the elements can be put together again in sciences and systems. Now sciences and systems are not themselves directly symbolized: only their parts are, but that is sufficient. The purpose of instruction is not augmented experience, but cognition through parts, of the whole. To teach is to make the parts that are warranties in the whole, together with their consecutants, relevant to a subject matter that is through and through the object of our experiences, fully known and explicit in the mind of the learner, who is by his actual experience and his potential understanding prepared to know.

THE ROLE OF THE TEACHER IN PROGRESSIVE EDUCATION *

Joseph J. Schwab

The new education proposed by Dewey differed fundamentally from common theory and practice. Its aims and methods took their meaning from a new view of intelligence or inquiry: a new conception of knowledge, of knowing and of that which is known. Thus his doctrine was, in two ways, something more than a theory of education. In the first place, it was not about education taken as something apart. It was about knowing, knowledge, and the known. Because of the view it took of these matters, it was also about human action and communication and human goods. In the second place, it was not a theory in the received meaning of the term. Its aim was not to explain and provide settled "understanding" but to persuade its readers to embark upon a practice.

This aim was inherent to the very view of knowledge which it proposed. For Dewey, any theory of practice, including his, finds its full meaning only as it is put into practice and gains its "verification" only as it is tested there. A theory includes a body of "logical forms," conceptions designed to embrace and relate to one another all the facts in a problematic situation which are seen as relevant to its resolution. These logical forms take part of their meaning from the facts they are designed to hold, and another part from what they do to the facts by way of making them signify actions to be taken. Hence, the theory cannot be understood until the facts are experienced in the form given them by the organizing conceptions of the theory; and "experienced" means that they must be seen and felt and that the actions they signify must be undertaken.

Further, the theory is "verified" only by such an undertaking, for a theory is good to the extent that it does take account of all the pregnant facts and leads to actions which resolve the prob-

* Reprinted from "The 'Impossible' Role of the Teacher in Progressive Education," *The School Review*, 67(Summer, 1959), 142–43, 147–55, 158–59. By permission of the University of Chicago Press. Copyright 1959 by the University of Chicago.

lem to the satisfaction of those who are caught up in it. Hence, the problem of pragmatic rhetoric is to move men to an informed and reflected practice.

Now, it must be remembered that this view of knowledge plays two roles. In part it is the conception of education which Dewey hopes to convey. At the same time, it represents to him the way it must be conveyed. Remember too, that it is a wholly novel view of meaning and of truth. To this day, it remains far from being generally understood. If these three points now be joined, something very like a paradox emerges.

Dewey seeks to persuade men to teach a mode of learning and knowing which they themselves do not know and which they cannot grasp by their habitual ways of learning. . . .

The significance to education of pragmatic rhetoric is twofold —corresponding to the two roles which the rhetoric plays for Dewey. As part of a conception of education, it becomes part of the meaning of "learning by doing." What one learns is considerably more than habits, attitudes, precepts and doctrines presently true and useful. These, yes. But they are only the first order of learning. Each such instance of first-order mastery is, in addition, the occasion for a learning of a second order, a learning of what it is to learn. And learning, for Dewey, is active participation in the pragmatic rhetoric—the recovery and test of meaning. Hence, the effective "learning situation" is not the one which leads by the quickest, most comfortable route to mastered habit and attitude, used precept and applied knowledge, but the one which is provocative of reflection, experiment, and revision.

As the means by which Dewey hoped to convey his view of education, pragmatic rhetoric points to the fact that Dewey's evangelists rendered him a poor service when they interposed between him and the teacher a series of deceiving simplicities which purported to contain the "new" view of education. This point applies to the present as well as the past. If teachers are effectively to guide their students through and to the exercise of intelligence, they cannot, themselves, be unreflective. The teachers college and the administrative structure of the school cannot afford, therefore, to repeat the error of the epitomists, to provide their teachers with fixed techniques, content to be learned by rote, and imposed curriculums. Teacher training ought, in some measure, to become teacher education despite the pressure of an expanding population. It ought to exhibit the material which their students will teach as matter for reflection rather than as matter for docile mastery. It ought to exhibit proposed ends and methods of instruction in some of their difficult, tangled, and doubtful connection with the imperfect and incomplete researches on society, the learning process, human personality, and similar topics, from which they stem. The schools, in turn, ought to be so organized that at least some of their capable and energetic teachers find in the classroom and in each other the opportunity to reflect on ends and methods and try alternatives which experience and reflection suggest.

Luckily, Dewey's influence penetrated areas other than education. He laid the ground for dynamic theories of personality. His criticism of the rigid Pavlovian notions of conditioning modified research into learning and thereby affected our views of human intelligence and its operation. His conception of human association influenced many sociologists and, through the results of their researches, modified the very social structure in which we live. By these means, Dewey created a learning situation much broader than the classroom. Out of that situation, many American scholars, including some educators, have moved into the region of pragmatic intelligence. Let us look now at the scope and character of that space.

Dewey's problem in constructing that space was to rejoin what decadent memories of ancient philosophies had struck apart, to re-establish circuits through which divisions of human thought and interest could find each other. There were the urgencies of human needs, the "practical," left, in their isolation from science and scholarship, to seek each its own means to satisfaction with indifference to the farther future and with frightened inattention to the consequences of taken actions on areas of other needs. There were the fields of science and scholarship, enjoying an integral character which the practical lacked but preoccupied each with the intricate relations among its own conceptions and growing sterile from lack of contact with the arena of human needs and with each other. There was the area of value—of duty and enjoyment—treated as something opposing or beyond the condition of man and the circumstances of existence. There was the area of fact treated as ultimately unresponsive to man's wishes and irrelevant to his highest aspirations.

Pragmatic Intellectual Space is Dewey's solution to these problems. The solution is remarkable in that these divided factors are placed in communication with one another without sacrificing the special character of each one. Science and scholarship retain their integrations; the practical, its competence to cope with urgency. Art and aspiration continue to look beyond the present and the presently possible. The anchoring recalcitrance of fact is not denied. But while each retains its special advantage, each can repair its lack by connection with the others. Science finds refreshment and new impetus in problems posed it by the practical. The practical finds organization of means and consequences and refinement of its aims in science. Art and aspiration find test, support, and material for realization in the world of fact and of the practical. Facts are made more pliable by science and placed in the service of art and the practical.

These connections are achieved by discerning new guiding patterns and outcomes for the exercise of intelligence, replacing the older ones. In older guiding views, for example, science consisted in the pursuit of one or another eternal stability: irreducible elements of which the world was supposed to be composed; or the ultimate formal patterns which organized each subject matter; or the system of natural classes to which each natural thing belonged. The very universality and ultimacy of these directive notions was what cut science off from the practical. Similar directives walled off art from "life" and ethics from ordinary affairs.

We can catch a glimpse of Dewey's revised channels of intelligence by examining briefly the topography of pragmatic intellectual space with special reference to theory and practice, science and daily problems.

The (literally) fundamental differentiation of pragmatic space from other views of intelligence lies in the discard of the notion of brute and given fact observed. The doubtful notion that facts are seen "objectively," without reference to the seeing thing, is replaced by the notion of "situation." The primitive intelligent act is apprehension of need, requirement, imbalance, in one's relation to surrounding circumstance. From apprehension of imbalance we move to specification of it—what there is about us and circumstance which is teetering, open, needful: we locate the problem which the situation poses. The process moves to its climax when we find a way of acting which promises to restore balance in the situation—a way to solve our problem. The process is completed when we master the pattern of action which does, in fact, resolve the problem by creating a satisfactory state of affairs.

If we look closely at this idea we can see what replaces "brute" fact and plants the germ of an integration of theory and practice. There is a primitive knowing here—a forecast of science. There is a primitive practicality—the resolution of an imbalance involving us. And the two are closely joined. What we know is not facts *sub specie aeterni,* but facts as parts of a practical problem and as means to its solution. In the opposite direction, what we achieve is not merely satisfaction of a need but a new condition in the world around us, an experiment, if you please, which will evoke new situations posing new problems which will present new facts for us to know.

The first level of pragmatic space is, then, a mastered pattern of action to an end. But, says Dewey, this is an artifact, an abstraction. No single pattern of action to an end exists alone —even in animals "lower" than man. No two situations are precisely alike; single, rigid patterns of action will not continue to master situations. So a second level must intervene before we can reach the level of reflection. At this level, we achieve, for each kind of problem and situation, flexible ways of acting, modified steps and alternative sequences designed to meet the flux of materials and events.

This state of affairs is a marked improvement; it is intelligent. But it is not yet reflective; we have not reflexed, looked back. On the side of means, we have not yet noted why certain actions were effective, others not. On the side of aims, we have not yet compared them with one another. We are *too* responsive to the flux of materials and events; too little its master.

The third level of pragmatic space—the first level in which reflection appears—fills this gap. At this level, we take note of

connections between different things done and different resulting consequences. Thus we compile a catalogue of means to
ends, a body of practical knowledge. Then we look to connections among differing consequences and the differing satisfactions which ensue, yielding knowledge of wants and their objects
—what there is that satisfies and in what degree. Thus reflection
provides us with tested means by which to meet similar situations in the future and with alternative aims by which to guide
the use we make of these situations. We become good, practical
animals.

This sort of practical knowledge suffices for some parts of
some lives, but it is too much chained to the past to anticipate
adequately the changing future. It is reflection on past means
and ends. It can serve to anticipate only such futures as are
notable in the past; but there is reason to be sure that the future
will pose problems markedly different. We have ourselves set in
train events which will change them. Each resolution of a past
situation has been successful because it changed something.
Very often, the change is small, and what follows from it is
equally small. But some solutions to problems are far-reaching
in their effects. . . . And while these changes take place on the
circumstantial side of situations, the other side—ourselves—
changes too. By the act of solving problems and by living with
their solutions, we alter ourselves. Our competence is enhanced,
and our wants are changed. When problems of mere survival are
overcome, we look for comfort. When this is found, we uncover
higher aspirations. From being satisfied with outcomes of our
acts, we turn to pleasure in the act well done; from being
satisfied with other men as henchmen, we look for men as
friends. So, in respect of both ends and means, the future poses
problems which may differ radically from those of the past.

If this condition is to be met, the pursuit of knowledge must
race ahead of practical problems posed and do without their aid.
It must be unchained from past experience, even from the
present. It must go on "for its own sake," for the future. This
process is the birth of the sciences—those which concern ourselves as well as those concerned with the surrounding world.
We now arrive at the fourth level.

We already have the makings of a modest science in the

form of known means to ends. But the linkage of each bit of knowledge as a means to an end is the chain to the past. It makes a catalogue of our knowledge which can be enhanced only as new problems permit us to discover new means. What we need is a way in which knowledge of means alone will point to sources for new knowledge. This is achieved when we disconnect each means from its end and invent a new form of organization which binds our bits together as coherent knowledge of some extensive part or aspect of the world. Where we knew before, for example, that heat hardens clay and eggs but softens meat, we are now to forget about dishes and stews and concern ourselves with heat and with the structure and states of matter. Thus we transform knowledge from knowledge of means to tentative knowledge of the world.

This reorganization, remember, is not invented to give more practically useful structure to what we already know but to point to new things to know and new ways of disclosing knowledge. There is a dual significance to this function of scientific structure. In the first place, it means that the organization is still instrumental (not "real" or ultimate or "true") as was knowledge when organized as means. Only, the end has changed, and the instrument is a new instrument. The end is knowledge, the instrument is an instrument of inquiry. It is designed to show us how to create problems deliberately instead of waiting on them and how to create just those problems which will create new experiences to enlarge our body of knowledge. This is the activity of experiment and research.

To say that scientific knowledge is organized instrumentally is also to suggest the second significant point: that its organizing forms (atoms, electrons, wave-motion, reflex arcs, cultures, civilizations) are not the forms of things, an ultimate or "true" picture of a static world, but the forms which serve us well, in the present state of our knowledge, as means for pursuing more knowledge. In consequence, the forms will change. As they succeed, they change the state of our knowledge. New forms become necessary as the potential of the old ones is exhausted. So science, like practical knowledge, is fluid and dynamic.

This last fact has explosive meaning for the conduct of the school. It points to the pervasive place of reflection in all educative experience. The pervasive dynamism of things and knowledge, practical and theoretical, means that at no level of pragmatic space can education rest on inculcation only. There are no dependable patterns of reaction, no permanent catalogue of means and ends, not even a permanent body of scientific knowledge, which, once known, can be the unreflective basis of all other action and reflection. We need to reflect on our acts in the light of knowledge of means and ends and to reflect on this knowledge in the light of what science has to offer.

But this reflective motion downward from above is only half the story. Since scientific knowledge is couched in terms corresponding neither to "reality" nor to immediate human needs, we need to reflect on the relations of its conclusions to its forms and evidence in order even to know what it is about. Its conclusions make sense only in the light of the way they were formed. And the *use* of the conclusions presupposes reflection which transforms both the forms of scientific thought and the requirements of felt problems so that the two can be brought together.

Mirroring these needs, pragmatic intellectual space supposes two sets of reflective motions. There are, first, the motions which make each level: the trying-out which yields patterns of effective action; the cataloguing which yields knowledge of means and ends; the inquiring which yields science. But these cannot go on (or, if pursued, be completed) without reflection that oscillates between each level and the others. Seeing problems in the practical freshens the forms of inquiry; seeing practical possibilities in the structure of scientific knowledge enhances the life of everyday. These are the dynamics which link the levels to one another and enable them to serve their function in the system.

With the fifth and sixth levels of pragmatic space we shall deal very briefly. The pursuit of new scientific knowledge is guided by the organization with which we structured the old. This structure, embodied in such "theoretic" concepts as atom and electron, organ and organism, culture and civilization, cause and kind, creates and constrains the methods of science. The effectiveness of each science is thus determined or limited by the adequacy of its forming concepts. These may be more or less effective for the purposes of inquiry. But effective as they may be at any given time, they may reach the end of their usefulness, require refreshment or replacement. Hence, there must be reflection on the means and ends involved in the discovery of knowledge, a reflection that judges and measures. This is the level called Logic.

Finally, there must be an activity of supremely creative reflection, a process dedicated to the invention of new concepts, new logical forms by which to restructure knowledge and guide its increase. This is the level of Mathematics.

Let us summarize the scope of pragmatic intellectual space in the diagram in Figure 1. This diagram omits two extremely important matters. One is the place of art. The other is the dimension of human association and communication. Perhaps also there is a seventh discipline, "Critic," combining logic and mathematics and applying to the entire space. This would be the discipline used by Dewey himself.

We turn now from knowledge and knowing to what is known —to the subject matter of reflection. Of the three factors we shall have discussed, this one is the simplest. It may be put bluntly thus: no dependable, anticipatory judgment can tell us that *one* of the terms into which a problem can be analyzed is its first, most proper, or only principle. *All* the terms that men severally have recognized should be considered as relevant, interacting factors. Reflection is the better as it puts together what other men have put asunder.

. . . What, then, is the "impossible" role of the teacher in a progressive school and curriculum?

It consists, first, in the fact that the teacher must be a learner —even unto the fourth level of Dewey's intellectual space. It is not enough for the teacher to master certain ways of acting as a teacher. This is only a capable apprentice. It is not enough to be master of flexible ways of acting. This is only to be a competent "hand" who can function well when told what to do but who cannot himself administer. It is not even enough to possess organized knowledge of ways and means. This is to interpret a policy and tend to its efficient execution but not to be able to improve a policy or change it as problems change.

Only as the teacher uses the classroom as the occasion and the means to reflect upon education as a whole (ends as well as

The Dynamics	The Activity	The Outcome	The Name
5th	Reflection on knowledge of discovery	Invention of means and ends of discovery	Mathematics*
	Reflection on the conduct of discovery	Critical knowledge of scientific method	Logic
4th	Reflection on ends and means; deliberate pursuit of experience	Knowledge organized for pursuit of further knowledge	Science, including the Social
3rd	Reflection on actions and consequences	Knowledge organized as tested ends and means	Technics; Practical Ethics
2nd	Sensitive mastery of variable problematic situations	Flexible ways of acting in each such situation	Flexible habit; Artfulness
1st	Mastery of problematic situations	A way of acting in each such situation	Mere habit

* "Mathematics," as used here, covers more than the number system, algebra, and geometry taught in schools. It includes all invention of formal devices and relations.

FIG. 1.—The levels and dynamics of pragmatic intellectual space

means), as the laboratory in which to translate reflections into actions and thus to test reflections, actions, and outcomes against many criteria, is he a good "progressive" teacher.

Meanwhile, he must be a teacher too. As a teacher, he must aim to carry all his students to the third dynamic of intellectual space, some to the fourth, and be alert to find those few who may go still farther. To aim for less than the third is to fail to test the possibility of a democratic society, to capitulate to the notion of Mass and Class—the latter managerial and manipulative; the former, managed servants, unaware.

THE DISCIPLINE IN DEWEY'S THEORY OF INQUIRY*

Dorothy J. Newbury

A search for a theory of discipline in Dewey's theory of growth leads one to think of discipline as synonymous with inquiry. The theory of inquiry, then, should give us insights into classroom discipline problems. To spell out such a theory of discipline from *Logic: The Theory of Inquiry* [1] is our present purpose: "The remedy for the evils attending the doctrine of formal discipline previously spoken of, is not to be found by substituting a doctrine of specialized disciplines, but by reforming the notion of mind and its training." [2]

Dewey rejects the old conception of mind as independent, isolated, "spiritual":

> Too frequently mind is set over the world of things and facts to be known; it is regarded as something existing in isolation, with mental states and operations that exist independently. Knowledge is then regarded as an external application of purely mental existences to the things to be known, or else as a result of the impressions which this outside subject-matter makes on mind, or as a combination of the two. Subject-matter is then regarded as something complete in itself; it is just something to be learned or known, either by the voluntary application of mind to it or through the impressions it makes on mind. [3]

These conceptions, says Dewey, "are mythical."

Mind is not something complete in itself. "It is a name for a course of action intelligently directed." [4] "Conceive mind as anything but one factor partaking along with others in production of consequences and it becomes meaningless." [5]

* Reprinted from "A Theory of Discipline Derived from Dewey's Theory of Inquiry," *Educational Theory,* 7(April, 1957), 102–11. By permission of the author and the editor of *Educational Theory.*

[1] John Dewey, *Logic: The Theory of Inquiry* (New York, Henry Holt and Company, 1938).

[2] John Dewey, *Democracy and Education* (New York, Macmillan Company, 1920), p. 155.

[3] *Ibid.,* p. 153.

[4] *Ibid.,* p. 155.

[5] *Ibid.*

These points in regard to the nature of mind Dewey says are demonstrated by the "facts of interest." [6]. . .

If "mind is a course of action intelligently directed," thinking is the process by which it is carried out. We have already defined discipline as the same thing. "Thinking *is* the method of intelligent learning, or learning that employs and rewards mind. We speak, legitimately enough, about the method of thinking, but the important thing to bear in mind about method is that thinking is method, the method of intelligent experience in the course which it takes." [7] Our investigation now brings us to the conclusion that discipline is thinking. What promotes thought, therefore promotes also discipline. For this, we have seen, the theory of interest is not enough. Discipline in the classroom requires purposive activity. A warranted conclusion at this point might seem to be that this must be provided by the teacher through carefully structured problems. Only in this way can mind be "a name for a course of action intelligently directed." In this way, discipline can be held synonymous with thinking. A disciplining situation, therefore, features the careful structuring of the teacher. . . .

This leads us to ask, what is knowledge, in the sense that it constitutes subjectmatter? Dewey's naturalistic logic points out three stages of knowledge. The first stage is the power to do, the ability to manipulate things in accordance with purpose. Following this is a higher stage in which one is able to communicate a report of what he is doing to others and to surcharge his power to do with information assimilated from parents, teachers, and books. The third and final stage of knowledge is that of logically organized material. This is the stage of science. [10]

Much traditional discussion of knowledge in education recognizes the final stages only. Knowledge consists solely of communicated information or scientifically formulated truths. It is cut off from its basis in the lower, manipulative stage. Without this basis it can only become a set of truths learned through memorization. The method of acquiring this knowledge, then, is formal

[6] *Ibid.*, p. 153.
[7] *Ibid.*, p. 165.
[10] *Ibid.*, p. 216.

discipline. The subjectmatter is thought to be disciplining in the sense that it compels the unwilling.

Since this subjectmatter is removed from the learner and his needs, it cannot function to sustain the learner's interest and attention over the period of time necessary for the solution of a problem. Because it does not so function, teachers following this theory exhort students to use their "will power." Also they resort to rewards and punishments.

With Dewey, interest and attention are sustained through the period of time necessary for problem solving, because the three stages natural in the formation of knowledge are appropriately recognized. But this does not mean that discipline is located in subjectmatter alone. For as we have seen the subjectmatter itself exists only in a problem situation which features a learner motivated by interest and purpose.

Progressive educators whose theory of discipline consists in the formula: "Give the child something to do which interests him," may well be begging the question. Unless their theory is further developed, they are placing discipline in the same locus as traditional teachers—in subjectmatter. Their discipline, like their subjectmatter, may be less formal. But it is still supposed to do a trick. Somehow or other, learning is supposed to be the result of exposure and application to subjectmatter. With the impetus that characterizes the swing of a pendulum from one extreme to another, traditional teachers emphasize a discipline of "mind" in the traditional, separate-from-the-body sense, while progressives emphasize a discipline of activity. When reviewed in relation to subjectmatter, the positions of traditional and progressive teachers exhibit elements strongly similar, if not identical.

Perhaps, then, it may be possible to reconcile such antithetical theories and practices as those of the traditional and the progressive teacher. Why not take from the traditionalists their emphasis on teacher guidance of subjectmatter and from the progressives their insistence on subjectmatter meaningful to the learner? Can something of this sort be done without merely eclectic combination? If so, it will require a new plan of educational operations. And this will in turn be derived from a new order of conceptions, proceeding from a level deeper and more inclusive than the level of present struggles.

If the hand of the teacher can be strengthened by structuring learning situations, guidance for the process may reasonably be expected from the pattern of inquiry, the process by which knowledge is made. Indeed, the foregoing discussion of the nature of knowledge and of subjectmatter required terms which find their fuller meaning in the theory of inquiry. This is true to such a degree that one cannot get an accurate understanding of the nature of these terms without examining the theory of inquiry.

No force has been more important in transforming theories of knowing and the known, than the development of the experimental method as the most successful practice for making knowledge and for making sure that it is knowledge. The pre-eminence which it has won justifies basing theory of knowledge upon it and trying to extend it to new fields in the hope of improving them.[11]

Among the "new fields" to be improved by application of the scientific method is the field of values, moral or social. As the experimental method produced a new material world, so it will also eventually produce a new mind. This sentence is put in non-transactional terms. It is better put in these terms: Thinking man, as he transforms his world, becomes increasingly conscious of his method and applies it to all phases of his activity, including the formation of values.

Education, ruled by value judgments, is a part of this field. Especially is the problem of discipline a part of it. In order to know how one ought to conduct classrooms and inquiries for the facilitating of learning, one has to make many value judgments. In saying that the guide for these judgments is found in the practice that best makes knowledge, one is saying that this guide is in the process of inquiry. When this inquiry is, by definition, the experimental (or scientific) method, one is saying that value judgments fall within the field of the experimental method.

So, in turning to inquiry for a pattern for discipline, one is

---

[11] *Ibid.*, pp. 393–95.

saying that the way to go about teaching people to solve problems (or make knowledge) is to copy the way knowledge is made. If this be true, discipline rests in inquiry.

Dewey has said that one of the chief issues in philosophy which concerned him and controlled his thinking was that of the relationship of value judgments to scientific knowledge.[12] This issue controls the present study, as attention is directed to the theory of inquiry.

This is sufficient reason for examining inquiry in its relation to discipline. But there is yet another reason: An analysis of the theory of inquiry facilitates the use of *transactional terms*. This is true because the theory of inquiry is unhampered by dualisms, by archaic views of mind, or by aims, goals, or purposes imposed from without by authority.

Inquiry is a process. In a naturalistic logic, it is continuous with previous processes which are not inquiry. In keeping with the principle of continuity, it ends in a state of affairs which is recognizable as a result of its process. If these states of affairs are considered as pre-inquiry and post-inquiry, a way is found into an analysis of the process of inquiry itself.

The starting point in inquiry is a situation. The clearest and quickest understanding of a situation can be had by stating what a situation is not. It is not an object, either single or multiple. It is not a single object, for inquiry does not recognize isolates. Inquiry always considers the single object or event in connection with other objects or events that constitute a part "of an environing, experienced world." [13] It is not a multiple object, in any sense in which "object" excludes the observer. For if objects are parts of an "environing, experienced world," an observer is necessary. An environment requires an organism,[14] and experience is an attribute of organisms, too. That is, a situation includes an observer and objects. The objects are events or facts of the existential world. A situation unites observer and objects in a transactional way. They affect each other and this effect is conditioned by their relationship in the situation.

[12] *The Philosophy of John Dewey,* ed. by Paul Arthur Schlipp (New York, Tudor Publishing Company, 1951), pp. 523, 578–79.
[13] John Dewey, *Logic: The Theory of Inquiry,* p. 67.
[14] *Ibid.,* p. 106.

What are the boundaries of a situation? What marks a situation off from the rest of the existential world? A situation is felt to be a contextual whole. The key word here is "felt." [15] If one did not have a feeling that the various objects, events and facts might fit together in some way, there would be no situation. As long as this relationship is only felt and not known, the situation is indeterminate. This is what is meant by a pre-inquiry situation. It is characterized by the adjectives vague, confused, obscure, unsettled, disordered. These adjectives describe all the factors in the situation, the existential facts as well as the "mental states" of the observer. The observer's state of mind is confused, because of the confusion among the existentials. There is nothing cognitive in the pre-inquiry situation.

The boundaries of the post-inquiry situation are *known*. We call this situation determinate, by which we mean that its parts are all related in an ordered and settled way. The "contextual whole" is now clearly evident. Confusion is gone from the existential facts and from the observer's state of mind. He knows, and what he knows is neatly recorded as knowledge. He has not "come out where in he went." The process of inquiry has changed things.

Problematic situation. A problematic situation begins with questions. One might call the pre-inquiry situation problematic. But this is to anticipate the process of inquiry, [16] for that which is problematic is no longer merely felt. It has moved into the field of cognition. This is the first step in the process of inquiry. The step consists in noting that questions must be asked and answers anticipated.

Institution of a problem. Inquiry begins with questions. The indeterminate situation is a questionable one. There is a unique quality about a situation which gives rise to particular questions. These in turn control the procedures of inquiry that are to follow. At the initial question stage, the situation begins to be cognitive. But the asking of a question alone does not constitute inquiry. For, as has been noted above, a situation unites observer and observed in a transactional way. The questioner must anticipate an answer and must take steps to check the accuracy

[15] *Ibid.,* p. 68.
[16] *Ibid.,* p. 107.

of his anticipation. This is inquiry. The key word in discussing inquiry is *problem*. When one sees that questions must be asked and answers anticipated, one has a problematic situation; when one has determined ways to check these answers, he has a problem. "A problem represents the partial transformation by inquiry of a problematic situation into a determinate situation." [17] The very conception of a problem must suggest solutions and ways to check them. In stating the problems, one tentatively decides what can be done to actualize the potentialities anticipated. Thus to have a problem is to be well along in inquiry. "It is a familiar and significant saying that a problem well put is half-solved." [18] A problem is, therefore, not the beginning of inquiry. Inquiry is, instead, the progressive determining of a problem, and the problem is finally determined only when it is solved.

Determining a problem-solution. The process of inquiry is here being viewed in its temporal aspect. Without violence to the principle of continuity, three phases of this process may be distinguished in analysis. First there is the noting that the situation is problematic, then the instituting of a problem, and finally the determining of a problem-solution.[19]

In this third phase of inquiry, viewed from its temporal aspect, two phases are to be noted.

The first phase in determining a problem-solution consists in finding the settled constituents of the situation or "the facts of the case." This means those constituents that are already ordered. As has been noted in the discussion of problematic situation, particular questions arise due to the unique quality of any problematic situation. It is the settled constituents that produce this unique quality. So a first phase in getting a problem-solution is to state all these settled constituents. These are

[17] *Ibid.*, p. 108.
[18] *Ibid.*
[19] This phase division is necessary for purposes of analysis. That there is overlapping is to be expected. The evidence of this overlapping can be seen by means of this phase analysis. Simplicity requires talk of "steps" coming "first," "second," etc., but more properly the analysis runs by phases, aspects or functions, and the order is analytical rather than literally temporal.

the "facts" of the problem, which serve to clarify it. They are obtained through observation.[20]

The second phase in determining a problem-solution consists in using *ideas,* or proposals of possible solutions.[21] There are again three phases noticeable in the use of ideas: (1) An idea, which is a forecast of what will happen when something is done, arises from observation and is born as a vague suggestion. (2) The suggestion turns into an idea by examination of how it will work. This second phase in the ideational process is called reasoning or ratiocination. (3) The idea turns into a judgment, a statement of "warranted assertability," when the idea does work. This judgment is the settled outcome of inquiry, a statement of the order replacing the confusion among existentials of the problematic situation with which inquiry began. With judgment the problem is solved.

The use of reasoning. It remains to clarify how the phase of reasoning (ratiocination) tests whether or not the idea "works." What does one mean when one says an idea works? One means that it institutes observation of other facts not previously seen which fit all the facts together into a coherent whole. How is this done? What is reasoning?

It is convenient in analyzing reasoning to chop the reasoning process into two parts. One views reasoning thus not from a temporal aspect but from the aspect of its existential and conceptual parts. This aspect forms a second dimension which can spread over the whole process of inquiry. One limits its use here to the analysis of ratiocination.

The existential constituents of reasoning are observed facts called perceptual data. The conceptual constituents of reasoning are commonly called ideas. They are possible methods of solution embodied in symbols and called propositions. These two divisions of reasoning, the existential and the conceptual, represent nothing more than a division of labor in a single process. In reasoning, existential and conceptual constituents are manipulated tentatively through their symbolization in propositions, until their relationships are thoroughly explored. This

---

[20] John Dewey, *Logic: The Theory of Inquiry,* pp. 108–9, 112–13.
[21] *Ibid.,* pp. 109–10, 112–13.

means that of the many possible relations that have been anticipated, one fits best and suggests operations to be performed—
not in reasoning through symbols but in fact—in order to check
its applicability.[22]

Reasoning thus provides the means of checking on itself.
Within the process of determining a problem-solution, it carries
trial facts and trial ideas symbolically, until it connects them
with experiment. It thus unites existential and conceptual material in such a way that both become ordered rather than disordered. The result is a determined situation (in general terms) or
a solved problem (in the terms of inquiry). Perceptual materials
provide the initial data and the final checking; conceptual materials provide in symbols the plan for relating all the parts.

Returning to a temporal analysis, reasoning is seen to take
place through a progressive determining of relationships. Exploring of intermediate relationships is necessary before a final
(for the present process of inquiry) "best" in the sense of most
unifying relationship is found. Only thus can a *judgment* (problem-solution) be made. Warranted assertability does not occur
at the beginning of the reasoning process, even if *the* best
relationship should be chanced upon first. For reasoning is the
exploring of many possible relationships through symbols. The
best relationship leads to an overt response, a checking or
solving of the problem which ends inquiry. If this is done before
many possibilities have been explored, inquiry is cut short.
Existentials might be ordered, but knowledge is not the result.[23]

Knowledge is the end product of inquiry. It is that warranted
assertability, that working judgment which results when competent inquiry is carried on. The use of this knowledge in future
experience is intelligence. Mediating between knowledge and
its use in intelligence is mind, constituted of habits built out of
previously attained knowledge. Meaning is a word used to refer
to perception of relationships.

Thus the process of inquiry gives fullest definition to terms
which we encounter in any theory of growth. The reason for this

[22] *Ibid.,* p. 112.
[23] *Ibid.*

is that these terms find their fullest use in the operations of inquiry.

Pragmatism has been interpreted as a theory of knowledge in which knowledge is subordinate to action or practice. Knowledge as instrumental has been taken to mean that knowledge is true or of value only as it is of use to the knower. The reference to instrumental here is mistaken. In Dewey's pragmatism, it should now be evident, action is necessarily involved in knowledge, but knowledge is in no sense subordinate to action. Instrumentalism is not concerned with the desires and satisfactions of the knower, but with the relationship of ideas and the connections of disorganized things.[24]

Corresponding to the mistaken theory of pragmatism as "knowledge is action that works," is the theory of discipline that motivated many activity programs: give the child something to do that interests him. When knowledge is understood as the conclusion of inquiry, this being that which resolves a problematic situation, then the place of action is seen within the contextual whole of inquiry. It is inquiry that controls action and not vice versa. Activity and interest are not significant for discipline in and of themselves but as they operate in inquiry. Controlling the whole context of inquiry is the problematic situation.[25] Discipline, like knowledge, rests in the resolving of this problematic situation.

For knowledge is not necessarily that which works. If a course of action works on first trial, it interrupts the course of inquiry and thwarts knowledge. Immediate knowledge may be the result of spontaneous activity in some theories of knowledge, but it is contrary to all that Dewey has written on the subject.[26]

Dewey's pragmatism will find discipline in a staying power that carries through to the resolving of a problematic situation. This necessarily takes time. Quick and easy solutions do not yield warranted assertability. "To know what to do and to move to do it with requisite means," Dewey's definition of discipline given previously, needs the context of inquiry to qualify its

[24] *The Philosophy of John Dewey,* ed. by Paul Arthur Schlipp, p. 528.
[25] *Ibid.,* p. 560.
[26] *Ibid.,* p. 527.

"do's." If not, it can be interpreted into a mistaken and superficial pragmatism.

If the problematic situation controls inquiry, if a problem does not appear until the mid-course of inquiry, then discipline cannot begin with a problem. If discipline is to follow the pattern of inquiry, it must begin with observations, activity and questions directed toward the institution of a problem. Time must be allowed for development of the problem. So, the pattern of inquiry implies for discipline more careful planning of learning experiences rather than less. It also implies that course charting, instead of being done with what are frequently called "educational objectives," can better be done with aims rather differently conceived.

The learning situation must feature detailed structuring with this delayed problem in view rather than as a starting point. And it must plan for a mutual interrelationship of subjectmatter, pupil and teacher in the planning: not just of teacher and pupil as was stated earlier, but of teacher, pupil and subjectmatter. Activity must be featured, but activity includes observation and ideational activity as well as overt responses. The mode of lesson planning indicated earlier in this study is strongly reminiscent of Herbart. The plan called for now is better named a flexible program of inquiry.

The plan called for, in view of the pattern of inquiry, must start out with an aim rather different from the sort which has come to be called "educational objectives." At least as frequently conceived, objectives are fairly rigid and specific. In inquiry, they correspond roughly to a problem already instituted, and they therefore should come in the mid-course of the learning process. The aim needed at the outset, on the other hand, is flexible and general. It corresponds to purposive questioning in the opening, problematic-situation stage of inquiry. It is nothing more than a plan for action, very tentative, a mere sketch at first. It can be called purpose, if purpose is understood transactionally as a plan for action.

The sort of aim needed differs from an objective in that it is not what ought to be accomplished; it is, at most, what probably can be done and possibly ought to be done. It is not imposed from without the learning process; it is a sketched plan for the process itself, rising out of the existing conditions and subject to change at any moment. It is not of value because of some sought-for goal at the end of the learning process; it is of value for itself alone as a guide to action. It does not exist for the sake of accomplishing thus-and-so; it exists because without it there will be no accomplishing.

This sort of aiming, or purposive questioning, is the starting point; tentative formulation of objectives, or of a problem, is the mid-point; learning, or knowledge, is the conclusion. The first of these terms applies in the learning process, the second in inquiry.

The replacing of objectives—specific, atomized and itemized —by this sort of aim as the starting point for the learning process is highly significant for evaluation. For when this sort of aim guides the learning process, the end has value only as the conclusion of a process of guided activity. The end is not valued as a separate result. Guided activity itself, liberating in the sense that more activities take on increasing meaning, is the prime value for its own sake and not as an unavoidable means of attaining some result. The significance of this concept for classroom evaluation should be apparent.

TEACHING, LEARNING, AND THIRDNESS*

D. Bob Gowin

It is a recognized fact that teaching does not always produce learning and that learning sometimes occurs in situations where there is no teacher or teaching. This state of affairs has prompted some philosophers of education to state that the teacher could not be said to have taught unless the pupil had learned (e.g., Dewey, Kilpatrick). A consequence of this postulated relationship between teaching and learning, however, seems to be that "teaching" and "learning" as terms are either synonyms or related in such a way that the process can only be meaningfully discussed in terms of the product. In the interest of clarity, some analytic philosophers of education (e.g., Smith, Scheffler) have sought to redefine the terms "teaching" and "learning" so as to separate their meanings and to make them more precise. Although clarity might be achieved by increased precision in separating "teaching" from "learning," the problem of the way they are related still remains. Separation of meanings of terms by use of distinctions and definitions does not in any way preclude a logical relation of the terms or an empirical relation of the things (events) to which the terms may be properly applied. . . . The relations of teaching to learning will be examined in terms of monadic, dyadic, and triadic propositions, and in terms of meanings. The thesis of this paper is that the relation of teaching to learning is triadic, that meaning is logical, empirical, and psychosocial, and that a defensible conception of teaching will be based upon distinctions and definitions consistent with such a relationship and meanings. . . .

Let us take another look at Dewey's original statement of the equation between teaching-learning and buying-selling. Dewey writes:

* Reprinted from "Teaching, Learning and Thirdness," *Studies in Philosophy and Education,* Vol. 1, No. 3 (1961), 87, 98–100, 103, 104–13. By permission of the author and the editor of *Studies in Philosophy and Education.*

Teaching may be compared to selling commodities. No one can sell unless someone buys. We should ridicule a merchant who said that he had sold a great many goods although no one had bought any. But perhaps there are teachers who think that they have done a good day's teaching irrespective of what pupils have learned. There is the same exact equation between teaching and learning that there is between selling and buying. The only way to increase the learning of pupils is to augment the quantity and quality of real teaching. Since learning is something that the pupil has to do himself and for himself, the initiative lies with the learner. The teacher is a guide and director; he steers the boat, but the energy that propels it must come from those who are learning. The more a teacher is aware of the past experiences of students of their hopes, desires, chief interests, the better will he understand the forces at work that need to be directed and utilized for the formation of reflective habits. The number and quality of these factors vary from person to person. They cannot therefore be categorically enumerated in a book. But there are some tendencies and forces that operate in every normal individual, forces that must be appealed to and utilized if the best methods for the development of good habits of thought are to be employed.[10]

"There is the same exact equation between teaching and learning that there is between selling and buying." This is the offending sentence. Taken negatively first, if the equation between selling and buying is grossly inexact, so then is the equation between teaching and learning.

The teaching-learning, and buying-selling statement of Dewey's may be clarified by a statement Dewey makes in *Logic: The Theory of Inquiry*. The main point of the *Logic* is to clarify the relations between the formal and the material, or the abstract and the existential.

Dewey states that there are two kinds of logical (as opposed to linguistic) propositions—dyadic and polyadic.[11] A dyadic proposition is "Justice is a virtue," a triadic proposition is "The point M is the middle point between A and B," a tetradic proposition reads "European nations owe the United States N dollars on account of war loans."

Any proposition having direct existential reference applies to

[10] John Dewey, *How We Think* (Revised ed.; Boston, D. C. Heath and Company, 1933), pp. 35–36. (Italics added.)

[11] John Dewey, *Logic: The Theory of Inquiry* (New York, Henry Holt and Company, 1938), pp. 312–13.

conditions or circumstances, and logically any existence has to be determined with respect to date and place.

" 'Man is mortal' is strictly dyadic, when it means 'If anything is human, then it is mortal,' for both terms are abstract, and the relation affirmed is of abstract nonexistential character. The proposition states a relation between conceptual contents." These propositions are "(1) independent of space-time reference, and (2) state a necessary relation betwen antecedent and consequent."

Now, when Dewey writes about the relation between teaching and learning he is not stating propositions about matters-of-fact. His terms have no space-time existential reference. Rather, it is a statement of necessary relation between antecedent and consequent. It is dyadic.

When Dewey attempts to specify *what* relations teachers have to learners the propositions take a different form. The teacher needs to discover something about the learner that is other and more than the relation of teaching-learning. The teacher needs to know something about the student's past experiences, not just the learning relation he sustains to the teacher. Hopes, desires and interests are important things to know about a learner, just as credit standing, upward mobility, status-seeking and political party may be important things for a seller to know about a buyer. But these additional points of contact are part of the existential matrix out of which the selling-buying or teaching-learning relations derive. . . .

What we need are cognitive propositions which are adequate to the process we wish to describe. Peirce's logic of relatives may appropriately supply a useful start in this direction. . . .

Charles Peirce states the simple triadic relation as "A is a sign of B to C." In his philosophy it does not remain simple, there being at least 10 trichotomies and 66 classes of signs (reduced from Peirce's one-time estimate of over 59,000). Two examples may clarify what Peirce is trying to demonstrate.

Analyze for instance the relation involved in "A gives B to C." Now what is giving? It does not consist [in] A's putting B away from him and C's subsequently taking B up. It is not necessary that any material transfer should take place. It consists in A's making C the possessor according to *Law*. There must be some kind of law before there can be any kind of giving—be it but the law of the strongest. But now suppose that give *did* consist merely in A's laying down the B which C subsequently picks up. That would be a degenerate form of thirdness in which the thirdness is externally appended. In A's putting away B, there is no thirdness. In C's taking B, there is no thirdness. But if you say that these two acts constitute a single operation by virture of the identity of the B, you transcend the mere brute fact, you introduce a mental element.[16]

If we substitute the statement "A teaches B to C," then teaching, as a form of thirdness, would not consist in A's putting something forth and C taking it up. A puts a book on a table; C takes it up; A writes a word on the board ("trieb"), C writes it down on a piece of paper; A says Kennedy will make a great president; C repeats the statement. In this dyadic relation, there is no thirdness. But when you say that these acts constitute a single operation by virtue of the identity of the B, you introduce thirdness or mediation—what Peirce calls a mental element.

Thus a criterion arises for specifying a necessary condition for teaching: *if there is no thirdness, there is no teaching.* What is thirdness? Peirce writes: ". . . Thirdness is the triadic relation existing between a sign, its object, and the interpreting thought, itself a sign, considered as constituting the mode of being of a sign. A sign mediates between the *interpretant* sign and its object." [17]

This criterion may be applied to the so-called teaching machines. The machine is programmed; this programming is like A putting B forth; the student works through the program; this working through is like C taking B up. Where is the thirdness? Unless there is mediation to the point of recognizing that the B was similar in both cases, there is no thirdness.

Of course, the psychologist will assert that there is a law

[16] Charles S. Peirce, *Values in a Universe of Chance,* ed. P. P. Wiener (Garden City, N.Y., Doubleday Anchor Books, 1958), p. 388.

On pages 389–90 Peirce makes clear that he is not trying to talk psychology: "What is the essential difference between a sign that is communicated to a mind, and one that is not so communicated? If the question were simply what we DO mean by a sign, it might soon be resolved. But that is not the point. We are in the situation of a zoologist who wants to know what ought to be the meaning of 'fish' in order to make fishes one of the great classes of vertebrates."

[17] *Ibid.,* p. 389.

operating—the law of effect, and therefore, being this law, there is mediation, or thirdness. But does the law pertain to A teaches B to C? Apparently this is not the case. Rather the relation is C learns B from X, the machine or the program. Is the program the student learns the same B the teacher intends? Yes, but only if the teacher intends for the student to learn by rote. If the teacher explains to the student that the B he intends to teach is to be learned by "rote learning," and the student identifies the program-learning as rote learning, then we move to a thirdness level, and to teaching.

Scheffler seems to imply necessity for a thirdness relation in his analysis of the standard example of teaching. Scheffler writes that,

> . . . if we are to decide whether or not Jones is engaged in teaching activity during a specified interval, we can neither rely merely on one momentary observation, nor can we rely merely on observations of Jones' movements during the interval in question. Rather, in the light of information that normally goes beyond the interval in question, we have to see whether what Jones is doing is aimed at getting someone to learn something, whether it is not unreasonably thought to be likely to achieve the learning aimed at, and whether it falls within the restrictions of manner peculiar to teaching as ordinarily understood—in particular, whether acknowledgment of the alleged pupil's judgment is made, whether, e.g. the pupil is not systematically precluded from asking, "How?" "Why?" or "On what grounds?" [18]

Thirdness may be seen in this quotation. The teacher puts something forth; the teacher does so in a way which acknowledges the alleged pupil's judgment in "asking 'How?' 'Why?' or 'On what grounds?' " While this conception of teaching seems cryptic as presented here, the necessary elements of thirdness are implied in that signs, objects and interpreting thoughts are necessary for such a relation to be established.

Using the machines as an example to clarify the point, most teaching machines systematically preclude the pupil from asking why, how and on what grounds. They present only a dyadic relation.

Machines using the scrambled book technique are closer than

[18] Israel Scheffler, *The Language of Education* (Springfield, Ill. C. C. Thomas Co., 1960), p. 68.

others to achieving a thirdness relation in teaching and learning.[19] These machines seem to incorporate a provision for explaining to the student why and how he made a mistake. They provide reasons why such a mistake is likely under the circumstances and acknowledge "clever errors." They explain what piece of learning is missing, how that learning may be sought ("turn to p. 94") and how the missing piece of information will help the student to overcome his mistake.

Some may object that the thirdness criterion begs the whole issue. It may be that the most important distinctions are to be found in neither teaching nor learning. The most important distinctions may lie in specifications of *what* is taught and what is learned (the B element of the paradigm).

Such phrases as "learning experiences," "organizing centers for learning," "learning laboratories" suggest strongly a context, an environment. The authors of such phrases apparently intend to de-emphasize the image of the teacher didactically pounding the learner with bits of content. They seek out an action arena —the play's the thing. The play of the learner over things and events, the play meaning the interplay of actors, and the play meaning the content written (as subject matter). This action arena might contain: a standardized comprehensive examination (to be taken whenever the learner thinks he is ready for it), a well-selected body of curricular materials, readings, films, records, provision for direct experiences, the option of coming to class or not, a team of teachers any one of which may at any time take responsibility for some part of the discussion. Thus is created a diffuseness in the image of "teacher" and the action of "teaching." "Who is the agent when" (the teacher teaching) becomes much less important than the action arena, the occasion or situation for learning experiences. The deliberate and deliberated manipulation of the environmental setting through various institutionalized devices becomes the "teacher teaching."

Likewise, with learning, "who is patient when" is made diffuse. The learning of one student, when observed by other

---

[19] Norman A. Crowder, "Automatic Tutoring by Means of Intrinsic Programming," *Automatic Teaching,* ed. Eugene Galanter (New York, John Wiley and Sons Inc., 1959).

students in the group, may generalize to the other learners. These other learners learn the same thing, but not in the same way as the student who learns it first. He, in effect, by becoming a "good" learner, "teaches" the other students in the process of his own learning. Such "teaching" is not deliberate.

We need not call all that contributes to learning "teaching." Students live in a social milieu of "learning." There are plays, films, social activities, competitions of various sorts (sporting and not so sporting), and the much belabored and idolized "bull sessions." Self-reports of students give us evidence that the environmental setting produces learning. We need not suppose that there happened to be either deliberate or incidental "teaching" ubiquitously present in all such occasions.

By the same argument, moreover, we need not suppose that the typical picture of Professor X lecturing to students in a classroom constitutes teaching. He may be merely submitting ideas, he may be urging the acceptance of ideas without debate. He may be teaching, putting forth an argument in such a way that it results in contemplation—the reasonable connection of one thought in some careful way to other thoughts.

What this means, it would appear, is that one should not confuse the context for teaching with the activity of teaching or the content taught. If there is a one-to-one relation between teaching and learning, it has not been found. The relations are multiple; the context contributes something, the individuality of the teacher contributes something, the students contribute something, and all these things may be variables, if not unknown factors, in some very complex phenomena.

Teaching may be construed as argument (philosophic). Following Peirce we find that argument may be related to firstness, secondness, and thirdness. As firstness, an argument may be submitted only to its interpretant, as something the reasonableness of which will be acknowledged. Firstness is the mode of being of that which is such as it is, positively and without reference to anything else. The teacher puts something forth; it is submitted *as is*. It is a quality, or a qualitative experience, a peculiar positive possibility regardless of anything else. Its impact on the student is a mere appearance, brute is-ness. It is an unanalyzed, total impression made by any complexity which is not thought of as actual fact but simply as a quality.[20] This is monadic.

Secondness as argument, is urged upon the interpretant by an act of insistence. There is action on the part of the teacher, but not necessarily reaction from the pupil. The teacher's action is determinate and fixed for the student. But the student's assent or intellectual acceptance of things taught is "indeterminate" for the teacher. That is, as Peirce writes, "indeterminancy belongs only to ideas; the existent is determinate in every respect." [21] The student has determinate existence; but assent to the ideas of the argument is indeterminate, in that the teacher does not create any reaction to the action he takes in urging the argument. This is dyadic. To call this kind of teaching indoctrination suggests too strong a criticism of dyadic relations. Indoctrination is probably most like secondness, most like insistence without waiting for reaction. But there may be other characterizations of this dyadic relation which would not necessarily be construed as indoctrination.

Thirdness, as argument, is presented to the interpretant for contemplation. It is not urged, nor merely submitted; its appeal lies in being interpretable in "thoughts or other signs of the same kind in infinite series." Such contemplation would seem to require a triadic relation—the argument presented, the acceptance or receipt of the argument (either in assent or rejection) by the interpreter.

Viewing teaching as thirdness implies comparison, combination and composition. And continuity, Peirce claims, represents thirdness almost to perfection. In bringing a first and second into relation, thirdness, like teaching, mediates between two subjects and brings about their connection. Peirce writes that any attempt to relate entities without reference to thirdness must meet with failure.

If the teacher puts something forth—an idea, a diagram, a proposition, a puzzle—the student responds to something more than the brute "putting forth." The student responds not merely to the chalk marks or to the noise patterns but to these movements as an index of something else. The student's response is

---

[20] Peirce, *op. cit.*, pp. 383–84.
[21] *Ibid.*, p. 385.

transferred from the teacher's direct movements to the object (idea, thing, event) to which the teacher points. Instead of regarding the object in an ordinary way, as the student might respond to any object as a stimulus, the student responds in a way which is a function of the teacher's *relationship,* actual and potential, to the thing. The characteristic of the student's response to the teacher's putting forth is that the student responds to the thing from the standpoint of the teacher teaching. He perceives it as it may function in the teacher's (and other students') experience, not just ego-centrically. Similarly, from the teacher's standpoint, the teacher has a conception about the thing not only in its direct relationship to himself, but as a thing capable of being grasped and handled by the student. He sees the thing as it may function in the student's experience.

This property of behavior in which something is made common in at least two different centers of behavior is the heart of communication which has meaning.[22] Put another way, meaning is the distinctive quality of behavior in relation to things such that response to another's act involves response to the thing as entering into the other's behavior. When this is achieved upon both sides, the event has a shared meaning. It is in this sense that we see how thirdness accounts for meaning. And it is also here that we can see how thirdness, in accounting for meaning, helps us to account for much that needs to be subsumed under a concept of teaching.

One of the chief purposes of teaching is to find, develop and test meanings. When a teacher views teaching in the light of the concepts of meaning, he may start in the middle—or muddle— of things. Meanings are vague, precise, ambiguous, clear, abstract, concrete, universal, particular, speculative, verified, consummatory, instrumental, symbolic, immediate, generated, given, logical, psychosocial, empirical. The list could be extended. This is not the place to offer a critique of the concept of meaning. Two points, however, are relevant to this discussion. The first is to specify three dimensions of meaning, calling attention briefly to their philosophical progenitors. The second

[22] John Dewey, *Experience and Nature* (Chicago, Open Court Publishing Company, 1926), pp. 178–79.

is to set this brief discussion of meaning in the context of teaching.

First, a teacher thinking about teaching in terms of meaning might well begin with psychosocial meanings, meanings that are an admixture of the personal and social, meanings evident in common usage and ordinary language. Here the first-hand, direct experience of the student is important. The teacher might try to tease out the vital, lively, energetic, pulsating immediacy of experience. He might try, as the existentialist philosophers try in all manner of expression—verse, plays, novels, sketches—to confront the person directly in an encounter. Peirce's firstness comes to mind—a peculiar, positive possibility regardless of anything else, a qualitative experience. Dewey's idea of pervasive and dominant qualitativeness of immediate experience and Northrup's esthetic dimension of experience perhaps refer to the same phenomena. Teaching, like philosophizing, must engage the person directly at some points or else remain the peddling of abstractions emptied of sustaining vigor. The appeal to common usage and ordinary language is an appeal through social convention to psychosocial meanings. This beginning point in teaching, as in philosophizing, is the connection of common meanings to more refined meanings. This connection leads to meaning in terms of analytic, logical meaning—contradiction, tautology, necessity.

Meaning conceived in this second sense (logic) moves from common usage and ordinary language toward more abstract concerns. Formal logic, symbolic logic—even that form of metaphysical logic characteristic of systematic philosophies which attempt to answer all of man's questions—could be considered here as treating of meaning. This conception of philosophy points a way in teaching toward the vantage point of wider perspective. One fails to understand a subject matter by seeking *only* to understand that subject matter (the fallacy of subject matter viewed as the only necessary element in teaching); some meta-level concerns are necessary. For students the value of seeking a meta-level understanding of a field of study is like the feeling of driving with your head above the traffic, or viewing the valley from the mountain peak, or figuring a balance sheet. All things considered the larger, macroscopic point of view is possible and valuable. The learner can gain the larger view if teaching, through the precision of meaning, progressively lifts him to higher levels of abstraction.

A third dimension of meaning can be related to these two. This is meaning in its operational, denotative, empirical sense. Meaning, as here referred to, is meaning as viewed by the verifiability (or testability) criterion of meaning. Evidence, warrant, and test come into play. Cases, contexts, practical procedures, operational definitions, inductive inference, and methods of inquiry so much discussed by the pragmatists and logical empiricists comprise meaning in this third dimension. Some may think of this dimension as applied logic; for others it has to do more with inquiry in its final stages. I use the term empirical meaning to refer to this third dimension of meaning.

In summary, meaning is here referred to in its psychosocial, logical and empirical dimensions. This conception of meaning does not imply an ontology. That is, no a priori assumptions are being made about the nature of reality as "meaning." Rather, meaning is seen as a concept which points three ways. Meaning is a midway station, perhaps a midwife to the whole and the part, the universal and particular, the large and the small, the psychosocial, analytical and the empirical. It suggests, in the context of teaching, that one can move (1) toward logical abstraction and a comprehensive view as well as (2) toward concrete experience of the open texture of psychosocial experience, and (3) toward concrete experience involving inquiry concerning matters of fact. This concept of meaning is somewhat like Plato's illustrations of the divided line and the allegory of the cave, Dewey's distinction of immediate and mediated experience, and the modern philosophers' concern with the analytic and synthetic distinction. . . .

It seems evident that much human behavior is a quest for meaning. Some kind of meaning will be made out of any situation. Northrup writes that: ". . . the spatio-temporal social habits and ordering of people in any culture, and its objective buildings, art forms, and positive legal procedures for settling disputes are the deposit of an implicit or explicit common set of *meanings* for describing, integrating and anticipating the raw data of human experience." [23] Northrup quotes the anthropologist Bateson to the effect that: ". . . the human individual is endlessly simplifying and generalizing his own view of his environment; he constantly imposes . . . his own constructions and meanings; these constructions and meanings are characteristic of one culture as opposed to another." [24] A person, in the quest for meaning, will not rest until the meaning or meanings, *for him,* become established.

Not only do humans continuously try to make sense out of experience through establishing meaning, but meanings are characterized by a quality of being extractable. To some extent they are to human affairs like the isotopes of physical science. A meaning created or developed in one situation may be extracted and "implanted" in another situation. This extraction of net meanings and their application in a different situation may be done intelligently through teaching. The relating of one meaning to another—psychosocial to logical, logical to empirical, empirical to psychosocial—requires thinking and reflection. It requires abstraction and extraction of meanings, plus the seeing of some relation. . . .

Some writers have referred to the ladder of abstraction of meanings. The ladder of abstraction of meaning is not linear nor sequential, as the image "ladder" might lead one to expect. The multiplier effect leads us to expect some progression other than by simple step-by-step progression up the "ladder." If an image is needed for the concept of the multiplier effect, perhaps pyramids will do. If we think of the apex of a pyramid as the point at which we begin to examine meanings, then we can imagine meanings spreading out in all directions down toward the base of experience. Meanings can move into a broad base of direct experience; moving up the pyramid we see a reduction in the variability of meanings and a gain toward specificity, a convergence toward an apex. Downwardly, meanings move into a divergence toward nuance, feeling, particularly although not specificity.

[23] F. S. C. Northrup, "Ethical Relativism in the Light of Recent Legal Science," *American Philosophers at Work,* ed. Sidney Hook (New York, Criterion Books, 1957), p. 444.
[24] *Ibid.*

Now, place an inverted pyramid on top of the one already constructed. Here the movement is upward, through the combination and recombination of meanings, words linking with words, sentences linking with sentences, signs coupled with signs ad infinitum. Meanings may expand through abstraction and gain a kind of richness different from the one of direct experience, a richness rather of expanded vicarious experience. Critics of progressive education criticize the aimless activity programs. Although often misinformed, the critics are right in their desire for expansion of meanings through abstraction, through the imagination of literature, logic and mathematics—through theoretic experience. This kind of meaning development abhors the foot-dragging immediate experience; it seeks to soar without the constant reference to direct experience. It has a place in education.

To teach is deliberately to change the meaning of experience. Teaching need not result in immediate behavior change. However, if meaning is changed, then, should the student act, he would act as if his experience had changed. But the dimensions of change are as broad as the dimensions of meaning. Change may occur in increased logical precision of meaning, in enhanced nuance of psychosocial meaning, in increased accuracy in prediction through operational meanings.

This discussion of teaching is not a literal description of teaching seen in the actual doing. There is more to observe in actual teaching than is presently caught in this view of teaching. But, as a proposed theory of teaching, Peirce's conception of thirdness captures what seems to be a logical criterion of a conception of teaching. And meaning, as one way to make thirdness explicit, comes closer to the practical context.

THE MEANING OF LEARNING AND THE LEARNING OF MEANING*

E. C. Weir

Educators have been increasingly engaged in recent years in discussion and experimentation which point to systematic thinking as both process and goal in teaching and learning. Some of our academic brethren—those who have finally come realistically to grips with the questions of what to teach and how to teach—are beginning to come around to the point of view that in teaching our emphasis should be not so much on assimilation of thought as it is on thinking. This discussion has centered largely on methodological approaches to helping students to discover (or create), analyze, and test ideas which they can use to solve problems and to explain and order the phenomena of existence. Emphasis is upon the "problem of warranted belief, and how teachers may help students determine whether there is any warrant for holding certain beliefs." [1] The methodology depends heavily on principles of formal logic. With regard to the organization of the curriculum, it is urged that ". . . the curriculum of a subject should be determined by the most fundamental understanding that can be achieved of the underlying principles that give structure to that subject." [2]

In what follows, it is not at all our intent to disparage this "new" focus in educational thought. We are most heartily receptive to any effort which conceives of the human entity as an awareness and a seeking after meaning, a disposition to order and control experience. Such efforts are especially fortuitous at this particular time when the behavior of rats is seriously being

---

* Reprinted from "The Meaning of Learning and the Learning of Meaning," *Phi Delta Kappan*, 46(February, 1965), 280–84. By permission of the editor of the *Phi Delta Kappan*.

[1] L. E. Metcalf, "The Reflective Teacher," *Phi Delta Kappan* (October, 1962).

[2] Jerome S. Bruner, *The Process of Education* (Cambridge, Mass., Harvard University Press, 1960), p. 51.

proposed as the model for explanations of human behavior and technological and curricular gadgetry as the nostrum for the ailments of education. In view of these developments, it is gratifying to realize that dedicated educational thinkers and researchers are working diligently and without the doubtful advantage of great fanfare under the assumption that humanness is a unique phenomenon in the world and that the potential of the human consciousness unfolds through continuing experiences in reflective choice-making with regard to the dilemmas of existence.

However, it is our feeling that, in giving attention to the development of a logicalistic methodology for teaching and learning, we may overlook the *person* who is to teach and the *person* who is to learn. We need to remind ourselves of the ultimately *subjective* nature of thinking and learning, of knowledge and meaning. Principles of logic do not objectively exist; they only exist in *persons* who understand, accept, and use them in their thinking and learning. Knowledge exists in someone knowing. Concepts exist in someone conceptualizing. Meaning is not objectively *in* the universe; it exists in a particular individual *person's* awareness as he perceives his own identity and relatedness. Reflective thinking, which is an attribute of the highest order of human behavior, obviously can only occur in persons who are *subjectively* disposed and able to think reflectively. Critical examination of one's beliefs and behavior is not merely an operation in logic; it is an operation requiring a high degree of psychological competence. By the same token, the reflective teacher is not merely a logician; he is a *person* who is able to function reflectively as a person within the intricate complex of meanings and motivations, dreams and disappointments, hates and hopes and fears and loves that exist in the persons he is to teach. If he is to teach—that is if he is to help his students to grow in their ability to function reflectively—it is important that he have competence in logic and that he have profound intimacy with the structure of his subject. However, it is at least of equal importance that he be the kind of human being who can relate personally to his students in such a way that they become psychologically free to create themselves, to engage themselves fully and courageously in the hazardous project of examining and reconstructing the meaning of their own living.

A man is an idea; he is what he perceives himself to be and what he perceives himself as becoming. An idea is a man; it comes into being as a man discovers it or creates it and employs it in shaping the essence of his living.

Translated into a concept of learning, this statement means that an individual has learned when he integrates into himself a new meaning, a meaning that has such personal significance in his awareness that the quality and direction of his existence are in some way different than they were before.

What do we mean by "meaning"? We suggest a subjective definition.

Meaning is the order imposed upon experience by the individual as he becomes aware of the interrelationships between the self and the phenomena encountered in his experience. . . .

It is true that the order I impose upon a given experiential situation may be an objectively illogical order, completely or partially out of conformity with reality. I may completely or partially misinterpret the relationship the event or object has with my goals and values, so that my behavior, as a result, will be seen by others to be inappropriate. But it is the relationship *I* see, the order *I* impose, and to me, therefore, my behavior will seem quite appropriate—until such time as my pattern of meanings takes on a new and perhaps more realistic configuration. Herein, of course, lies the task of education—*to help the young to discover and take into themselves increasingly more realistic and encompassing meanings with concomitantly increased efficiency of behavior.* Rigorous application of principles of logic, together with understanding of the fundamental structure of organized knowledge, are essential in the development of a pattern of subjective meaning that is consistent and whole, but one must also be psychologically consistent and whole if he is to recognize the inappropriateness of his perceptions of reality.

If it were not for the fact that personal meaning can be distorted and inconsistent with reality, it would be almost a tautology to say that the task of education is to help the young to discover and incorporate increasingly more adequate meanings into their experience. Meaning, as we have defined it, is present in some degree in all learning. And conversely, if the individual can find no meaning in a situation, he will learn nothing in that situation.

In the often-used example of the child touching the hot stove, the evidence of learning lies not in the fact of withdrawal from the source of pain but rather in the subsequent consistency of the child's avoidance behavior with respect to the stove. From this subsequent consistency of behavior, we can infer that for the child the stove has taken on a new meaning. The stove signifies pain, and sharp physical discomfort is the quality of relationship which the child "sees" between the stove and himself. He thus discriminates the stove from other objects in the room; it takes on a more precise configuration for him. He also generalizes about the object he has thus discriminated, and, for this reason, is able to behave appropriately with respect to the object when he encounters it again. The world has become a little more meaningful for the child. . . .

The relationship that the child has discovered and the order he has imposed on his experience are not the results of "systematic reasoning." The new meaning was acquired at a relatively low level of cognitive activity. Nevertheless, there was a "sensing" of, a conscious awareness of, new relationships, and this meets the requirements of our definition of meaning.

The phenomenon of intuitive creation of new meaning, however, is not always evidence of childishness of thought. A powerful new idea frequently emerges in the consciousness of the creative thinker prior to the application of logic and often in the face of what appears to be logical. The procedures of logic are needed to test and validate the new idea, but perhaps we need to give more attention to the pre-logical processes which operate so mysteriously in our children and in our Einsteins and Beethovens to produce a new richness of meaning where no meaning existed before.

All learning, then, involves an increase in the learner's store of personal meanings or a shift or re-patterning of perceptual structure and is accompanied or followed by relevant changes in behavior. . . .

In our definition of meaning we emphasized the individual's awareness of the interrelationships *between the self and the phenomena encountered in experience.* Such self-identification with phenomena is necessary not only in a learning situation; it is equally necessary in a transfer situation. The individual must see that the new situation has relationship to his own self-concept, to his own life purposes, values, and interests. If the student memorizes the facts of the history assignment or dutifully repeats the formulae of logic in order to accomplish the purpose of pleasing a teacher he likes, or merely as a titillating intellectual pastime, he is unlikely to transfer this learning to other situations in which the teacher is not present or intellectual titillation not his urgent concern. The individual must *see* the applicability of the learning in the new situation, and he must *want* to make the transfer.

In summation, what we have been saying is that learning is the self-incorporation of meaning into the subjectivity of the learner. The more deeply personal the meaning acquired through a learning experience, the more effective and lasting the learning will be. If allowances are made for the "intuitive hypothesis," the processes of systematic thinking are probably productive of the most highly dependable and fruitful meanings. We need to remember, however, that learning occurs only to the extent that these processes are internalized into the personality structure of the learner as an integral part of a way of living. The objective, in other words, must be subjectivized. This is not to imply a dichotomy between the objective activity of systematic thinking and the subjective activity of perception. It is rather to suggest that, since these two types of activity are inseparable in the dynamics of teaching-learning, there is need for exploring the possibilities of merging the thought and efforts of the proponents of both approaches to the study of the problems of teaching and learning.

ORDERED PLURALISM – 2*

George E. Barton, Jr.

How can we tell what changes in students we ought to aim to effect? We need an inventory of the student as he is, an ideal of the student as he ought to be, and a judgment of which gaps are most serious. We need an assessment of which gaps we could close if we tried hard enough, and what it would cost in all kinds of resources and sacrifices to close each. We need practical judgments saying, "In the light of all the foregoing, emphasize this, go once over lightly on this, and skip that entirely." At every stage, from planning the descriptive inventory to making the plan of action, we need the cooperation of philosophy, science, and common sense.

But who are "we," who decide what objectives should be sought? At the outset, we are parents, teachers, and schools. But in the end . . . the student decides for himself. There is a gradual preparation for what is eventually a Copernican revolution in education.

And what do "we" look at to help us decide? At students, world, knowledge, teacher—always at all four. But there are two cautions:

(1) In this context, "the teacher" is not really a fourth factor; he is the sum of the other three. Any human being may, through weakness, get his roles mixed up and try to change students in order to release his own tensions. But the teacher in his role of teacher always aims to improve his students. To prepare for this role, he tries to internalize all the cues from student, world, and knowledge. To perform his role, he tries to speak as their summation incarnate.

(2) While we must always look at all four factors, we cannot and should not emphasize all four equally at all times. Focus should change. In any given situation, one factor is central, and in sharpest focus. The others do not disappear, but they are seen

---

* Reprinted from "Ordered Pluralism: A Philosophical Plan of Action for Teaching," *Educational Theory*, 13(October, 1963), 266–70. By permission of the author and the editor of *Educational Theory*.

only peripherally. Let us turn the kaleidoscope through a human life, and watch the emphases change. . . .

Seen in its temporal evolution, teaching may be observed to run through cycles—little cycles for little learnings, great cycles for great learnings, with the great ones including many little ones. Each cycle may be taken to involve four distinguishable functions, derived from corresponding phases in learning. By contrast with the Herbartian five formal steps, these are not five, not formal, and not steps. A closer parallel might be the phases in reflective thinking, distinguished by Dewey. Yet there is no sense in denying that these tend to come in a certain order, and therefore tend to be actual steps. Of course, they may interpenetrate. The words used to baptize them are bound to be inadequate; but this need not matter if people will interpret each word by the accompanying exposition. . . . Commonplace words are then as good as any others; and we may suggest that teaching proceeds by inducing (1) Exploration, (2) Conversation, (3) Resolution, and (4) Consummation.

1. Student-centered teaching
The Age of Exploration calls for student-centered teaching.

During the Age of Exploration, which is also the age of universal education, the decision about what changes ought to be made in students rests largely with parents, teachers, and schools. To prepare for an eventual Copernican revolution, they should from the start invite the student to take as much responsibility as is appropriate for deciding what should be done. But . . . the Copernican revolution is still a long way off, and the amount of responsibility he can appropriately take for major decisions almost forces others to "play God."

Toward what criterion should parents, teachers, and schools mainly look in setting educational objectives during this period? Mainly to the knowers themselves—to the students. (It cannot be too frequently said that they must not lose sight of the known, knowledge, and knowledge-inducers. Anyone deciding on objectives must always look at all four, but during this Age, the focus is on the student himself, and the others are seen peripherally.)

In *any* teaching situation in which needs of the student cry for attention, the teacher should give it. Is the student, in this situation, more than usually plastic and vulnerable? Is he, in this situation, so poised that the teaching act may start him moving with cumulative inertia either toward happiness or toward misery? If so, we should focus on the student himself in deciding what to try to accomplish.

Teaching situations frequently have this character in the Age of Exploration. Besides reaching out to the world with imagination and wonder, the child is integrating himself ("his self," may I say?). The basic structure of his personality and character is likely to be formed now, and likely never to be really re-formed in the future. Hence the objectives of education should be student-centered.

These student-centered objectives call for purposive order.

The organization of knowledge in the early years is likely to be informal and *ad hoc* (Whitehead), about centers of use and enjoyment (Dewey), whether we like it or not. But I think we should like it. What better way to help a child toward integration than to help him build a structure of purposes—*his* purposes, always, in the psychological sense, but gradually reaching out to unselfishness and self-transcendence in the moral and spiritual sense? What better centripetal force, to give a core to centrifugal explorations? What better focus for a core curriculum? Or for the work of an ungraded school?

Recommendation: From exploration to student to purpose.

Overriding considerations, however, may frequently call for change. Does social crisis threaten? Unique social opportunity beckon? Does an exciting breakthrough in knowledge suddenly fix everyone's attention on mechanism? Is your school a special kind of school, with a special mission? Do you have a teacher uniquely qualified to do the job another way? Yours be the practical judgment! You may decide, "All rules are off!"

2. World-centered teaching

The Age of Conversation calls for world-centered teaching.

During the Age of Conversation, which is also the age of general education, deciding what changes teaching should aim to achieve still remains largely the responsibility of the school authorities. But the underground movements toward revolution get stronger. We may still appropriately make the entire curriculum "required" courses. But in each course, there is conversation—give and take in which the student gives substantially, and does not merely take. The student's more or less silent aims for himself begin deeply to influence the changes which really get aimed at with any effectiveness.

Toward what criterion should school authorities (and students) mainly look in setting educational objectives during this period? Mainly to the known—to the world. In any situation in which the student's selfhood is firm enough to take care of itself, it may be sentimental to insist that all education remain student-centered. Even by emphasis, we should not too long cut development of self from its natural concomitants—development of the citizen, the child of nature, or the child of God. What better spirit can there be for general education than that in which the teacher makes an introduction: "Student, I want you to meet the world!"

World-centered objectives call for organic order—an order of internal relations.

The point is not to treat everything as an organism (although the student may well seek to know himself and his mind in organic terms). The point is more the importance of exploring to the limit the interconnectedness of things, and doing it in the spirit of conversation, or dialogue. I would organize the curriculum divisionally, with committees cutting across the other way. We have got a set of matters and a set of forms to consider. We have got humanities, social studies, natural sciences, and integrative studies. We have got purposive study, organic study, mechanistic study, and classificatory study. Let us make one set into Divisions, and cross-cut it with Committees to take care of the other. But throughout everything, let us aim for the spirit of conversation, examining all sides of every question, all relations of every thing—the civilization of the dialogue.

Recommendation: From conversation to world to internal relations.

Overriding considerations, which might call for change: Same as before.

3. Knowledge-centered teaching

The Age of Resolution calls for knowledge-centered teaching.

During the Age of Resolution, which is also the age of special education, responsibility for deciding the desirable objectives for teaching is pretty well shared. This is the age of specialization, and students decide for themselves what they want to specialize in. But once they have decided, teachers lay out the program of the specialty with considerable precision, and keep some would-be students from beginning or completing the program. During this Age, the students propose; the teachers dispose. But the Copernican revolution in education has almost arrived.

Toward what criterion should the students and teachers mainly look in determining the proper objectives for teaching during this period? Mainly to knowledge—to the arts, sciences, professions, technologies, crafts, or trades in which students specialize. When a student's selfhood is firm, and when he has been introduced to the whole system of the world, what better service can a teacher perform than induct him into the mysteries of a specialty? The main thing any specialty has to contribute is its discipline—its molding of the ways a man thinks or acts to give him self-control and power. Such discipline—which involves thorough mastery of a conceptual structure, either for understanding or for action—cannot be had by every man in every field. But in whatever fields a man makes central, whether by choice or by drift, he must master the discipline in order to resolve matters. During the Age of Resolution, teaching should be guided by the logical structure of subject-matters.

Knowledge-centered objectives call for mechanistic order— an order of external relations.

The point is not to treat the internal structure of every discipline mechanistically. But the establishment of any precise explanatory system, whether of cause and effect or of functional intercorrelation, involves its separation, at least for practical purposes, from the whole rest of the world. At least for these practical purposes, then, we assume externality of relations. Where we do not quite get it, we can still make laws which hold true, "all other things being equal." Some fields come out clean. Others come out bleeding, as if from vivisection. But come out they must, for practical purposes of specialization. And even within fields, we normally achieve better and better understanding and control as we manage to describe in smaller and smaller steps the path from cause to effect or from independent to dependent variable: the basic trend is mechanistic.

Recommendation: From resolution to knowledge to external relations.

Overriding considerations, which may call for change: Same as before.

4. Teacher-centered teaching

The Age of Consummation calls for "teacher-centered teaching." But this is not what it seems: in fact, it is absurdly different. Forget, if you will, the reflexivity which will give it its queer meaning. Forget, if you will, the idea itself. Remember, if you will, only my hymn to adult education (not as it is, but as it should be)—the continuing education of an educated man.

The adult—the educated man—is the student. Having resolved the problem of the general kind of life he means to live, he has begun to find his real vocation in the living of it. He is at last complete, as "the compleat angler" was complete—not dead and done for, but at last fully developed and ready to go. He has reached "the last of life for which the first was made."

The adult—the educated man—is also the teacher. With the Age of Consummation, which is also the age of individualized education, comes a Copernican revolution: each student takes over responsibility for his own education. He takes the helm and steers himself—master of his fate, captain of his soul, director of his own self-realization. That is what it means to be an adult. And so, who now decides that, in the adult student, there will be some changes made? The adult himself, playing the teacher's role. For that matter, who goes about inducing the changes? The adult himself, playing the teacher's role. It is finally true that all true education is self-education: those of us who call ourselves adult educators are really helpers, counselors, tutors, guides.

The Age of Consummation calls for "teacher-centered teaching." But first this means that, in guiding his own life, the adult looks within himself. And second, it means that what the adult finds there is his own best internalization of all the factors one can look at, for we have seen that—in this context—"teacher" is a summation term. He looks, then, at student, world, knowledge, and knowledge-inducers; but he sees them as he has internalized them, with their cues for the living of the kind of life to which he is dedicated.

This queer kind of self-teaching calls for classificatory order.

The adult—the educated man—is by now, in a sense, the knowledge. For by now he is disciplined in the use of purposive, organic, and mechanistic forms: they are part of him. The problem of his maturity is to know which to use for any given problem. Not that some one of these is always uniquely right! But the chances of using the most useful are enhanced if one asks himself: What kind of situation do I face? What kind of problem do I face? What kind of forms of thought are likely to be most useful? Classification offers a meta-inquiry, which assigns each form of inquiry to its best functions.

The adult—the educated man—is by now, in a strange sense, his own world; and what he inquires into is an extension of himself. From the perspective of external relations, education is education is education; and adult education is pretty much like all the rest. The one independent differentiating factor is the adult himself: he is not like less mature men. But from the perspective of internal relations, the differences to him entail differences in everything else. At long last, the very world he lives in is *his* world—made up of helps and hindrances to the kind of life to which he is dedicated. And it is this life for which he seeks help in the Age of Consummation.

When men are mature, education has a chance actually to be what it should always work toward being: *counseled, self-directed self-realization.* We who teach are the counselors. The kind of self (and world) a man builds is ultimately his business, or God's. We do the best we can to help, each of us guided by his own philosophy. And to make help effective, we must make help orderly and cumulative. But you must counsel in your way, and I in mine. And it is good that we offer differing counsel in differing ways. This leaves man-making where it belongs: we would not want to pre-empt what is the student's job, or God's.

INDEX

Ability, as a *Ding an sich,* 139–141

Ability grouping, illustrative of knowledge relevant to policy, 135–137

Actualization of potentialities, 34

Adjudication, in settling policy disputes, 95

Adler, Mortimer J., 155

Aims: inadequate conceptions of, 10, 13–14; relative to society, 113, 116–117

Alexander, Samuel, 50, 54, 56

Alienation, 131–132

Aristotle, 39, 61, 62, 156–160

Ausubel, David, 214

Autonomism as educational doctrine, 15–17

Autonomy of educational process, 26–27

Berkeley, George, 60

Blanshard, Brand, 47

Bode, Boyd, 182

Brameld, Theodore, 121, 124–127

British empiricists, 60, 62, 238

Broudy, Harry S., 176–177, 179–180, 182

Bruner, Jerome, 174–175, 178, 189, 214

Classificatory relations: in curriculum, 216, 218–219; in teaching and learning, 298

Cognitive experience, 40

Common education, 66

Common schooling, 133

Conant, James B., 194

Concepts, as organizing experience, 63

Conceptual system, as heart of a discipline, 192

Condillac, Etienne de, 100

Consciousness, 61, 63

Copernican revolution in education, 292, 293, 297

Descartes, René, 61–62

Dewey, John: concern for effect of knowledge upon conduct, 42; contrasted with Aristotle, 163–164; problems as integrative principle, source of, 171; exposition of his learning theory, 252–261; comparison of teaching and selling, 274–276; mentioned, 39, 72, 86, 96, 121, 155, 172, 181, 182, 210, 227–228, 230, 242, 257, 283, 284, 293, 294

Discipline, 189

Education, as a practical activity, 30

Educational process, as locus of problems of philosophy of education, 23–24

Educational science, as dependent upon psychology, sociology, and philosophy, 21

Einstein, Albert, 212, 290

Emerson, Ralph W., 166

Epicureans, 61

Essential attributes of man, 36–37

Ethics, as presupposed by philosophy of education, 37–38

Eton, 49